The social democratic parties we in Europe. Today, however, they less, crucially lacking the ideolog vitality which underpinned thei landscape.

Electorally marginalised, seemingly ideologically exhausted and often out-of-step with the contemporary zeitgeist, European social democracy is currently in profound need of revision and renewal – potentially its very existence as a political force is under threat.

This book marks a serious attempt to forge the intellectual backbone of a renewed social democracy fit for the twenty-first century. Bringing together leading academics, political thinkers and policy experts, it offers a new and original perspective on ideological and policy innovation and will be invaluable reading for anyone interested in the future of social democracy.

Edited by Olaf Cramme and Patrick Diamond

after the third way

The Future of Social Democracy in Europe

I.B. TAURIS
LONDON · NEW YORK

Published in 2012 by I.B.Tauris & Co Ltd
6 Salem Road, London W2 4BU
175 Fifth Avenue, New York NY 10010
www.ibtauris.com

Distributed in the United States and Canada Exclusively by Palgrave Macmillan
175 Fifth Avenue, New York NY 10010

ISBN: 978 1 84885 992 0 (HB)
ISBN: 978 1 84885 993 7 (PB)

A full CIP record for this book is available from the British Library
A full CIP record is available from the Library of Congress

Library of Congress Catalog Card Number: available

Typeset in Minion by MPS Limited, a Macmillan Company
Printed and bound in Great Britain by T.J. International, Padstow, Cornwall

MIX
Paper from responsible sources
FSC® C013056
FSC
www.fsc.org

About Policy Network

Policy Network is a leading thinktank and international political network based in London. We seek to promote strategic thinking on progressive solutions to the challenges of the twenty-first century and the future of social democracy, impacting upon policy debates in the UK, the rest of Europe and the wider world.

We organise debates and conduct research on policy and political challenges that present all governments and political parties with urgent dilemmas, either because sustainable solutions remain elusive, or because there are political barriers to their implementation.

Through a distinctly collaborative and cross-national approach to research, events and publications, we have acquired a reputation as a highly valued platform for perceptive and challenging political analysis, debate and exchange. Building from our origins in the late 1990s, the network has become an unrivalled international point-of-contact between political thinkers and opinion formers, serving as a nexus between the worlds of politics, academia, public policymaking, business, civil society and the media.

Contents

Contributors *ix*

Preface *xiii*

The Guiding Purpose of Centre-Left Politics

1 From Fatalism to Fraternity: Governing Purpose and the Good Society 1
Patrick Diamond

2 Social Democracy in a Global Era 29
Luke Martell

Policy Predicaments

3 Debt and Deficits: The Quest for Economic Competence 45
Andrew Gamble

4 The Mechanics of Markets: Politics, Economics and Finance 61
John Kay

5 Social Democracy at the End of the Welfare State? 75
Peter Taylor-Gooby

6 Equality, Social Trust and the Politics of Institutional Design 95
Bo Rothstein

7 Progress and Social Policy: Two-and-a-Half Cheers for Education 111
Lane Kenworthy

8 Social Cohesion, Culture Politics and the Impact of Migration 125
René Cuperus and Mark Elchardus

9 Identity, Community and the Politics of Recognition 143
Michael Kenny

Governance and Politics

10 The Power of European Integration: Choice and Purpose for Centre-Left Politics 157
Olaf Cramme

11 Back to the Future: Towards a Red-Green Politics 175
John McTernan

12 Globalisation Challenges to Centre-Left Internationalism 187
John Lloyd

13 The Squeezed Middle and the New Inequality 203
Liam Byrne

14 Citizen Engagement and the Quest for Solidarity 219
Henry Tam

15 Co-operation, Creativity and Equality: Key Concepts for a New Social Democratic Era 235
Tobias Dürr and Robert Misik

16 Afterword: The New Social Democracy? 251
Olaf Cramme and Patrick Diamond

Notes *255*

Index *273*

Contributors

Liam Byrne is the UK Labour party's shadow secretary for welfare and pensions, MP for Birmingham Hodge Hill and coordinator of Labour's national policy review. Previously, he has served as shadow chief secretary to the Treasury and minister for the cabinet office, responsible for the co-ordination of policy across Government. He helped to write the 2009 Pre-Budget Report and 2010 Budget, and led Labour's reorganisation of public services. His other posts have included chancellor of the Duchy of Lancaster, and minister of state for borders and immigration.

Olaf Cramme is director of Policy Network and a visiting fellow at the London School of Economics' European Institute. He is also a member of the General Assembly of the Lisbon Council for Economic Competitiveness and Social Renewal, and co-founder and vice-chairman of Das Progressive Zentrum, a Berlin-based political thinktank. Olaf publishes widely on the future of the European Union and European social democracy, and is editor of *Rescuing the European Project: EU Legitimacy, Governance and Security* (2009), and co-editor of *Social Justice in the Global Age* (with Patrick Diamond, 2009).

René Cuperus is director for international relations and senior research fellow at the Wiardi Beckman Stichting, the thinktank of the Dutch Labour Party (PvdA). He is a former member of the Basic Values Commission and the European Policy Review Commission of the PvdA, and served as senior policy adviser to the chairman of the PvdA, as well as to the party's parliamentary group. He is a member of the Friedrich Ebert Foundation's international team and a member of the Scientific Committee of the Paris-based thinktank Terra Nova. His latest book is *De wereldburger bestaat niet* (2009). He is also a columnist for the Dutch newspaper *de Volkskrant.*

Patrick Diamond is senior research fellow at Policy Network, Gwilym Gibbon fellow at Nuffield College, and visiting fellow in the Department of Politics, University of Oxford. He is a former head of policy planning in 10 Downing Street and senior policy adviser to the prime minister. He has served as a special adviser at the heart of British Government, including the Cabinet Office, the Northern Ireland Office and the Equality and Human Rights

Commission. His publications include: *Beyond New Labour* (with Roger Liddle, 2009); *Social Justice in the Global Age* (with Olaf Cramme, 2009); and *Global Europe, Social Europe* (with Anthony Giddens, 2006).

Tobias Dürr is a political scientist and editor-in-chief of the German political journal *Berliner Republik*. He is also co-founder and chairman of Das Progressive Zentrum, a Berlin-based political thinktank, and speech writer for Matthias Platzeck, Minister President of Brandenburg. He regularly contributes to newspapers including *Die Zeit* and *Die Welt*, and is the author of several books and essays. His works include *Die Heimatlosigkeit der Macht: Wie die Politik in Deutschland ihren Boden verlor* (2000) and *Die CDU Nach Kohl* (1998).

Mark Elchardus is professor of sociology at the Vrije Universiteit Brussels, founder and former director of the research group Tempus Omnia Revelat (TOR). Until last year he was also chairman of the National Union of Socialist Health Services and is chairman of the P&V Foundation. His main research interests include cultural sociology, the sociology of time structuring, and the role of education and the media in relation to political and social policy. His key works include *De Symbolische Samenleving* (2002) and *De Dramademocratie* (2002).

Andrew Gamble is professor and head of the department of politics at the University of Cambridge. Before that he was professor of politics at the University of Sheffield, where he was a founder member and subsequently the director of the Political Economy Research Centre. He is joint editor of *The Political Quarterly*, and a fellow of the British Academy and the Academy of Social Sciences. His books include *The Spectre at the Feast* (2009); *Between Europe and America: The Future of British Politics* (2003); and *Politics and Fate* (2000). In 2005 he received the Sir Isaiah Berlin Prize for Lifetime Contribution to Political Sciences from the UK Political Studies Association.

Peter Taylor-Gooby is professor of social policy at the University of Kent and chair of the British Academy New Paradigms in Public Policy programme. He is a fellow of the British Academy and a former adviser to Prime Minister Gordon Brown's Strategy Unit. His research focuses on cross-disciplinary work on risk, comparative cross-national work on European social policy and work on theoretical developments in social policy. His books include: *Reframing Social Citizenship* (2008); *Risk in Social Science* (with Jens Zinn, 2006); *Ideas and the Welfare State* (2005); and *New Risks, New Welfare* (2004).

John Kay is a visiting professor of economics at the London School of Economics and a fellow of St John's College, the British Academy and the Royal Society of Edinburgh. He is a director of several public companies and has previously been director of the Institute for Fiscal Studies, and director of Oxford's Said Business School. He contributes a weekly column to *The Financial Times* and is the author of many books, including *Obliquity – How our Goals are Best Pursued Indirectly* (2010); *The Long and the Short of It: Finance and Investment for Normally Intelligent People who are not in the Industry* (2009); and *The Truth about Markets* (2003).

Michael Kenny is professor of politics at Queen Mary University London and an associate fellow at the Institute for Public Policy Research. Previously, he was head of politics at Sheffield University, and was a charter fellow at Wolfson College, Oxford University. His research focuses on political ideologies and the role of the idea in public policy. His recent works include *The Politics of Nationhood in England (forthcoming)*; *Reassessing New Labour: Market State and Society under Blair and Brown* (with Patirck Diamond, 2011); *The First New Left in Britain, 1956–64* (2010); and *The Politics of Identity* (2004).

Lane Kenworthy is professor of sociology and political science at the University of Arizona. He publishes widely on the causes and consequences of poverty, inequality, mobility, employment, economic growth,social policy, taxes, and public opinion in the United States and other affluent countries. He is the author of *Should We Worry About Inequality?* (forthcoming); *Progress for the Poor* (2011); *Jobs with Equality* (2008); *Egalitarian Capitalism* (2004); and *In Search of National Economic Success* (1995).

John Lloyd is a contributing editor to *The Financial Times.* He is a supernumerary fellow of St Anne's College and an associate member of Nuffield College, both of Oxford University. He is a visiting professor at City University, an associate of Demos, a member of the editorial board of Prospect and a member of the board of the Moscow School of Political Studies. His publications include: *Loss without Limit: the British Miners' Strike* (with Martin Adeney, 1985); *The Future of Work* (with Charles Leadbeater, 1987); *Birth of a Nation: an Anatomy of Russia* (1998); and *What the Media are Doing to our Politics* (2004).

Luke Martell is professor of political sociology at the University of Sussex. He publishes widely on political sociology, especially globalisation, socialism and social democracy, New Labour and the third way, and environmentalism. He is also is co-editor of *The Journal of Democratic Socialism.* His recent books include: *The Global Left* (forthcoming); *The Sociology of Globalization* (2010);

The Third Way and Beyond (co-edited, 2004); *Social Democracy: Global and National Perspectives* (co-edited, 2001); and *New Labour, and Blair's Britain* (both with Stephen Driver, 1998 & 2001).

Robert Misik is a journalist and independent political analyst based in Vienna. He is a regular contributor to German and Austrian magazines and newspapers including *Profit, Falter, Die Tageszeitung* and *Der Standard.* His work centres on the consequences of globalisation, cultural politics and political philosophy. He has twice received the Bruno-Kreisky Prize for Political Books (1999 and 2000), and in 2009 won the Austrian State Prize for Cultural Journalism. His key works include *The Politics of Paranoia: Against the New Conservatives* (2009) and *The Cult Book: The Glory and Misery of Business Culture* (2007).

John McTernan is a commentator and political strategist who works internationally. He is currently communications director for Australian Prime Minister, Julia Gillard. Previously, he was senior policy adviser and director of political operations to former UK Prime Minister Tony Blair and has been an adviser on health, welfare, and defence. He has also served as head of policy at the Scottish Executive and special adviser to the Secretary of State for Scotland. He writes regularly for *The Scotsman* and *The Daily Telegraph.*

Bo Rothstein holds the August Röhss Chair in Political Science at the University of Gothenburg. He has been a visiting scholar at the Russell Sage Foundation, Cornell University, Harvard University, Collegium Budapest Institute for Advanced Study, University of Bergen, Aalborg University, the Australian National University and the University of Washington. His main publications in English are: *The Quality of Government: The Political Logic of Corruption, Inequality and Social Trust* (2011); *The Problem of Trust* (2005); and *Just Institutions Matter: The Moral and Political Logic of the Universal Welfare and Social Traps* (1998).

Henry Tam is director of Cambridge University's Forum for Youth Participation and Democracy, a visiting professor at Birkbeck College, London University, and a fellow of the Globus Institute for Globalization and Sustainable Development at Tilburg University. He is a specialist in the development of inclusive communities and has headed up government initiatives in Britain in support of civil renewal, community empowerment, and equalities. His most recent books include: *Against Power Inequalities* (2010); *Progressive Politics in the Global Age* (2001); and *Communitarianism: A New Agenda for Politics & Citizenship* (1998). He blogs at Question the Powerful.

Preface

This book is intended for anyone who wishes to develop their understanding of the changing nature and context of social democracy in Europe. It is aimed at expert commentators and students of politics alike. We take ideas to be of central importance in our analysis, structuring the electoral strategies, political identities and policy agendas of centre-left parties. There is a vast historical literature on European social democracy which explores the role of ideologies, institutions and interests. Although ideas are referred to in passing and are closely related to ideologies, institutions and interests, for many authors they remain of secondary concern.

Our contention is that ideas are at the core of social democratic strategies and programmes. According to Daniel Béland, ideas 'shape the way we understand interests, are the inspiration for the construction of political and social institutions, and are the currency of our discourse about politics'.[1] The changing context of ideas in the advanced capitalist democracies has fundamental implications for the future of social democracy. Our mission is to bring ideas back in.

Of course, the relationship between the world of ideas and the world of action is a complex one, and the transmission of ideas between the policy and political worlds is far from straightforward. If the development and application of new concepts and theories provides the focus for this book, it emphasises that all centre-left parties in Europe have been forced to come to terms with major structural transformations since the 1980s. If 'new' Labour in Britain has moved furthest and fastest from the state to the market over the last 30 years, similar attitudes are to be found among almost all European social democratic parties.

It is important to acknowledge, as the authors do in this collection, that contingency is at the core of social democratic politics.

Contingency means not just being alive to accidental and unexpected events in a world characterised by global shocks and structural change. It is also about preparing for the future, demonstrating that social democracy has the capacity to face up to long-term challenges. This argument will be elaborated further throughout the book.

In this vein, the volume takes a distinctive approach to much of the scholarly debate since Ralf Dahrendorf's depiction of the 'end of the social democratic century'.[2] Countless quantitative and qualitative studies gave support to this thesis by analysing the diminished role of trade unions, the erosion of class-based voting, altered party competition and coalition-building constraints, as well as the impact of economic and socio-cultural changes such as globalisation. Lately, the constraints imposed by European integration have been added to the list. They have reinforced a disposition towards fatalism, rooted in the belief that social democracy in the global age has lost its distinctive sense of purpose and governing élan. The forward march of labour, as the historian Eric Hobsbawm put it, appears to have been abruptly halted.

There is not one pre-ordained future for the left, however, but a range of options and strategic choices in the face of profound upheavals in the global economy and domestic politics. These have the potential to open up an infinite array of outcomes and futures. We refute the assertion that centre-left parties are in a state of terminal decline. Apocalyptic claims about the end of social democracy do not stand up to wider scrutiny. While ambiguity and contingency present distinct challenges to the social democratic agenda, they are also a precondition for charting a new, more radical direction for left-of-centre politics.

Social democracy therefore needs to attain a new vibrancy and a new radicalism. Transformations in the intellectual and cultural climate can have a major impact on the thinking and assumptions of politicians and policymakers, who too often remain prisoners of their own outdated assumptions and ideological shibboleths. Instead, social democracy must be the subject of constant innovation and experimentation, relentlessly confronting new challenges and reconnecting with the contemporary context of prevailing ideas.

The chapters in this volume are the product of precisely such an enterprise: held under the aegis of the international think tank Policy Network and the Wiardi Beckman Stichting (the think tank for Dutch social democracy), and attended by serving ministers and politicians, senior experts and policymakers, and a host of academic commentators and social scientists, a series of working group meetings throughout 2009 and 2010 offered the unique opportunity to map out new terrain in the field of social democratic ideas, doctrines and strategies.

We are very grateful for the commitment and support of all the authors and participants. We would also like to thank the many people who have helped in the preparation of this book. In the Policy Network office, Michael McTernan has worked tirelessly in helping to organise these meetings, liaising with authors, editing early drafts and co-ordinating the production of this volume. Without his dedication and professionalism, the book would never have been possible. Thanks are due to Roger Liddle, Kathryn Skidmore, Jade Groves and Robert Tinker for their wholehearted support. We would also like to thank all the staff at I.B.Tauris who have been efficient and helpful throughout.

Olaf Cramme and Patrick Diamond
December 2011

CHAPTER 1

From Fatalism to Fraternity: Governing Purpose and the Good Society

Patrick Diamond

'The past really is another country; we cannot go back'

—Professor Tony Judt[1]

Despite the worst global economic crisis for over 80 years, it is christian democracy which is ascendant in today's Europe, as the political tide has turned sharply towards the centre-right. The shattering of confidence in global capitalism and the return of the activist state has done little to revive support for parties of the left. In the face of growing economic turbulence and escalating public debt, many now question whether social democracy is even capable of renewal.[2] The centre-left appears to have no persuasive electoral or ideological programme. Social democrats are floundering not just because they are losing elections: they appear to lack any credible governing vision for the future.

Of course, the electoral performance of centre-left parties has been relatively weak for more than a decade. Most Scandinavian countries are led by the centre-right, where social democracy has been the natural party of government for over 60 years. The 2009 European parliamentary elections could scarcely have been more dismal: social democrats were behind the centre-right in 21 out of 27 EU member states, including Austria, Belgium, the Czech Republic, Finland, France, Germany, Italy, the Netherlands, Poland, Spain and Britain. The European Parliament has a smaller centre-left representation than at any point since 1979.

In recent elections, the SPD and the British Labour Party flirted with disaster, achieving among their lowest vote shares since universal suffrage. The shock of defeat has been all the greater because, having experienced the worst financial crisis since the 1930s, the return to government activism and Keynesian stimulus had done little to bolster social democracy. The prospect of a centre-left renaissance is more distant than ever, while the historical achievements of post-war social democracy in Western Europe – universal welfare, high-quality public services, the social investment state – seem imperilled as never before.

Taking stock of these recent developments, this chapter proceeds in the following sequence. The electoral performance of social democracy in the recent period is considered, reflecting on the various modernisation strategies developed by social democratic parties since the mid-1990s. It then proceeds to consider the 'neo-revisionist' analysis of social democracy. The chapter argues that the founding assumptions of post-war social democracy have to be re-examined from first principles, in particular the nature of economic and political power, and the scope and scale of the state in relation to the market and civil sphere. The implications of this analysis for the ideological and programmatic development of social democratic parties are then spelt out. The remaining question is whether the centre-left can regain the capacity for adaptation in a world where many traditional practices and institutions are increasingly obsolete.

The Politics of Nostalgia and the Politics of Despair

Electorally, social democrats are on the back foot, but this chapter warns strongly against the view that history is stacked inexorably against the left: the long march of progress has not gone into reverse. Social democracy does face testing times in Europe and across much of the world, but the pessimism can be overdone. We should refuse to succumb to what Andrew Gamble characterises as the politics of nostalgia and the politics of despair.[3]

This interpretation of history is pervasive among many European social democrats. It begins with the claim that third way social democracy has achieved little since the late 1980s, in the face of increasing acquiescence to neo-liberalism. Many of the traditional social democratic values have been abandoned, so the argument goes, as governments everywhere seek to roll back the state. Having asserted social democracy's capitulation to economic liberalism, what follows inevitably are the politics of nostalgia. The period between 1945 and the early 1970s is hailed as a 'golden age', in which social democracy fought to entrench universal social citizenship encapsulated in the welfare state and a model of regulated capitalism that protected national populations from misfortune. In Britain, the post-war Attlee Government is still regarded as the pinnacle of social democratic achievement.

This narrative might appear persuasive, but it radically overestimates the efficacy of neo-liberalism during the 1980s, and gives a false impression of social democratic durability during the years of the long boom. In the 1950s, for example, many Western European countries were dominated by parties of the christian democratic right, having skilfully captured the post-war settlement promising a new model of social market capitalism. It was only in Scandinavia that the centre-left was capable of sustained electoral hegemony.

Another weakness of the politics of nostalgia is that too much ground is conceded to the free market right. The ideology of neo-liberalism became highly influential in the early 1980s as the post-war settlement collapsed. Indeed, many of its guiding assumptions live on, even in the wake of the global financial crisis. But the state has hardly been rolled back or systematically dismantled, as critics of third way politics often allege. Even in the UK, among the most neo-liberal of the Western European countries, the struggle to rein in public expenditure after 1979 was far from successful. Welfare spending as a proportion of national income, for example, was substantially higher when the Conservatives left office in 1997. Across the industrialised economies, expenditure on the welfare state and social protection as a proportion of GDP increased from 1980 to 2005 by over 6%.[4]

The fundamental weakness of the politics of despair and the politics of nostalgia is their emphasis on the preservation of existing ideals and institutions, instead of engaging radically with the challenges of the future. Social democracy has to adjust to new challenges in order to encompass the needs of the present. That requires sustained reflection about the strategic aims and guiding purpose of centre-left politics, alongside the specific institutional mechanisms required to enact social democratic policies and strategies in power. This chapter addresses those questions directly, beginning with an assessment of the various governing programmes that social democrats have sought to develop in power since the late 1990s.

The Electoral Performance of Social Democracy

In the wake of the capitalist crisis that engulfed the West in the mid-1970s, political scientists predicted the inevitable decline of social democracy in the face of Margaret Thatcher and Ronald Reagan's dominance of the political landscape. The sociologist Ralf Dahrendorf foresaw the 'end of the social democratic century'.[5] Neo-liberal globalisation and the integration of the European market had severely constrained the options available to centre-left parties. The obstacles that they faced were exacerbated by the fiscal crisis and voter resistance to higher taxation; long-term demographic trends that added to the pressures on the welfare state; and post-industrialisation which decimated many long-established industries and led to spiralling unemployment. Pessimism about social democracy's survival seemed wholly justified.

By the end of the twentieth century, however, Europe was witnessing social democracy's magical return. Secular trends in Western Europe had not destroyed the left's governing authority. There was a renewed spirit of historical confidence, as most social democratic parties embraced their own form of ideological revisionism.[6] Astonishingly, 13 out of 15 Western European countries were governed by parties of the centre-left.

By the end of the next decade, the trend had come full circle. The left was once again on the wrong side of history, and the decline of social democracy was seemingly irreversible. The historic defeat inflicted on the centre-left in the 2009 elections in Europe was hardly new. In France, for instance, the Socialist Party (PS) has not won a national election since 1997. The PS vote share in the first round of legislative elections has never recovered to the level achieved in the early 1980s.

Similarly, the PvdA in the Netherlands has failed to exceed the 30% threshold in every election since 1989, with a run of historically poor results in 2002, 2006 and 2010 where it has fallen close to 20%. In Germany, the SPD has achieved only one convincing election result since reunification, winning 41% of the popular vote under Gerhard Schroeder in 1998. In 2009, the SPD endured their worst electoral performance since the First World War, declining to just 23%. And even the Swedish SAP, historically among the most successful social democratic parties, appears destined for a long spell in opposition having suffered its first consecutive defeat since the Second World War.

The rebirth of the centre-left in Europe at the turn of the millennium proved to be neither sustainable nor enduring. The new wave of revisionism did not provide the basis for long-term electoral recovery. An important explanation is that centre-left parties struggled to come to terms with the structural causes of defeat, and did not develop alternative election-winning strategies. They were trapped in the politics of evasion, in which they sought to pin the blame for defeat on anything other than their programmatic commitments and ideological ideals.[7] What followed were short-term fixes, tactical adjustments and the search for new political alignments, all of which obscured the imperative of understanding the fundamental causes of electoral decline.

More importantly, the drive to embrace new methods and governing approaches that characterised the European left in the 1990s was insubstantial and, at times, alarmingly superficial. The process of doctrinal modernisation was primarily concerned with the abandonment of obsolete commitments relating to nationalisation and public ownership, and the rejection of traditional Keynesian economic orthodoxies.[8] Yet the centre-left struggled to envisage what was the guiding purpose of social democracy in a world of lost ideological certainties. Many existing assumptions were taken for granted, even the durability of global financial capitalism itself, confidence that perished with the economic crisis of 2008–9.

Since then, explanations for defeat have shifted to the fundamental structural tension within social democracy, caught between a world-view based on liberal cosmopolitanism on the one hand, and solidaristic communitarianism on the other. The inexorable rise of globalisation, strongly embracing values of liberal diversity, appears to conflict with the decline of social solidarity and the erosion of traditional forms of community and cohesion. The centre-left's core constituency is irreparably divided between the professionalised middle class and an alienated base of traditional working-class support.

This implies a clash of material interests as the beneficiaries of globalisation in high-value, tradable sectors are increasingly set apart from the 'losers', relatively low-skilled workers whose real wages have fallen sharply since the late 1990s. It relates, at the same time, to themes of identity, belonging and nationhood, and to the capacity of social democracy to go beyond its traditional concern with the economy and the welfare state. This new electoral cleavage poses a powerful set of dilemmas and constraints that are explored throughout this volume.

Social Democracy as Hybrid Ideology

As a backdrop to the strategic debate about the future of centre-left politics, it is important to clarify what is meant by social democracy as a form of political ideology. Most social democratic parties in Western Europe espoused a particular notion of class politics. Electorally, they were rooted in the manual working class and organised labour, which provided the bedrock of their political support and the core of their identity. After 1945, this coalesced around a commitment to the welfare state and the managed market economies of Western Europe. In particular, Keynesian political economy provided the theoretical justification for redistribution.[9] Although originating in the British liberal tradition, J. M. Keynes's ideas came to be an important influence on the labour movement more generally.[10]

This provided social democracy with a coherent identity, as a fixed set of values and practices that included the strong commitment to redistribution, democratic control of the market through state intervention and the guarantee of citizen's welfare throughout the life-course, from cradle to grave in Beveridge's phrase. That was closely linked to greater equality of income and wealth achieved through redistributive tax and benefit policies, and according priority to full employment.

The tendency to treat social democracy as a fixed doctrine proved counter-productive, however, particularly given the upheavals of the 1960s and 1970s, and the need to come to terms with the rise of economic and social liberalism. It was wiser to conceive of social democracy as a 'hybrid' political ideology, one that retained strong revisionist tendencies with the capacity to reinvent itself in the light of changing conditions.

Over the last 30 years, social democrats have forged new economic and political institutions, consolidating existing arrangements such as welfare universalism, as well as coming to terms with new risks and needs. This has inevitably involved a significant degree of national variation and experimentation. The founding assumption is not just that government intervention can alter the distribution of assets, rewards and opportunities. A consistent thread is the combination of economic efficiency and greater equality, where social justice is closely linked to the prosperity arising from a capitalist economy.

Social democracy is defined, then, not as a fixed approach to economic management and the role of the state, but as a set of changing programmatic commitments informed by an enduring framework of ethical values. The American philosopher Irving Kristol has described neo-conservatism as a persuasion, not a fixed doctrine. Social democracy combines a set of normative ideals with the determination to eradicate human misery and suffering. It sees conscience, not class, as the key to radical politics. Social democracy is strongly imbued with narratives of progress, underlining the commitment to radical political action. That requires the centre-left to attain power by winning elections, and to act as a responsible party of government.

The Social Democratic Project Across Europe

The previous section has charted the evolving character of the social democratic project since 1945. This should not obscure the fact that there are, of course, a sweep of divergent social democratic traditions in Europe and across the world, each of which has diverse roots and ideological concerns.

Since the end of the Second World War, there has been striking variation in the policies pursued by centre-left parties, as each has sought to evolve a particular model of welfare capitalism.[11] In Britain and Austria, for example, there has been particular emphasis on a large-scale, nationalised state sector. In Sweden, however, public ownership was always incidental to the strategy pursued by the social democrats. There was no single, overarching corporatist model.

The reformist turn continued this pattern of national variance and institutional diversity between social democratic parties. The British Labour Party, for example, evolved a distinctive, market-orientated path to power. That process was heavily influenced by the American Democrats, who offered ideological inspiration as well as new policy instruments such as tax credits and welfare reform. In Scandinavia, there had been a long tradition of reformism stretching back to the mid-nineteenth century. Both Germany and France updated their distinctive traditions of state-orientated social democracy. Inevitably, no single, uniform model emerged.

In fact, three particular modernisation strategies were discernible. In France, a state-centric model was developed; the German SPD evolved a new form of consensual corporatism and social partnership; and in Britain, a model of globalised social democracy was readily embraced. Each party fought to contend with structural and circumstantial constraints which helped give shape to these particular strategies. They occupied different positions in their respective societies, faced with political rivals and resources that varied from one country to another. Not all made the same ideological concessions in the process of programmatic renewal. It is this assessment of available margins of manoeuvre that provides some of the clearest ways of drawing distinctions between social democratic parties in government.

The state-centric model in France, for example, is predicated on making full use of limited policy autonomy. The centrality of ideological choice and the capacity of politics to shape markets are repeatedly emphasised. As such, economic imperatives are counter-balanced by social cohesion and solidarity, encapsulated by the former Prime Minister Lionel Jospin's belief in 'a market economy, not a market society'. However, New Labour's globalised model focuses on increasing labour market flexibility and employability, firmly embracing globalisation and market competition. This seeks to demarcate the party clearly from the perceived defeats and bankruptcy of British social democracy in the 1960s and 1970s.[12] The German model lies somewhere between the French and the British approaches. It is rooted in the post-war settlement, based on a co-ordinated market economy with strong orientation towards consensus between the social partners, including the trade unions and business.[13]

The impact of each model on economic efficiency and social justice is inevitably contested. For example, the British model is widely portrayed as strong on efficiency and weak on equity, although this is rather misleading. Merkel, for example, has shown that German corporatism ranks comparatively poorly on measures of social mobility and social justice.[14] However, the UK has experienced among the sharpest falls in income inequality among the industrialised nations since the late 1990s,[15] although inequality and relatively high rates of deprivation remain a major structural weakness in British society.

The alternative approach to defining the national pathways of social democracy is envisaged by Wolfgang Merkel, drawing on the political scientist Peter Hall's framework of first, second and third order policy changes.[16] Merkel has examined the performance of six Western European social democratic parties in power over the last 20 years. The focus is how centre-left governments are adapting to changing circumstances, and how they seek to retain traditional social democratic values and goals in the light of new challenges.[17]

Merkel defines three categories of 'traditional', 'modernised' and 'liberalised' social democracy across Western Europe. According to his typology, the traditional social democratic parties in France and Germany have stuck to previous objectives, leaving their policy instruments (which include a heavy emphasis on state intervention in the economy) largely unchanged. In Sweden and Denmark, they held fast to traditional goals, but developed new governing instruments and approaches such as welfare to work. However, in the Netherlands and Britain, not only are new methods employed but also new objectives and political priorities have emerged. Social inclusion, for example, replaced the traditional emphasis on equality and redistribution. In this political context, core ideological values and commitments are not regarded as untouchable, but are worthy of constant revision and renewal.

Stephen Padgett argues that the very process of adaptation in an era characterised by the ascendancy of economic and social liberalism has been unsettling for those of a centre-left disposition, given the extent of market liberalisation and the challenge to the traditional levers of state power.[18] Brokering a new relationship between market and state, reconciling the individualism of markets with the traditional concern for social solidarity, has proved politically testing.

It is hardly surprising that the various national models of social democracy across Europe have not proved to be equally successful. The central issue raised by Merkel is whether shifts in policy inevitably entail the dilution of core values. Because globalisation limits the potential for traditional social democratic intervention within a unitary national economy, those values have to be examined afresh. The acknowledgement of constraint in the 1980s and 1990s prompted fresh approaches to the pursuit of economic growth and social justice. It is important not to exaggerate the degree of discontinuity since the impact of such constraints has been a feature of social democratic governance throughout the twentieth century, although it was far greater after the economic crisis of the mid-1970s.

In assessing the fate of European social democracy, it is also essential not to lose sight of the historical experience of centre-left parties in the former Communist countries of Eastern Europe. In East, Central and Black Sea Europe, resurgent centre-left parties were eagerly supported following the collapse of the Berlin Wall. They now appear to be on the brink of collapse. Entire regions of Europe such as Hungary and Romania no longer have a solid democratic left presence, as centre-left governments struggled to cope with harsh economic realities and rapidly lost power.

European social democracy since the late 1980s has been defined by the programmatic response to changing economic and social conditions. All major Western European parties were increasingly revisionist, but their underlying orientation and ideological approach varied markedly.[19] These strategies produced significant, although short-lived, electoral success. They also created structural dilemmas and trade-offs that centre-left parties repeatedly struggled to resolve. Some suggest that social democracy faces an unenviable tension between ultimate ends and electoral realities. It has always faced a conflict between adherence to the ultimate goal, the achievement of a social democratic society based on fairness and social justice, and securing mass electoral support.[20]

The scenario envisaged by Przeworkski is shatteringly bleak. Where centre-left parties do attain electoral success, it is claimed that they have ceased to be social democratic at all. Only by adapting to become catch-all parties of the centre-ground does the left attract a sufficiently wide coalition of electoral support, uniting its traditional working-class base with new middle-class voters. In charging to the electoral centre, however, these parties inevitably fail to meet the expectations and demands of their core supporters. What results is a constant cycle of raised expectations, retreat and disillusionment, followed by inevitable defeat.

This interpretation of social democratic politics is excessively fatalistic. It underestimates the extent to which centre-left parties historically have been able to form inclusive progressive coalitions that unite many constituencies and classes. And any credible governing party must have the capacity for constant structural adaptation to changing voter expectations, and political and economic conditions around the world. The next section will summarise the key issues that social democrats need to address in the coming years.

The Rise of Neo-Revisionism

In reality, most traditionalist and modernising social democrats agree that the basic framework of social democracy ought to be revisited. The disagreement concerns which ideological and programmatic commitments should be regarded as untouchable and how deep and fundamental the task of rethinking ought to be. The third way rapidly emerged as the dominant governing strategy for the centre-left because there were very few credible or persuasive alternatives.[21] Nonetheless, the third way was primarily concerned with jettisoning moribund ideological principles, rather than furnishing social democracy with a compelling strategic vision and guiding purpose. The argument of this chapter is that modernisers and traditionalists alike have resisted any fundamental re-examination of centre-left politics. They have avoided going to the roots of what social democracy is, and what it might become in the future.

This is highlighted by the increasing prominence of 'neo-revisionist' ideas within European social democracy. Neo-revisionism is not a coherent doctrine or programmatic alternative, but an approach to rethinking centre-left ideas. It is strongly rooted in traditional forms of social democracy, but is prepared to grapple with new questions such as identity and nationhood that social democrats have historically avoided, and it has set the pace of the debate on the left so far. Neo-revisionism is exemplified in the writings of academic commentators such as Tony Judt and Thomas Meyer.

These writers do not explicitly subscribe to the revisionist method. What they seek to understand is the relationship between the programmatic means and philosophical ends of social democracy. At the core of 'neo-revisionism' is the proposition that centre-left parties have become alienated from their traditional base of working-class support, promising neither to defend that constituency from the impact of rapid economic and technological change, nor to affirm the sense of national identity and belonging.

These writers seek to underscore the importance of a class-based, 'majoritarian' social democracy. They argue in turn that the long-term sustainability of the welfare state is dependent on a widely constituted tax base. This is generated by ensuring full employment among the working-age population, including women with children, who in turn depend on the collective provision of caring services. The right to comprehensive care from cradle to grave, together with universal social insurance against the vagaries of sickness and redundancy, helps to cement support for the welfare state across all classes, as well as fulfilling the social democratic aim of a society based on equity and justice.

Inevitably, this chapter cannot do justice to the full sweep and historical range of the arguments put forward by neo-revisionist thinkers. The key points, however, are as follows:

- Social democrats must urgently address economic insecurity and anxiety within their core electoral constituency. There is considerable evidence that neo-liberal globalisation has eroded the real wages and living standards of the 'squeezed middle'. The downgrading of post-war corporatism and government activism in the face of global market competition has exposed those in the middle and lower segments of the income distribution. Much of Western Europe has witnessed growing structural unemployment and worklessness. Income and wealth inequality have soared, with runaway rewards for those at the top. Social democracy has appeared increasingly defensive in the face of these changes fuelling cynicism and disengagement from politics itself.
- Another claim is that social democrats have to recognise the limits of the European Union as a form of economic and political co-ordination. The drive towards further economic integration since the 1950s has hardly protected EU member states from the impact of globalisation and industrial restructuring. Many traditional social democratic voters are increasingly sceptical about the EU, which appears far removed from the political realities of national politics. Europe lacks a political anchor, and the gap between institutions and citizens has grown wider since the advent of the single market and the Euro. The Greek sovereign debt crisis has also heightened fears about the sustainability of monetary union. European integration was tolerated during a period of rapid economic growth and high employment. However, the EU appears to offer precious little reassurance in the aftermath of the financial crisis. It may indeed be the moment to rehabilitate the nation-state as the decisive agent of social democratic reform.
- This is combined with growing scepticism about the egalitarian potential of education reform. The centre-left has increasingly accorded education and investment in human capital central status within its economic and social policy. But this utopian reverence

for education has further alienated social democracy from its traditional support base. Investment in education would increase efficiency by expanding the productive potential of the economy, and advance social justice by nurturing talent regardless of background or circumstance. These expectations have been dashed, however, as the class divide remains intact in many European countries. In fact, social mobility has improved markedly little since the late 1950s, despite significant state-led investment in school-based education and post-16 learning.[22] In the meantime, the Asian economies have fuelled an educational and technological revolution, producing increasing numbers of highly competent and skilled graduates, particularly in science and mathematics. As Asia moves rapidly up the economic value chain, Europe will increasingly struggle to compete in the global economic race.

- At the same time, social democrats have to acknowledge the turn towards socially conservative values and beliefs in post-materialist Western societies. After the late 1960s, social liberalism was in the ascendency across Europe, but there is now increasing evidence of respect for more traditional ways of life including the importance of religious faith, marriage and the dual-parent family, the ties of neighbourhood and community, and nationhood and belonging. It is social democratic voters who have become sceptical of lifestyle individualism, and who are most concerned about diversity in the absence of strong pillars of solidarity and social cohesion. This includes the vexed question of ethnic diversity and the sustainability of an open immigration policy.
- Finally, the centre-left has yet to deal with the challenges of integration in the face of large-scale migration and labour market mobility. Weak integration results in marginalised minority communities, particularly 'pariah' Muslim groups who resent the majority population,[23] itself increasingly aggrieved at the loss of traditional identity. This amplifies fears among the native population about not only the dilution of national symbols of belonging and nationhood, but also the impact of immigration on living standards, employment and social welfare.

The neo-revisionist case outlined above is analytically wide-ranging and admirably perceptive about the structural dilemmas that social democratic parties across Europe now face. Centre-left politics has long been predicated on a model of inclusive economic growth and fairness in the structure of the wage distribution that would protect the interests of its skilled, blue-collar constituency. It was confidently assumed that the rising tide of economic prosperity would lift all boats. But rapid technological and economic change, combined with global market competition, has destroyed the founding premise of that model. The new growth theory initially pioneered in the United States has restricted government's role to supply-side investment in human capital, infrastructure and Research and Development.[24] The balance between manufacturing and the service-orientated economy was expected to shift inexorably in favour of the latter.

The new growth model accepted many of the foundational assumptions of economic liberalism that were destroyed by the financial crisis. But it was under severe pressure well before the shocks that hit the world economy with such force in 2008–9. The result has been an Anglo-American economy where real wages have grown less than personal debt, reflecting the squeeze on living standards. The latest ILO report on global wages, for example, shows that wage-levels in the industrialised countries declined by 0.6% in 2009.[25]

Overall, wage share as a proportion of national income has declined sharply since 1980 in the EU15, Japan and the United States, implying that average wages have failed to keep pace with labour productivity, as Figure 1.1 underlines below. In 17 out of 20 countries in the survey, earnings at the top of the wage distribution rose sharply relative to those at the bottom after the early 1990s. There is also evidence of higher levels of income volatility and wage instability in the major industrialised countries.[26] This is graphically illustrated by the American economist Jacob Hacker in his recent work *The Great Risk Shift.*[27]

Neo-revisionist ideas seek to address defining issues of income and wealth distribution in the light of globalisation and major structural changes in the world economy. At the same time, they acknowledge that for all the economic and cultural benefits of liberal cosmopolitanism and diversity, rapid migration has led to strains and

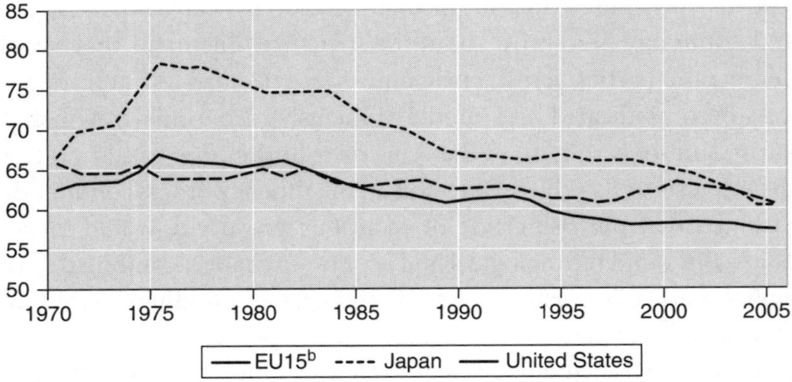

FIGURE 1.1 Wage share as a percentage of national income in EU15, Japan and the United States (1970–2005)[28]

tensions within the fabric of Western societies that were not previously anticipated. And the neo-revisionist emphasis on the promotion of solidarity and reciprocity goes with the grain of apparent residual support among Western electorates for welfare universalism and the strong social safety net.

Neo-revisionism does not explicitly reject 'third way' social democracy, but it does identify serious flaws in the modernisation strategies that developed with increasing vigour in the 1990s. Many of these criticisms are well founded, but neither modernisers nor traditionalists are well placed to resolve the current crisis of European social democracy. For all its originality and willingness to challenge emergent orthodoxies, neo-revisionist writing evokes the politics of nostalgia rather than engaging directly with the changing realities of global and domestic politics. It is quite legitimate to challenge the emphasis within the third way on the discontinuity wrought by globalisation and the economic and communications revolution since the early 1990s. The danger, however, is that genuine transformation is significantly underplayed or rarely acknowledged.

There are major challenges to nation-state social democracy in the industrialised countries relating to citizenship disengagement, weakening of governmental accountability, and the rise of complexity created by technology and new forms of knowledge.[29] Taking each in turn, interest in electoral politics has diminished exponentially in Europe and the United States over the last 60 years, weakening the class base of social democracy and leading to declining participation in the formal political system. The capacity of national governments to deliver for citizens has also weakened, and many actors such as markets and networks are increasingly outside the control of the state. Finally, complexity threatens the basis of participative politics, removing many decisions from deliberative engagement by resorting to technocratic expertise, pulling citizens and politicians further apart. If national democracies are increasingly neither representative, responsible nor participative, the development of a cosmopolitan, transnational, global polity appears ever more remote.[30]

This raises serious dilemmas for centre-left politics. Social democrats have always perceived themselves to be essentially progressive, on the side of radical political change. But electorates increasingly view centre-left parties across Europe as rather more 'conservative', associated with the preservation of the status quo. The basic concern of left parties is perceived to be the defence of current privileges, shielding insiders from any move to restructure existing social rights.

At the same time, the various social democratic modernisation strategies that emerged in Europe were a legitimate, if incomplete, attempt to face up to changing strategic realities on the left. In the halcyon days of the post-war social democratic state, the foundations of the centre-left's power were the nation-state, a relatively homogenous working-class base and a benign international framework. All of those foundations were steadily undermined in the post-war years, and now lie in tatters. The basic strategic paradigm of social democracy has been gradually weakening since the late 1970s. Of course, social democrats have worked to rebuild the enabling capacities of the state, while struggling to come to terms with the changing composition of their electoral base. The imperative of international leadership and co-ordination of policy at European and global levels has also been acknowledged.

But the drive to modernise social democracy has to extend far more widely, addressing fundamental dilemmas. Many of the institutional arrangements and political certainties of the post-war world have been drastically undermined.[31] The fate of centre-left politics will increasingly depend on how it responds to the three great post-crisis challenges: how institutions are adapted to accommodate the changing role of women in society; how effectively children and young people are prepared for the challenges of the knowledge economy; and how social democracy responds to new demographic trends and an ageing society. There is little to be gained simply by retreating to the tried and tested methods of post-war, egalitarian social democracy.

The Limits of Revisionist Social Democracy

If neo-revisionism is an important but inadequate basis for thinking seriously about the future of social democracy, this applies to the revisionist tradition as a whole. Modernisers emphasise the importance of revisionist strategies that compel progressive parties to reconsider the efficacy of particular policy approaches. There are, however, three central flaws in the revisionist framework of social democracy.

The first is superficiality: adapting policies in the light of changing circumstances still leaves many fundamental assumptions untouched. Revisionism, at the same time, inevitably entails jettisoning obsolete programmatic commitments and ideological identities, but it may leave social democratic parties without a coherent guiding purpose. Finally, revisionist social democracy has concentrated on the reformulation of policy programmes, rather than revising and renewing ultimate ends, the enduring values of centre-left politics. But this remains the great challenge for the contemporary left.

There has been a strong revisionist tradition on the European left for at least two centuries, led by reformist thinkers such as Bernstein and Kautsky. Social democracy is envisaged not as a fixed doctrine, but as a constant process of adapting means in the light of changing circumstances. There are close similarities to the model of second and third order changes outlined by Peter Hall. In fact, revisionism has influenced each of the traditionalist, modernising and liberalising strands of European social democracy since the early 1990s.

The claims of reformism have foundered, however, and revisionist social democracy is under renewed challenge. In part, the values that inspired the 'golden age' of post-war social democracy are increasingly contested, both on the right and on the left. The debate about the relationship between the values of equality and solidarity illustrates the point. The goal of economic egalitarianism was eagerly embraced by social democrats in the 1950s and 1960s, as redistribution offered a clearer route to the just society than nationalisation of the means of production. The traditional socialist concern with public ownership and the share of productive assets held outside the hands of private capital was superseded by an emphasis on welfare universalism, strong social services, redistribution through a progressive system of taxation and so on.

The structural context in which the value of equality is to be interpreted, however, has changed beyond all recognition in the last 50 years. For example, women are now the majority of the workforce across Western Europe. Absolute poverty among those in employment has largely been eradicated, but there is still a significant gender pay gap, and young families often struggle to reconcile the pressures of work and care. At the same time, there is evidence that greater diversity of culture and ethnicity erodes support for reciprocity and collectivism through the welfare state and contributory social insurance, albeit vigorously contested.[32] Then there is the fragmentation of state capacity and the emergence of new forms of governance. The central tenets of the post-war, egalitarian, social democratic settlement seem increasingly imperilled.

It is hardly surprising that in this new structural context, overarching and universal egalitarian principles are increasingly difficult to sustain. Social democrats certainly need to carefully consider this possibility, as the political theorist John Gray has elaborated.[33] The norms of fairness and equity still have political purchase, but need to be treated as locally specific and contextual.

One important dimension of egalitarian politics is the language and value of 'fairness'. This was once held to be a clear and succinct expression of political faith, but fairness has since become a hotly contested political ideal. There is increasing interest in the notion of a fairness code, although the implications have yet to be clearly spelt out. This emphasises the rejection of passive citizenship rights, underlining the reciprocity of entitlements and duties as central to the legitimacy of collective provision.[34] What is clear is that egalitarian social democracy will not be reconstituted as it was 30 years ago.

A host of other strategic challenges confront centre-left politics that further invalidate past normative approaches. The list is a formidable one: climate change, nuclear proliferation, global financial instability, migration and demographic change, the rebalancing of the global economy away from Europe and America, the persistence of global inequality. These make past programmatic and ideological commitments appear quite inadequate.

The task ahead is to think seriously about the fundamental nature of economic and political power, the relationship between state capacity and social democracy, and the durability of politics itself in an age of greater cynicism and disengagement. Strategically, social democracy has to become a movement of the future again. If it is to develop radicalising energy and élan, social democrats have to revisit, and if necessary tear up, many previously cherished assumptions and beliefs. They need to elaborate a coherent guiding purpose that aligns their political strategy with a credible governing approach.

British Politics and Thatcherism

In this respect, it is worth briefly considering the British Labour Party's response to Thatcherism after 1979. The left in Britain was confused and unsettled by the advent of Thatcherite Conservatism. The party refused to address why a significant segment of working-class support defected to the Conservative Party. The strategies of monetarism and welfare state retrenchment diminished the living standards of those on middle and lower incomes. Electoral opinion surveys conducted during the 1980s and early 1990s indicated that the electorate remained sympathetic to the traditional social democratic priorities of welfare, full employment and redistribution. Yet the Conservatives under Margaret Thatcher and John Major achieved four consecutive election victories in 1979, 1983, 1987 and 1992. Late twentieth-century British politics was dominated by the centre-right.

The reasons for their electoral dominance run deep, but one powerful factor is that the Conservative Party had a far clearer sense of the epochal changes sweeping the world, namely the break-up of the old post-war settlement and the emergence of a more variegated and fragmented society. Thatcherism sought to appropriate this new world of technological and economic change. The collective identities forged through the traditional institutions of work and factory, the trade unions, neighbourhood and community were in rapid decline. Of course, new electoral constituencies subsequently emerged that paved the way for the New Labour hegemony of the 1990s; but Labour's recovery was laborious and unsteady.

The Conservatives had successfully aligned themselves with all of the prolific growth sectors in the British economy including the City of London and the burgeoning financial sector. This was complemented by the strong emphasis on law-and-order policies, stressing their cultural attachment to the traditional values of family, duty, patriotism and nationhood.

As such, the right in Britain mobilised what Andrew Gamble has described as the free economy and the strong state.[35] The success of Thatcherism did not lie in the immediate popularity of its programme, but its ability to command the cultural landscape of Britain. The Conservative Party was poised to shape the future, rejecting the politics of national decline. The right's governing approach was far from uncontested, and there was strong commitment to the ideals of public service and recognition of a society based on reciprocal obligations, with protection for the most vulnerable. But the Conservatives were able to bequeath not just a policy and institutional legacy. They drove a cultural shift in the nature of British society as the basis for an election-winning strategy.

The New Social Democratic Reckoning

Future generations of social democrats across Europe ought to recognise the potency of the Thatcherite approach. The most enduring threat faced by the left is not only to be perceived as an incompetent manager of the economy, but to be out of touch with major cultural advances and the contemporary zeitgeist. There is an immediate danger that much of the momentum in global progressive politics will come from Green parties and the anti-capitalist movement, with social democracy relegated to the status of yesterday's ideology.

The shape of the world economy, of course, remains paramount. Across Europe, escalating national debt and budget deficits are at the centre of political debate. All countries are restructuring their finances and making sharp fiscal adjustments. The average budget deficit in the Euro-zone as a proportion of GDP, for example, stands at nearly 7%.[36] The reputation of social democracy as a strong custodian of fiscal discipline and economic stability has to be quickly restored.

Social democrats need to demonstrate that they are capable of managing public expenditure competently, reining in a whole sweep of public sector activity. This is not a process of incremental 'salami slicing' across different areas of government activity. It means rethinking the role and purpose of the state itself, while elaborating how the marriage of economic efficiency and social justice might be sustained. This includes new ways to define the public realm and the public interest, rediscovering the internationalist world-view that was the hallmark of social democracy at the turn of the twentieth century.

Political Economy and the Common Good

The unprecedented economic turbulence of 2008–9 has torn up many cherished ideas that have guided policy since the late 1970s. While neo-liberalism has been discredited, no systematic, progressive, social democratic alternative has yet emerged. Developing a new growth strategy in the context of a deep global recession is unlikely to be straightforward. The emphasis needs to shift towards developing a political economy model which is both resilient and capable of sustaining the common good.

This should include rebalancing the economy, addressing the distribution of power within different sectors, and nurturing new jobs and industries. It means addressing power imbalances between management and workers by reforming corporate governance models, as envisaged in earlier thinking about the stakeholder economy.[37] That relationship will determine whether public or private organisations are vibrant, dynamic and productive. This is the moment historically to cast aside orthodox constraints and guiding assumptions about the future direction of economic policy.

That also has to mean addressing the distribution of assets and wealth in the economy. The Swedish Meidner Plan, for example, provides important programmatic inspiration when few workers have an adequate stake in the modern productive economy. It includes a proposal to invest union pension funds in the stock market, making the distribution of ownership fairer and encouraging long-term investment in the productive capacity of the economy. Most importantly, the Swedish workforce would gradually acquire a substantial, collectively owned asset stake. The plan has never been implemented due to strong opposition among the private sector in Sweden. But social democrats need radical approaches of this kind to inform their political economy approach.

The inevitable focus on rising economic inequality is centrally important, but across the industrialised world, economic instability is also rising at a rapid rate. This refers to growing income volatility which is a product both of increased labour market insecurity and a weakening in the framework of economic protection. It afflicts those on middle-incomes as well as the poor and unskilled. The workforce as a whole has grown richer since the 1970s, but is prey to greater risk at the mercy of the global economic roller coaster.

Social democrats need to mould new risk-pooling institutions, from unemployment insurance and state-backed pensions to family-leave provisions and universal savings accounts. They should recognise that individuals will only be capable of participating fully in the economy and society, taking risks and looking to the future, where they are protected against misfortune, able to access the basic foundations of financial security.[38]

In recent decades, the centre-left focused on the assets, skills and human capital investment available to the workforce, as the cornerstone of new growth theory. This approach neglected the importance of economic institutions, however, and the values and ethos which are transmitted to the wider economy. Institution building is essential to rebalance national economies and achieve greater co-ordination, with the aim of breaking out of the low-wage, low-skill, low-productivity equilibrium that has produced wage stagnation across much of the industrialised world.

This should not imply that regulated competitive markets ought to be discarded by social democrats. For one, markets are necessary for growth and help to generate tax revenues, which are invested in public services and social goods. There is evidence that social mobility and opportunity would be weaker in centrally planned rather than market-based economies, as John Kay has described in his account of disciplined pluralism.[39] Social democrats ought to favour market competition within a clear framework of public interest principles and regulated norms of responsibility and trust.

Social Democracy and State Power

The most profound shift in thinking that needs to be undertaken by social democrats, however, relates to their conception of state power. After the financial crisis, it was widely seen as legitimate to undertake strong government intervention, stabilising the banking system, supporting the wider economy and protecting citizens from global economic storms. At the same time, the state continues to play a major role in socio-economic affairs.[40] It is far from clear, however, that the state is back as a major actor in the world economy. In part, citizens are concerned about the encroachment of centralised bureaucracy and its damaging effect on productivity and growth. At the same time, globalisation partially erodes the steering capacities of the nation-state. As a result, the role of the state has never been more contested.

The debate about the scope and scale of the state cannot be considered in isolation from other social institutions, namely markets and the private domain of the family. In fact, three pillars determine the shape of the economy and social welfare: not only the state, but the strength of markets and the extent of the familial domain. The real world of welfare is determined by how the three pillars interact (Esping-Anderson, 2009). The central question concerns which institution is most capable of fulfilling socially desirable responsibilities and duties, without producing adverse trade-offs between equity and efficiency. In other words, if the state shrinks back, the family or markets must be capable of stepping in to fill the void.

Of course, social democrats have a traditional preference for collective remedies based on state power. They distrust market-based institutions and tend to regard the family as inequitable. But now a critical approach to government's role is urgent and necessary. The state needs to have very specific and effective steering capacities if it is to contribute to public value, at a time of intense pressure stemming from the financial crisis, as well as long-term technological and demographic change.

The assumption that the goal of social democracy is to win power over the central state, using it to build society from the top down, is untenable. This has encouraged politicians to claim and promise too much, especially when they increasingly lack an effective grip on the levers given the dispersion of power and the emergence of multi-level governance. It will lead to often violent swings between unrealistic hope and unfounded disillusionment.

Achieving state power, of course, remains an important objective for social democratic parties. What is needed is a politics that is able to face up to intractable dilemmas and trade-offs, acknowledging the complexity of problems in a way that engages citizens. In his recent work, Anthony Giddens has encapsulated this point well:

> Our civilisation could self-destruct – no doubt about it – and with awesome consequences. Doomsday is no longer a religious concept, a day of spiritual reckoning, but a possibility imminent in our society and economy [. . .]. No wonder many take fright. Let's go back! Let's return to a simpler world! They are entirely understandable sentiments and have practical application in some contexts. Yet there can be no overall going back – the very expansion of human power that has created such deep problems is the only means of resolving them, with science and technology at the forefront.[41]

Social democrats must show far greater capacity for ceaseless renewal and reinvention. The historian Tony Judt has made a powerful case for the preservation of existing social citizenship rights gained over the course of the twentieth century. This is an essentially defensive approach to safeguarding the accomplishments of post-war social democracy. The next generation of centre-left politics cannot simply retreat to a defence of the traditional welfare state, not least because it would leave untouched a vast array of injustices and new social needs.

In the future, parties that are both electorally successful and governmentally competent will be capable of seizing the agenda, driving new forms of institutional innovation and devising new mechanisms through which such strategies might be implemented. This will occur against the backdrop of unprecedented shocks to the global economy, the changing nature of social citizenship and threats to the very survival of the planet. It will demand a new relationship between state and citizen which is neither laissez-faire nor paternalist.

This also has to mean ceasing to conflate collective action with state power, finding alternative approaches to promoting the public interest and delivering public goods. The state's role in relation to the market and civil society has to be redefined, rebuilding state capacity to deal with the fragmentation of governance since the late 1970s without reproducing the deficiencies of hierarchical, state-centric social democracy.

The emancipatory politics of democratic engagement and solidarity building has to be seized by the centre-left. Widening and deepening democracy through an extension of Proportional Representation (PR) in electoral systems, for example, ought to be fundamental. Protecting citizens from arbitrary abuse by state and market power is equally imperative. Governments have to be responsive and accountable, rather than promulgating a 'take it or leave it' culture. This chapter has emphasised that there is a rich inheritance of ideologies, institutions and ideas on which to draw. Most powerfully, this includes the European republican tradition which emphasises the autonomy of citizens, and the imperative of dispersing power as widely as possible.

Giving people real control and responsibility, as well as breaking with the commitment to centralised government, should be the test of the social democratic society. The centre-left has traditionally focused on reforms of the market and the state, paying too little attention to the vibrancy of the civic sphere. This should be combined with a new model of political economy, as well as a renewed commitment to internationalism, involving real engagement in global and world politics.

The aim of social democracy ought to remain the long-term transformation of society. But this will only be attainable if social democrats engage in serious strategic debate about the scope and scale of the state, and the nature of economic and political power. The ultimate purpose is to forge an enduring social democratic politics for the global age, aligning renewed electoral success with credible strategies for governing in the name of a fairer, more equal society.

CHAPTER 2

Social Democracy in a Global Era

Luke Martell

In the triumvirate of capital, labour and state, capital has long been a problem for the other two. Social Democracy has historically represented labour, especially in the UK where the Labour Party was born out of the trade union movement, and used the state as an agency to achieve its aims. But social democratic goals of redistribution and regulation are often not in the interests of capital, or not seen to be. And capital has pressured social democratic governments to restrain policies that involve such ends.

From the 1970s onwards capital's power has grown. Increased its power of exit as well as its voice. It can threaten social democrats that it will leave the country if governments pursue policies too much against its interests. This has been facilitated by political and technological changes that have expanded the possibility of capital flight. Relaxed regulations on the movement of capital and developments in information technology make it easier to move huge amounts of money in and out of countries very quickly. Governments that want to ensure a buoyant economy with investment, jobs and revenue they can tax to support welfare and public services are under pressure to moderate egalitarian and welfarist policies and acquiesce to capital to make sure it stays in the country. States compete with one another to offer the policies most amenable to capital to tempt it to come to them. Such policies tend to be neoliberal. A number of consequences follow: competition amongst states; preferences for neo-liberal over social democratic policies; convergence as states orient around the same sort of neo-liberal policies to attract capital; and an erosion of democracy as governments make policy choices in response to the wants of unaccountable capital rather than the voters who elect them. For some this involves a 'race to the bottom' – low taxes, weak regulations to protect labour and wages, a reduction in welfare and public services funded by tax, a rolling-back of redistributional policies, and restrictions on reflationary economics which are seen to damage financial confidence and deter investors. In short, a reduction to a lot of what defines social democracy, and the least social provision possible in order to persuade businesses that a low-cost location is being provided for them.

Global Capital and National Social Democracy

There is no doubt that capital, and increases in the possibility of capital mobility, put strong pressures on governments who want to pursue social democratic policies. This pressure should not be underestimated, but it can be exaggerated and there are reasons to believe there is space for national social democracy. For some on the right and centre-left it has become common sense that social democracy has to adapt to a politics of low taxes, limited redistribution, prudent public spending, a more marketised public sector and deregulation. But the argument does not stand up as well as at first it seems.[1]

It is important to test theories against empirical evidence, and the argument that social democracy requires modernisation in the face of globalisation – which means moving away from historical forms of social democracy – is less powerful when you look at what actually happens.

There are some very globalised countries in the world where classical tenets of social democracy continue very well. Countries such as Sweden, Germany and France may be vulnerable to the movement of capital abroad but maintain bigger welfare states, higher rates of tax and social spending, less inequality, stronger trade unions, and stronger cultures of respect for the state and public sector than their European counterparts and the USA. Yet they do not suffer major losses of capital overseas, and their economic performance is comparable to and, in some respects, better than that of countries with more neo-liberal policies like the US and UK. Not only do they maintain social democratic institutions and retain capital, they have some of the best standards of living in the world. Such countries also run up deficits without damaging financial confidence. Where governments are cautious about inflation and deficits there is often less reluctance about increasing social spending and the taxation needed to support it.

Beyond Europe, countries like Argentina and Venezuela have defaulted on loans, nationalised major companies or had substantial programmes of social spending, often talked up with left-wing anti-globalist rhetoric, yet attracted large amounts of foreign investment from countries like the US. In these European and Latin American countries, globalisation is overridden by domestic cultures and politics that support more social democratic policies. Furthermore, states in these regions have things that are attractive to mobile capital – education and infrastructures of health and social support which reduce costs for business, advanced technology, skilled workers, consumer markets, networks of suppliers and so on.

Exposure to the global economy – whether through reliance on external investment and finance, integration into networks of imports and exports or the involvement of multinational corporations – may lead electorates to call for more, not less, social democracy, to provide compensation for the social effects of globalisation. These effects include instability, insecurity and the potential risk of heavy shocks such as the global financial crisis. Here state intervention is needed economically to bail out capitalism, regulation to guard against phenomena like undue risk taking and support for people who suffer the social effects such as unemployment.

Having a healthy social infrastructure is not just good for people feeling the effects of globalisation. It is good for businesses looking to harness its advantages for their own gain. Investment in education and training, in health, social support for those unskilled, excluded or unemployed are all beneficial for companies. They ensure a skilled, healthy workforce, provided by the state, and take away the need for direct provision of such infrastructure by businesses themselves. In addition, such policies boost employment and so also tax revenues, which is good for social democracy that relies on tax for public spending.

Amongst rich country lefts there is much that is social democratic that can be done in a context of mobile capital. But many of the attractions mentioned are less possible in developing countries, especially those in the lowest tiers. There is less to offer and so the pressure to pursue neo-liberal policies to attract investment is much stronger there. For social democracy, this means there is a need for international solidarity across the global left. Social democrats in richer countries should build links with the left globally to support social democracy in poorer places. Internationalism, which used to be central to left thinking, is now more out of the picture, and behind the globalism of capital. Social democracy needs to be more international. But, as we shall see, this does not necessarily mean global politics at central institutional levels. So, the theory of mobile capital eclipsing social democracy seems plausible but, in better-off countries, fails empirical tests. Yet as Bourdieu has argued, this understanding has become common sense for both the right and the centre-left, such that anyone who argues against this perspective is seen to be out of touch, unable to 'get real' and be forward-looking.[2]

There has been a shift from a belief in a mixed economy, markets alongside welfare, redistribution and Keynesian economics to a view that sees these as no longer feasible under conditions of globalisation, or even that desirable. This model of new, modernised social democracy is typically one of more markets and private provision in the public sector, and deregulation, with inclusion of the worst-off in society replacing egalitarianism as a goal. The distinction between new social democracy and the new right becomes less a qualitative one and more an issue of the degree and extent of neo-liberalism rather than the questioning of it. What marks social democracy off as distinctive – equality, regulation, public welfare and reflationary economics – is eroded and space for a mainstream alternative to neo-liberalism begins to look empty of occupants. Globalisation is an external justification for this.

Global Social Democracy

But even if there is scope for social democracy at the national level, there are still reasons why it should be pursued internationally. The question is, how? Is there space for social democracy globally, to unite with the left in other parts of the world beyond the UK and Europe, and in global political institutions where international problems such as economic regulation and climate change can be tackled?

Global problems like international economic instability, inequality between the 'global North and South', and climate change require global political solutions. Citizenship, constitutional power and democracy are based at national levels yet national governments are increasingly incapable of tackling such problems alone. It is argued that global levels are where governance needs to operate. Consequently such features of democracy need to be moved from national to global institutions. From this perspective, we need inclusive global governance organisations, like the UN, perhaps combining those that currently exist in fragmentary form, from the UN to the World Bank and IMF. Global fora could be composed of all national actors, given formal global constitutional status, with lines of democracy and even citizenship. It is at this level that effective decisions on global problems of insecurity, inequality and environment can be made.[3]

Given its historical role as an egalitarian and regulatory politics, social democrats should play no small part in this, and they need to make sure that their beliefs achieve majority or hegemonic status in such institutions. To do this it is argued that social democrats have to shed their attachment to change purely at and through the national level. Regulation for social ends, greater equality, social welfare and stimulus economics are good nationally so should also be good globally. Responsibility to others should not extend just to our nearest and dearest but to humans across the world. There is nothing in social democracy that requires charity to be confined to the home.

However, we should also ask whether the most effective way to achieve social democratic *values* at a global level is through social democratic *politics* at a global level.

Are there social and cultural bases for global social democracy? Social democratic values are long-standing, and have become mainstream in many places, beyond social democratic parties – the importance of state welfare, health and education, a belief in greater equality, and the need to regulate, for instance, unaccountable finance. British Social Attitudes surveys show that such values survived in Britain through the neo-liberal Thatcher years. Moreover, for the elected left to maintain power and enact policies, a major shift to left values across the public does not seem essential. An image of Latin America in recent years is of a region through which a wave of leftism has spread. But left parties there have pulled on non-left as much as left values amongst the public.[4] Many who support the left are not of the left, but vote for it because it seems competent and effective and delivers policies that tackle problems like poverty. So there is a social basis for social democracy, consisting of values of traditional social democracy, and support that can be won across the board by political effectiveness.

But are there social or cultural bases for a *global* social democracy? World values surveys indicate few people hold global, cosmopolitan values. They identify with local or national identities more frequently than global identities or with those more distant from themselves.[5] Attitudes to immigration in rich countries are frequently hostile in a way that is out of touch with evidence on its positive benefits.[6] Social democratic politicians foster this prejudice when they attribute problems such as housing shortages or low wages to immigration, rather than to social democratic concerns such as the rundown of state housing or weak labour protection. The cultural basis for social democracy may be holding up but it is less clear what cultural basis there is for a more globalist and cosmopolitan form of this.

Even if there were a worldwide cultural basis for more global and cosmopolitan governance, this might well not be replicated in politicians' behaviour. Attempts at inclusive, formal, institutionalised global politics often break down over the competing material interests of different states, or result in agreements which are effectively unbinding and not honoured. This happens in talks on world trade, climate change, debt relief and nuclear proliferation in fora such as WTO talks, COP15, the G8 and the Nuclear Non-proliferation Treaty. Furthermore, some states in such fora have far more influence – even if formally all are equal – and can counter globally or social democratically minded policies. The US and China, for instance, wield much greater power in world trade and climate change talks than most other nations.

For global politics to take a social democratic direction there would have to be a coinciding of social democrats in a majority of states across the world, or of agencies willing to put forward social democratic norms in global institutions. For Andrew Gamble, social democrats have to ensure 'that the global polity, and not just the national polity, is governed by social democratic values and norms'.[7] But this prescription is made in a context in which social democrats find it hard to get into national governments, let alone many at once in global governance. When they do manage to be elected, they find it difficult to deliver social democratic programmes because of internal battles, revisionism away from social democratic values, electoral pressures and perceived external constraints.

Even in a restricted transnational forum such as the regional EU, the dream of national social democratic parties in power simultaneously has rarely occurred. When it did in the late 1990s, social democrats spent much of their energy facilitating a more economically liberal union rather than a 'social Europe'.

From the 1980s on, social democratic parties in Europe began to converge around more market-friendly policies, the British Labour Party being slow to keep up and then, under Blair in the 1990s, overtaking the rest with its enthusiasm for deregulation and free markets. But despite a theoretically common ideological and programmatic logic, social democratic parties vary across Europe and globally, according to factors such as national traditions, economic pressures and political contexts. Responses to the financial crisis have stretched from Greek austerity to Obama's quantitative easing. Some in Latin America, such as Lula's Workers' Party in Brazil have had elements of a third way approach, whereas others are more like old social democratic parties of Europe, leaders like Chavez being anti-neo-liberal and in favour of nationalisation and redistribution. The Latin American left has come towards European social democracy, with a shift from revolutionary roads to greater acceptance of democracy, but European social democracy in return remains suspicious.

So, across social democracy there are divergences in ideology and interest that make unity difficult, and for this reason alliances need to be selective and sought where commonality exists, rather than inclusively and across all. A more realistic and, therefore, more productive international social democracy, then, would be one where international social democrats form alliances with other social democratic and left parties and movements across the world when they share common aims. This moves away from all-inclusive, institutionalised, global fora where it would be hard to build a majority with a social democratic ideology which could be sustained against powerful opposition from other actors and from within.

There could have been hopes that the election of Obama, espousing interventionism and government action as answers to the global economic crisis, would inspire centre-left parties more globally. By rejecting American unilateralism in favour of more multilateral approaches, a global social democratic approach could have appeared more realisable. Any such hopes were not borne out. Obama's focus was often on domestic challenges – the deficit and recession in the USA and health care reform. He pursued social democratic routes, a reflationary approach to the economy and greater universalisation of health care, but on a domestic rather than international front. Obama held out the hope of bilateralism at home and multilateralism, instead of hard power, abroad. But the Republicans didn't play ball with bilateralism. And multilateralism was as much about security issues as pursuing social democracy. While the US made progress on nuclear disarmament with Russia, states such as North Korea and Iran did not respond to the hand of friendship with agreements to counter nuclear proliferation. Copenhagen was not a success for multilateralism and the old ally Israel was unwilling to do what was asked to secure peace in the Middle East. Obama may well have been too hopeful about overcoming fundamental conflicts of ideology and interest, so pointing to the need for more selective alliances where you can get them, with those like-minded and with interests in common.

Social Democracy in International Politics

Formal global governance, inclusive and top-down, allows for multiple clashes of interest. Consequently, a conflict understanding of politics is as good a route for social democracy as a dialogical approach that aims for agreement at a central, global level. Conflict-based approaches recognise clashing material interests, inequality and power.

They are compatible with participation in central, global institutions, but on the basis that social democratic ends will have to be pursued against opposed forces that have anti-social, democratic objectives and power, as much as through agreement between actors who have contradictory interests.

There are often not effective means for enforcing of policies above national levels. Equally effective for pursuing social democratic goals is building up from existing initiatives, from national laws that can be enforced more easily and bilateral agreements on social democratic policies where there are fewer parties involved, so more chance of things being achieved. In addition, the other side of competition between conflicting interests is collaboration in selected alliances with actors who are like-minded and have similar interests. This is below-global but still international, because it involves reaching out beyond nations to wider links, if not inclusion of all. It is bottom-up – alliances with the like-minded lower down rather than everyone at a global level. It is not inclusive. You ally just with those you can get agreement with. Leaders of the Latin American left have tried such an approach. International social democracy requires finding lefts where they are and building links between them, a global left rather than global government.

Bottom-up internationalism begins with local and national activities and generalises up to the global level, rather than creating global deals in an impossible situation of inclusive, conflicting interests and going down from there.

The former includes civil society. Global justice movements have been important in pushing social issues onto the political agenda – for example, the exploitative practices of multinational corporations, third world debt and proposals for taxes on financial transactions. Greater engagement with social movements in civil society will require social democrats to reach back to their roots in the workers' and trade unions movements and crossways to places like Latin America where the left has social movement bases such as trade unions and movements around indigenous people's rights.

At the same time, the state is an important part of the traditions of social democracy. An anti-statist approach which leaves everything to civil society will endanger social democratic concerns such as equality and wider collectivism. The state can be overarching and for the collective good of the people, taking into account needs not met by the market and redistributional questions. Handing state activities to civil society means that people have to look after themselves through voluntary associations when sometimes it is good for the government, democratically accountable with collective goals, to help rather than leave people to it alone. Some people want a democratic government to provide equality and security. An associational society needs mechanisms to maintain equality and collective provision across it, and this involves central state government.

International social democracy needs to be multi-dimensional, operating at a number of levels below formal global institutions. It can also be experimental – building from initiatives already in play bottom-up, including from civil society, rather than from abstract agreements top-down which may not be tried or tested, and are often effectively unbinding. Examples of ideas or practices from below which are in tune with social democracy and have or can be acted on include: (a) forms of taxation to fund development, environment or the public sector, such as the Tobin or Robin Hood tax; (b) debt cancellation; (c) co-operative types of ownership; (d) examples of the regulation of markets in different states; (e) environmental and climate change initiatives which go beyond targets and involve actual practices such as electrical vehicle and turbine innovations, deforestation and solar power developments; (f) social programmes like Lula's *Bolsa familia* in Brazil and Chavez's missions in Venezuela; and (g) minimum, social or living wage ideas. These have emerged from civil society, the private sector, social movements and states, not global governance.

Global institutions, then, may not always be the most effective means for globally minded social democracy. However, being sceptical about global institutions for social democracy does not mean scepticism about globalist social democratic ends, such as international equality and responsibility and global issues to do with the economy and environment. The development of world capitalism calls out for a global social democracy in ends, pursued through below-global means.

The Content of New Social Democracy

If social democracy is possible, nationally and internationally, in a globalised era, what should it be about? New social democrats argue that social democracy has lost its ideological direction. It is hooked on outdated ways of thinking and needs to renew its ideas in order to be applicable to the important issues of the day. Central to this is open-mindedness about the interpenetration of market and state, including the role of the market in rejuvenating the state and public sector. This follows the third way's emphasis on balancing economic efficiency with social justice, rather than valuing the latter over the former, and seeing the market and state as not opposed but increasingly difficult to differentiate, the market being needed to shake up and revive the public sector, the traditional concern for social democracy.

But social democracy's emphasis should not be on allowing the market into the state. It should be on regulating markets. Revisionist centre-left arguments about the role of the market are for a time when it was perceived that social democrats were too fixated on the state and dogmatically against the market. In fact social democrats have always been more anti-market in rhetoric than practice. Furthermore the time of anti-market dogmatism has passed and neo-liberalism has become the hegemony or common sense. In this context, talk should not be about balancing economic efficiency and social justice. This has become a given and the driving force is economic efficiency over social justice. What makes social democracy distinctive from liberalism and conservatism has been its emphasis on regulating the market. Now that the market has centre stage and is widely celebrated, the thrust of social democracy should be on regulation of markets by the state in pursuit of the public good, rather than on balancing state with market or allowing the market into the state.

Instead of mixing them up, social democracy needs to keep state and market separate. It should emphasise their distinct logics. It should keep under control the logic of the market (which is individualistic, inegalitarian and profit-driven) in favour of state logic, which, in social democratic hands, is about equality, social justice and human goals. It is sensible to see that the state is not always the best type of organisation, and that the market is often best for many areas of production and distribution. But it is also important ideologically to maintain boundaries between state and market so that the former can be seen as something that regulates and constrains the latter, and steps in where it is not the best form of organisation. Where boundaries between state and market are seen as very permeable, and breaking them down a virtue, the danger is that the market intrudes into areas of state activity, introducing inegalitarian dynamics and commercial criteria where the state became involved to promote equality and the collective good.

Take the case of UK higher education. Public funding from taxation is declining and private finance from students is increasing, a process that started with New Labour's introduction of student paid fees. A new breed of manager is being introduced, whose approach is authoritarian rather than consensual, and with a business rather than a public good perspective. Means and ends are being reversed: universities are changing from institutions that raise money to provide quality education for the collective good, into business machines where education is a commodity used to produce profit.

Areas of higher education are cut or expanded on economic rather than educational grounds, promoting inequality between universities, students, social classes, and management and employees. There is restructuring within universities, with directly commercial areas expanding and critical and humanistic areas under threat. The progressive incursion of the market and private consumer into UK higher education, rather than providing resources to enhance the public sector, is changing the meaning of education from the aim of the public good to private profit, with consequences for its structure and content.

Whilst it is important not to be dogmatic, there are dangers with making the boundaries between state and market too porous, so that the intrusion of market logic into the public sphere dilutes objectives of equality, regulation and community. New social democracy argues for deeper interpenetration of state and market and less distinct boundaries between them in the name of open thinking. But this runs the risk of eroding the distinctiveness of what social democracy is. The consequence is that as the historical actor occupying the mainstream political space in which equality and collective public institutions are advanced, and the market is regulated and restrained, this space is left empty. It does so in a context where the market and private sector are the norm, on the up and eroding collective and public values, exactly where social democracy is needed as an antidote. This is not an argument against open-minded thinking about the role of the market. But in the context of deregulation and the rise of neo-liberalism it is important to have a perspective that stresses where the market is limited and needs to be constrained and regulated.

If social democracy does not take on such a role in a post-Thatcherite, neo-liberal era, no-one else in the political sphere will. Those who want to defend the public good will have to take to the streets, which is what has happened in relation to the marketisation of UK further and higher education.

Nevertheless, in the case of the 2008 financial crisis, the problem was one of regulatory failure as well as lack of regulation. And there are myriad legal and illegal ways of avoiding regulation that companies and finance pursue. So, as well as defending regulation, social democracy needs to find better means of regulation. At the same time, a classic social democratic view is that government should go beyond regulation to the rebalancing of national economies through industrial policy. In countries like the UK, the economy has become reliant on finance and services to the detriment of manufacturing so that crises in the former impacted especially hard, leaving little else to fall back on. So facilitating markets and balancing them with regulation is not sufficient. Some type of planning is called for which evokes social democracy of old, but may need new thinking for changed circumstances and attitudes. Governments should not try to construct an economy, but they can try to compensate for risky imbalances through industrial strategy.

Social Democracy's Global Political Rudder

Social democracy has not so much lost its ideological rudder. If social democracy has gone astray somewhere, it is more accurate to say that it needs to find the right political rudder. As an ideology and practice, social democracy has a long history that has been successful in improving the conditions of working-class people. It has had a credible approach to government, part of building welfare capitalism. It remains more relevant than ever in a situation of rising inequality and lack of regulation of the economy.

The question is: what are the political bases and spaces for pursuing a regulatory and egalitarian social democracy, which must be more about the state and public good than about the market, or it loses what is distinctive about it and the values it aims to pursue, equality and the collective good over individualism?

The problem is a politics of support and government, as much as a new ideology for these. The question is not revising what ideologically demarcates social democracy from its alternatives in the name of modernisation; it is about finding the right places and alliances it can build social democracy from. Global levels offer some chances for this, but only some, heavily contested by more powerful forces. However, global left alliances offer chances that global government does not. National levels have not been swept away. And local initiatives on the ground offer existing bases that can be built upon.

One example where there is ideological insight but has been less political traction is the financial crisis. Lack of adequate financial regulation was part of the problem. As a historically regulatory politics, social democracy is well placed to bring in such an approach where it is needed, and where there has been a process, the financial crisis, that provides a basis for regulatory arguments. An ideological identity for social democracy is not lacking here, and it is not, in such circumstances, out of date. What have been missing are the political will, leverage, effective rules and cross-national co-ordination to implement this.

Another classic social democratic approach is reflation. Reflation worked towards saving capitalism during the financial crisis. Governments poured money into national economies to keep them afloat, while global regulation was bypassed. Ideological principles – reflation and regulation – are present and relevant, but the issue is the political will and spaces to carry them out. After neo-liberalism and the financial crisis, how is the ideology of equality and regulation out of touch and social democracy losing its way ideologically? The problem is not ideology but political leverage. Making the problem ideology takes us down a path that leads away from social democracy, what makes it distinctive and counters the right.

Governing strategy is in part about starting where social democracy is possible or working. This may be in civil society, with the state doing things for people, with the market and exploiting or regulating it, or with state provision and democratising it. Social democracy can seek initiatives which are being developed or work, which have a regulative or redistributional element to them, and work with them, maybe local initiatives being generalised or developed nationally or internationally. *Going downwards*, this involves looking for these in civil society, in associations and social movements (e.g. the Robin Hood tax which started with ideas in the ATTAC movement). *Going sideways*, it involves looking at other states and developing their ideas (e.g. from the Latin American left), or building links with them so policies can be carried out cross-nationally, limiting the possibilities for capital flight. *Looking upwards*, it involves fora at a global level where such initiatives can be slotted in, although, while such spaces and initiatives should be used where possible, contending and conflicting forces at this level make this a less propitious area for the development of policy. Internationally policy is best pursued with those most like-minded and co-operative where you can find them, rather than across a table with the more powerful who have diametrically opposed ideologies and interests.

Conclusion

Does globalisation mean that we need to construct a new and global social democracy? Globalisation, neo-liberalism and markets expanding into the state have not shown the need for reconstruction towards a new social democracy. They have shown the effectiveness of a reflationary approach, and the necessity of a regulatory, egalitarian social democracy oriented to the public good. Social democracy may need to think about how to do regulation effectively but not to discard the idea that it should be doing it. We need to go back to go to the future. If we do not, then important goals of equality and collectivism are lost, social democracy loses what makes it distinctive, and the political space which protects such values is left empty and without a political actor. Agents in civil society will have to take matters into their own hands.

And while globalisation has shown the importance of social democracy as an ideology, it has not shown social democracy in global governance to be the level where it should operate. Here the prospects for left success are dim, consisting of powers opposed to it, and unlikely prospects for social democratic power and unanimity coinciding across the world to make a majority. Under globalisation, the best prospects for social democracy are with building from experiments shown to work on the ground, at the national level where considerable leverage is still available and in the international collaboration of a global left between social democrats and other like-minded forces amongst governments, parties and social movements. Social democracy needs to seek out a global left more than global government.

CHAPTER 3

Debt and Deficits: The Quest for Economic Competence

Andrew Gamble

Economic competence is increasingly recognised as a vital component of political success, and political parties devote great effort to secure it. It has become one of the critical battlegrounds between political parties. Any viable political economy has to address a strategy for achieving it since if a government or a political party comes to be seen as economically incompetent its chances of holding on to power or winning elections are seriously diminished. Economic competence is not a fixed, tangible thing. It depends heavily upon perceptions, those of markets, media, politicians and citizens, and these arise in particular economic and political contexts, and are expressed through the narratives which form to make sense of them.

There are nevertheless some common elements which help define economic competence. As a minimum, it involves the ability of government to provide economic stability, security and opportunity for its citizens. The most important indicators of economic security are full employment, stable prices and effective public services, while the most important indicators of economic opportunity are economic growth and rising living standards. To earn a reputation for economic competence, national governments must show they can deliver these things for their citizens. However, governments operate not just within a national but an international context, and they must navigate the pressures of both. They have to decide on not just internal questions of the balance between state and market but external questions of the degree of openness of the national economy and the extent of its integration in the wider international economy.

National governments must therefore be aware of both the internal and external factors which help generate perceptions of economic competence, and link them together. They have to develop a credible external economic policy, a credible domestic stabilisation policy and a credible growth policy. This is what successful social democratic parties have done in the past and will need to do again.

Centre-Left Strategies for Achieving Economic Competence

There is no single blueprint for success in this respect. National circumstances are very different, and so are the contexts in which successful strategies have been developed. It is nevertheless possible to identify three principal strategies which have been followed on the centre-left for achieving economic competence during the last hundred years. The first is associated with planning, the second with welfare and the third with markets. All are social democratic in the sense that they have been employed by social democratic governments and have been aimed at advancing social democratic ends. Attempts to limit social democracy to one particular strategy have never been very rewarding or historically accurate. These three strategies have waxed and waned over the years, but they are not exclusive, and social democratic government programmes have always contained elements of all three. It is the mix that has varied.

For much of the twentieth century, social democrats became particularly associated with the first two strategies, and these have fuelled the image of the left as being associated with Big Government. In the last 20 years, however, social democratic parties have become much more associated with market strategies, particularly in the different variants of the third way. It is inaccurate to draw too sharp distinctions between these three strategies, however, or to suggest as is commonly done that only the first two strategies are social democratic, while the third is neo-liberal. All three are strategies for achieving the core social democratic aim of creating societies that are more equal in their distribution of wealth, income and opportunities and are best judged on results rather than on their conformity to principles. The opposite error is to suppose that market strategies are intrinsically better at delivering results and that all other strategies should be discarded. The evidence is very mixed on this.

Planning

The first strategy pursued by centre-left parties aimed at replacing the governance of the economy by bureaucratic rather than market co-ordination. It sought to replace market mechanisms by the application of direct controls and the public ownership of productive assets, on the grounds that markets were inefficient and wasteful, led to inequality and exploitation, and destroyed communities and social solidarity, for all of which there was an abundance of evidence from the experience of capitalism in the nineteenth century.

The enthusiasm for planning in the first half of the twentieth century was not only confined to the left, but also found many advocates on the right. Free market capitalism came to be regarded as anarchic and wasteful, unable to provide the kind of security and stability which was needed for political legitimacy. Industrial societies, it was argued, had grown beyond their liberal phase, and now needed to be organised and planned. Socialist political economy went further in proposing that this would be best done by replacing capitalism entirely with a fully socialist economy. But planned capitalism also attracted many adherents.

The advocates of planning regarded it as a method of co-ordination that was superior to the market, based on rational decision making for the entire economy. The principles of planning could be applied to all areas of the economy and society, and led to the creation of substantial public ownership of productive assets, in particular public utilities and also key parts of manufacturing industry. It was also extended to manpower planning, land planning, trade planning and many other sectors. It was inspired by the conviction that public initiative was generally better than private initiative because it was more rational, more likely to serve the public good and more likely to achieve the best outcomes for citizens.

What is common to all forms of collectivist political economy, socialist and anti-socialist, is the combination of a vision of the desired economic order (the moral economy) with an analysis of the actual economic order. It is possible for a government to be thought economically competent in a narrow, technical way, without any wider moral claim being made. Often such a claim is implicit, and the power of a narrative about economic competence often rests on the idea that what a government is trying to achieve is not only economically beneficial but also morally desirable. It is sometimes thought that the two kinds of claims have to be disentangled, but in practice in everyday politics they run seamlessly into one another, so that moral and technical arguments are often presented as one. The most common form this takes is claims for reconciling social justice or fairness and economic efficiency. This is not a new phenomenon. All forms of collectivist political economy, again both socialist and anti-socialist, claimed to have ways to manage modern economies which would combine social justice and economic efficiency.

Bringing these two goals together has always been at the heart of political economy and therefore also of perceptions of economic competence. It would be a strange political economy which deliberately set out to focus on only one. But in practice, particular strategies in political economy have been criticised for emphasising one more than another, and this has often led to alternative strategies being explored, particularly when the existing strategy is seen as damaging a party's reputation for economic competence and credibility.

Welfare

This was one reason why planning began to lose its hold as the master narrative on the left, and why a second strategy developed, one concerned less with replacing capitalism and markets by an alternative economic system as with setting limits to the way in which capitalism operated, by establishing countervailing powers and institutions – a framework of rules which sought to control and channel the forces which capitalism unleashed.

One of the key elements of this strategy was to protect those sectors of the economy which were not commodified, and to extend them into areas that were. The aim was to create a parallel economy which was not subject to market exchange but financed from taxation by the state. The expansion of welfare programmes, and in particular the provision of universal benefits and universal provision in health and education, became the key symbols of this strategy. This was a public sector which existed alongside the private sector, and could be conceived of as complementary in function to it, and also in some sense antagonistic, since its ethos and method of co-ordination and finance were so different.

What also emerged with the idea of constructing a socialist enclave within capitalism, which would not be subject to the same laws as the private sector, was the idea of the state itself as a guarantor of a non-capitalist sphere, including the public sector, parts of civil society and the family, and as the regulator of the private sphere in which market forces ruled. Such regulation could take both direct and indirect forms, imposing constraints on what might be done in the private sphere (e.g. health and safety legislation on hours and conditions of work) as well as measures to influence the framework in which economic activity was carried on, such as measures to manage demand and reduce the oscillations of the business cycle associated with Keynesian thinking.

The chief purpose of this kind of social democracy was to tame the wildness and wilfulness of the market, and prevent its forces from creating inequality and insecurity. It envisaged not the complete replacement of capitalism but the emergence of a more pluralist and balanced economy, in which the different principles would be recognised as appropriate in different spheres.

Markets

The third strategy emerged partly as a result of the vicissitudes of the former two. The strategies for delivering planning and welfare suffered setbacks, and in the major restructuring of capitalism which took place in the 1970s, many of the ideas and programmes associated with planning and welfare became marginalised following the rise of an aggressive form of neo-liberalism. This pro-market ideology redefined the terms of the political economy debate, and the way in which economic competence was defined. It encouraged social democratic parties to rethink their strategy because of the significant changes that had been brought about not only in the international economy but also in the changing division of labour and balance of productive activities in capitalist economies, with the dwindling of labour-intensive manufacturing industries and the working-class communities dependent on them.

This third strategy, which in some countries became known as the third way, aimed at overcoming the traditional dichotomy between states and markets in social democratic thinking and practice, by emphasising how states were intimately involved in creating and sustaining markets. Markets needed regulating but were recognised as the primary source of dynamism and innovation in the economy, with states playing an enabling role, steering the economy rather than directly controlling it. In this way, the strategy sought to reconcile the pursuit of social justice with the achievement of economic efficiency. The more successful the market economy became the greater the resources that could be deployed to expand the provision of welfare, health and education. Social democratic governments did not need to fight markets, but could utilise them as a means to secure their objectives.

Collectivist social democracy had united social justice and economic efficiency through the imposition of a rational plan from the centre. Welfare social democracy had separated social justice and economic efficiency by making the first the preserve of the public sector and the second the preserve of the private sector. Market social democracy sought to restore the unity, by giving priority to market mechanisms in both the public and private sectors, within a framework of public interest determined by the state.

The Illusory Hopes of the Golden Age

One might expect that these three strategies either separately or in combination offer more than enough options to social democratic governments to achieve success in managing economies and acquiring the mantle of economic competence. During the long upswing in the international economy in the 1990s, it seemed that this was being achieved. Centre-left parties were in office in many parts of the world, and had acquired a new confidence in handling the economy. They had learnt to adjust to the neo-liberal framework of this international economy, and to pursue within its rules traditional social democratic objectives, raising public expenditure to improve public services and redistribute income and opportunities. Fifteen years ago a new golden age of social democracy seemed to be emerging.

These hopes have proven illusory. For many critics they were always illusory – the new reputation for economic competence was bought at too high a price, and conceded too much to social democracy's opponents. Many of them refused to consider these governments social democratic, measured against the criteria of what social democracy had been in the past. But even if this argument is set aside, it remains true that the reputation for economic competence has not been sustained. Most social democratic Governments pursued social market policies during the boom of the 1990s and 2000s, but once the financial crash took place in 2008, they have once again appeared on the back foot, trying to find a credible response to the recession. Although by no means all, right of centre parties typically find it easier to adapt to recessions, and often appear to relish the tough policies that come to be prescribed.

Why should this be so? There are relatively few examples of centre-left Governments gaining the political ascendancy during major recessions and periods of economic reconstruction, the two exceptions being Sweden and the US in the 1930s. During the present recession, a familiar pattern has asserted itself, with many social democratic governments losing office. The Obama Administration is a major exception, but its touch has been uncertain, and it too is now on the defensive – control of the House of Representatives has been lost, and Obama faces a tough fight to be re-elected. The economy has become the central battleground and the Democrats have not established their ascendancy over it.

Combining Political Economy with Moral Economy

The challenge facing the centre-left is complex. It needs a political economy which can suggest ways of handling the issues of stabilisation policy, growth policy and external policy, but one which can also fit that strategy into an argument for a new moral economy as well. There has to be a vision of a different kind of economic order which can enlist the hopes and aspirations of a new electoral majority.

The financial crash of 2008 began as a banking crisis, but soon changed into a fiscal crisis, and by 2010 had transformed into a sovereign debt crisis. This is a familiar progression in a capitalist economy, but the centre-left has found it difficult to cope. In the course of this development, government, and particularly Big Government, has been singled out for blame. Unfortunately, if not always accurately, Big Government has been associated with the parties of the centre-left. After trying so hard for 20 years to dissociate itself from the ideas of Big Government and promote the ideas of smart and enabling government, the centre-left has found itself on the defensive, unable as yet to produce an alternative narrative which commands widespread support and credibility.

The consequence has been that policies which give priority to reducing the deficit at the expense of the public sector have gained the upper hand. In this respect the centre-left suffers two major hits on its reputation for economic competence. It is accused of not being serious about reducing the deficit, and therefore losing control of the public finances, with serious implications for future levels of debt and the well-being of the entire community. Second, it is accused of seeking to protect the public sector, which is treated as an unproductive sector and a burden on the wealth-creating sectors of the economy. The public sector is portrayed as a sink of inefficiency and waste, which deserves to be cut back radically to allow the private sector to breathe.

This is of course a morality tale, but a very powerful one. Many of these arguments are familiar from the 1930s, and it is remarkable that 70 years on they retain such force and can be resurrected with such ease. In the way they frame the crisis and what should be the remedies for it, these arguments prioritise the need for sound money and fiscal rectitude above all else. For Hayekians, the key requirement is to bring down the deficit, bring monetary values back into line with real ones, liquidating inflated costs and prices and valuations in the process. The quicker this is done, the sooner will the economy return to health – economic and moral. Against this, Keynesians argue that deficits should not be reduced at all until the recovery is well under way. They dispute the Hayekian claim that public spending crowds out private spending especially when the economy is a long way below full employment.

The weakness of the Keynesian position has always been that it can seem too clever by half. However correct its analysis may be, it flies in the face of everyday experience. It seeks to treat the national economy and the national budget differently from the individuals managing their personal finances. Yet the simple message that the national budget should be managed as though it were a household budget reappears in every crisis, as though Keynes had never written *The General Theory*. The centre-left has never managed to counter this with a similar analogy to explain the necessity of deficit financing in a recession and make it a form of common sense. Deficit financing gets represented as profligacy, and public expenditure is declared to be out of control. Governments that practise deficit financing in a recession get accused of not cutting the deficit fast enough. High deficits are presented as immoral, blighting the chances of recovery and loading burdens on to future generations.

The difficulty the centre-left has in defending its stance on the deficit is symptomatic of a deeper problem. The deficit is transformed into a symbol of Big Government, the fact that government has expanded too far and too fast and has become too intrusive in the economy. A purging of the excesses of the state becomes necessary, cutting it back to allow the healthy forces of the private sector to bring forth new growth. In this narrative the state always features as obstructive, inefficient, wasteful and restrictive. Government is captured by special interests and exists to frustrate new developments and hold back the spontaneous dynamism of the private sector. In seeking to defend the role of government and its spending levels, centre-left parties are identified as allies of the forces that are preventing economic recovery and new growth.

The reason why the centre-left struggles to retain a reputation for economic competence is closely related to its relationship with the public sector. Its past associations with planning and welfare come to the fore again in a recession, and eclipse the more recent association with social market policies. By identifying so strongly with the need for cuts in public spending, the right taps into a deep sense of how the economy is ordered and should be ordered. There is a bedrock of common sense which it can always fall back on, using moral arguments about the evils of excess, and the need to retrench in order to make the economy healthy again. Cutting the deficit is a process of purification, which at the same time reaffirms the primacy of the market and market relationships, and reinforces the message that the public sector is unproductive, is always subservient to the private sector, and must always be sacrificed to help the private sector.

Again, this narrative splits the moral and the political economy of the centre-left. By forcing the left to defend the public sector over the private, the right is able to present the centre-left as making a moral argument for public provision without indicating how the resources are to found from the private sector to sustain it. The attempt made by the left in the last 20 years to show that it now gives equal priority to the public and the private sectors falls apart. If the left can once more be identified just with the public sector, the right can seize the mantle of economic competence, as the party which alone understands how prosperity can be restored.

Escaping from the Right's Moral Trap

How might the left escape from this trap? It cannot simply reproduce one or more of its past strategies. It must rethink its political economy in the light of the new circumstances of the financial crash. There are a number of strategies it could adopt: market conforming, market complementing, market resisting, market substituting and market transforming.

Market Conforming

According to this strategy – which might be called the Philip Snowden solution – social democrats should become as orthodox as the most orthodox central banker in its economic policy. Snowden was a strong advocate of the gold standard and sound money, and was undeviating in his endorsement of the Treasury View that public spending was unproductive and only affordable if the health of the private sector allowed. Socialism had to be built on fiscal prudence or not at all. He famously described the rather moderate manifesto of his former Labour colleagues in the 1931 election as 'Bolshevism run mad'. Such a stance would mean centre-left Governments leading the way in cutting the deficits, outdoing their right counterparts for fiscal rigour. In this way no risks would be run with the economy, the confidence of the markets in the government would be secure.

Several centre-left Governments have attempted something similar in the last two decades, working within the constraints of the market rather than seeking to challenge them in any way. Yet it is a different matter to take this approach in a major recession. Instead of protecting its core supporters who work in public services or rely on public services, this strategy would put the burden of adjustment on them. However, if a left Government can hold its support through the crisis, it emerges in a strong position to restore spending once growth resumes.

The drawback of such a policy is that while it may work in a boom and lay the foundations for a large expansion of public spending, in a recession it can lead to disaster, a major fiscal contraction which risks turning the crash into a depression, as it did in many countries on both sides of the Atlantic in 1929–32.

Market Complementing

The main alternative that emerged at that time was a market-complementing strategy of the kind that Keynes proposed, halting the downward spiral and encouraging a recovery through a combination of monetary and fiscal interventions. But experience shows that it is very difficult to win the argument for a Keynesian approach in a recession, the moment when it is needed most of all.

Keynesian remedies were applied in 2008–9, but the Governments that adopted them have come under strong attack and have not been able to win long-term consent for continuing them. In many countries there has been a strong reaction to the bailouts, the fiscal stimulus and low interest rates – that is, for the policies which prevented complete economic collapse. The deficits which were the price of preventing the crash turning into a deep depression have been framed as the problem which now threatens recovery, and which has to be tackled as quickly as possible. In the United States, Obama delayed for a long time in proposing a deficit reduction strategy, but after the Republicans captured the House he was forced to do so in April 2011. His strategy is no longer Keynesian but a deficit reduction on European lines, with a ratio of public spending cuts to tax increases of 3:1. For Republicans even this is too much, and many of them are refusing to accept any tax increases at all. Rather, they target government expenditures on the poor and the elderly.

Further examples of market-complementing strategies are policies which put much greater emphasis on targeted assistance to particular regions and sectors, essential if Governments are to reassure those most affected by economic change, but often hard to do within EU rules. There are also possibilities in major investment in programmes designed to encourage green growth, permitting the economy to grow but in an environmentally sustainable way, to cope with the challenges arising from climate change. Arguments for green growth assume that there is ultimately no choice to be made between maintaining capitalist growth and protecting the environment. If the trade-off is indeed benign, or can be made so, then green growth offers enormous opportunities for reconstructing and rebalancing the economy, and for redesigning cities and lifestyles without too much pain. But the assumptions that it can be benign are very large ones, and the time for effecting change is quite short.

Market Resisting and Market Substituting

These strategies normally involve some kind of national protectionism. Here the centre-left becomes the champion of national economic sovereignty against the global market. This is achieved through the imposition of controls on capital, labour and goods, which at the extreme involve the suppression of market arrangements altogether. Such policies are attractive because they appear to safeguard the core electoral base, but they carry a heavy cost in terms of economic growth and living standards, and are very unlikely to prove electorally successful in the long term. At times the centre-left has flirted with such policies, but has rarely been seriously tempted because of the dependence of living standards and growth on continued participation in the international economy. The dilemma facing centre-left administrations is reconciling the strong domestic pressures for controls, particularly during recessions, with maintaining an open and liberal international order.

To avoid giving priority to market resisting strategies, the left has to find a language to express the complexity and the interdependence of modern economies and societies which will resonate with voters, while simultaneously convincing them that it can protect them and is governing in their interests. The reason why the right often scores more highly than the left for economic competence is that it has colonised two political narratives which are particularly strong in Western democracies at the present time, one around nations and nation-states and the other around free markets.

The right combines these narratives effectively to marginalise and outwit its political opponents, an example of which is currency union. The world is dividing up into large currency unions, and countries are being forced to choose between being part of a large currency union with some political influence over how it conducts its affairs, or to be a satellite of a currency union with no political influence at all. But it is often hard to make a case for joining or remaining a member of a monetary union without being attacked for surrendering national sovereignty. Posing as the guardians of nation-states and free markets simultaneously often produces inconsistent policies, but it is a strong position to defend. It can make the centre-left appear as cosmopolitans who are not rooted in the nation-state. They are depicted as allowing too many immigrants to enter the country, supporting transnational agreements on currency and trade, and at the same time are attacked as advocates of the Big Government opposed to economic dynamism and prosperity by protecting welfare dependents and inefficient public services.

Many of the left's problems are rooted in these dilemmas, but abandoning openness in its external policy would be a huge setback for a credible social democratic politics. It would quite rapidly become something else.

Market Transforming

These strategies involve experiments with radical decentralisation and redistribution. It is a programme of policies which have been hinted at but not fully developed since the 1990s. Advocates of this approach argue that public services have to be transformed so that they are delivered as efficiently as the best services in the private sector, and that the way to do this is to dismantle centralised, top-down forms of delivery. This would mean fully embracing the human capital and assets-based welfare approach to welfare and public services. Further, it would mean finding ways to encourage a more diverse ecology of institutional forms in the public and private sectors: mutuals, co-operatives, non-profit companies.

Such an approach has the potential to give the initiative back to the left by lifting the negative burden of its association with the existing public sector, and identifying it with dynamic and innovative sectors of the economy. The main drawback is the controversy over whether the human capital agenda can be a left agenda. This focuses on the issue of financialisation, the regulation of the financial sector, the feasibility of redistributing assets, and the wider social and political implications of treating individuals as financial subjects.

The Left Needs a Distinctive Moral Vision of the Economy

The left needs to find ways to turn financialisation to its advantage and make it serve a left strategy. If it cannot do so it may be difficult in the present stage of development of the international economy for the left to achieve a reputation for economic competence, since to have a credible growth strategy, the left has to find a way to link its goals with the interests of the leading sectors of the economy.

What the left needs above all is the confidence to develop long-term thinking about the frameworks that are appropriate for managing the economy. This is not just a question of political economy but of moral economy. Questions about, for example, the size of the state, the composition of state spending, the degree of decentralisation, the capacities and institutions required for a modern economy, the commitment to a liberal, international economic order and economic co-operation all need to be considered together to create a convincing and credible set of principles which can both provide guides to policy and be expressed as popular common sense. But none of this works unless the left can also set out a distinctive moral vision of the kind of economy and society it values, and find the policies that can express it.

CHAPTER 4

The Mechanics of Markets: Politics, Economics and Finance

John Kay

The banking crisis of 2008 offered the centre-left a once-in-a-generation opportunity. For three decades, market fundamentalist ideologies had framed argument and influenced economic policies. Intellectual leadership in economic thinking, historically led by the political left, had been seized by the political right. But then the financial sector, the principal advocate and the principal beneficiary of such market fundamentalism, imploded.

As Patrick Diamond explains in his Introduction, the political opportunity offered was comprehensively missed. The centre-left offered no diagnosis, no new ideas and gained no electoral advantage. The political parties which had waited a century for capitalism to collapse under its own contradictions congratulated themselves that the collapse had been staved off by the injection of simply incredible amounts – trillions of dollars – of taxpayer funds into the banking system. The financial sector not only emerged unreformed, but successfully transferred most of the consequences of its own failure to governments and the non-financial economy.

The core argument of this chapter is that to acquire economic competence, the centre-left needs to engage with the mechanics of markets: to escape from an essentially absurd polarisation between 'pro-market' and 'anti-market' positions. That Europe will be, largely, a market economy is a fact of life; but without a careful, informed appreciation of the strengths and weaknesses of markets, the incidence and design of interventions are likely to be inept.

As it has been in the financial crisis, the centre-left has been prominent in calling for 'more regulation'. But such calls are without significance or substantive content in the absence of diagnosis of the underlying problems which led to the crisis, or specification of the public policy objectives that such regulation might hope to achieve. Stabilisation of failed financial institutions may be a necessary emergency response; but it is not an economic policy.

Andrew Gamble has identified the three broad traditional economic strategies of the centre-left – planning, welfare and the social market.[1] Planning, as he describes it, 'was aimed at replacing the governance of the economy by bureaucratic rather than market co-ordination. Its bias was to replace markets by the application of direct controls and the public ownership of productive assets, on the grounds that markets were inefficient and wasteful and led to inequality and exploitation'. That taxonomy is central to understanding the micro-economic issues the centre-left faces today.

The Centre-Left Predicament

The reason the centre-left is today on the back foot in micro-economic matters is easily explained. Although markets are, as Gamble describes, inefficient and wasteful, and lead to inequality and exploitation, planned economies in which co-ordination was attempted through bureaucratic process rather than by market co-ordination were even more inefficient and wasteful. Planned economies did not even score highly in avoiding inequality and exploitation.

Although the negative verdict on the performance of centrally directed economic systems is unequivocal, that verdict took some time to emerge. Even in the 1960s, observers on the right feared that the technological superiority of the Soviet Union would lead to its economic dominance. Planning would enable developing economies to achieve Western standards of living without the painful transitions which the West had experienced.

In Western Europe itself, governments of both left and right favoured some sort of national planning framework. The apparent successes of central direction of economic activity in the Second World War, and the post-war development of operations research and information technology, lent support to an almost universal expectation that industrial structures would become more concentrated and would operate in close relationship with a guiding state.

This consensus on the direction of travel was reversed in the 1970s and 1980s. The two largest centrally directed economies abandoned planning, with the collapse of the Soviet Union, and the opening of China to the market. At the same time, reaction in the US and Britain against what was seen as increasingly sclerotic corporatism led to the rise of the radical right under Reagan and Thatcher. In the developing world, success in achieving economic growth was broadly correlated with enthusiasm for capitalist models of economic development.[2]

And so the right, which had often dominated the levers of economic policy, came to dominate the terms of economic debate. A market fundamentalism which had only a short time before been advocated only by an extremist fringe became a mainstream ideology. The terms 'globalisation' and 'privatisation' were central to the language of those who resisted these developments as well as those who welcomed them.

In the face of this onslaught, the centre-left essentially withdrew from the argument, accepting the empirical and intellectual triumph of the market with bad grace. The post-war era saw a steady retreat in Britain from controlling the commanding heights in the 1940s, to formulating a national plan in the 1960s, to seeking some planning agreements with individual firms in the 1970s, to light-touch regulation after 2000. In the rest of Western Europe, the Communist left, which had seemed close to power in several countries, ceased to be an electoral force, but the socialist left did not make corresponding gains. The progressive watering-down of unsuccessful policies failed to attract voters or inspire supporters.

So when the banking system collapsed in 2008, the political left readily acquiesced in the process by which the governments provided much of the capital and underwrote all the liabilities of major banks. The British Labour Party was so frightened of the word 'nationalisation', let alone its reality, that it would not contemplate discussion of the issue: although the moment was one at which many people on the political right would have been easily convinced that a period of nationalisation provided the best means of restructuring banks and securing continuation of their essential functions during that restructuring process.

Markets and Planning

Market fundamentalism rests on a range of assumptions. Greed is the dominant motivation in economic affairs. Markets populated by self-interested individuals are the only efficient form of economic organisation, and interference with markets is justified only to accommodate a limited class of defined 'market failures'. The role of the state is appropriately limited to the enforcement of contracts and property rights, and perhaps the provision of a minimal welfare safety net.

Despite the many deficiencies of this doctrine, the ideologues who set it out were prescient in understanding why planned economies would fail. Hayek, in particular, recognised that the informational requirements of a central administration which sought to plan a complex modern economy were unmanageable. He also argued that bureaucratic structures were ill-equipped to handle the processes of experiment and discovery which lead to innovation in product and business processes.[3]

Events proved him right. Centralised and inflexible, the planning process responds inadequately to changing technology and consumer needs. The ineffectiveness of centrally directed controls and targets in the face of differences in the information available to the centre and the periphery leads to frustration, and endless complication and proliferation of controls and targets – hence the seemingly inevitable association of the planned economy with authoritarian politics.

The common response is that what we need is better planning. This is a difficult argument to counter because an infinitely omnipotent, omniscient and benevolent planner would always find outcomes superior to those achieved by unco-ordinated mechanisms of economic organisation. But a comparison between inefficient and wasteful market competition is not relevant: the inevitable reality is that planners are only intermittently benevolent, are very far from omniscient, and must operate in a democratic society which is wise to be intolerant of omnipotence. The failures of planning have been sufficiently widespread to require proper modesty about what can be achieved in practice. And – I shall return to this – the same humility is required, and for the same reasons, in considering what can be accomplished through regulation.

The Right and Market Fundamentalism

The failures of planning make a case for the market economy, but not for a market fundamentalist ideology. Market fundamentalism is a travesty of how market economies, of which there are many varieties, really operate.[4] Markets function only because they are embedded in a social context. Property rights and contracts are social constructs. The pursuit of greed destroys both the organisations that exemplify it and the legitimacy of the system that supports it, as the events of 2008 proved. The organisation that 'makes nothing but money' (Bear Stearns's notorious self-description) proved in the long run not even to make that.

Most important risks in society – including, we now see, the risk of dislocation in risk markets themselves – are handled not through markets, but by social institutions. Complex modern economies require far more co-operative activity than a market fundamentalist account would allow, and so on. If the term 'free market' is a description of a market free of government regulation and social control, it is an oxymoron.

True believers in market fundamentalism were never more than a small minority. Business interests were ready to espouse the rhetoric of market fundamentalism: it offered ready-made arguments against any government action they disliked, but did not constrain their approval of government actions that helped them. The subtle but important distinction between policies that support markets and policies that support the interests of established large firms in these markets was not widely appreciated by policymakers on the right or the left. 'Free market' policies could therefore be interpreted as the promotion of a wish list for corporate lobbyists.[5]

In 2008 the market fundamentalist doctrine – that failing businesses should be allowed to collapse – conflicted with the practical fact that these failing businesses included the largest and most politically well-connected corporations in Europe and America. The fundamentalist view did not last long – at most, 48 hours from the collapse of Lehman to the rescue of AIG. The most strident business advocates of market fundamentalism made clear that the doctrine had never been intended to apply to them, or at least not in the way that more intellectual proponents of the doctrine had suggested.

Government support for free markets meant exactly that. If markets became illiquid, it was the responsibility of government to support these markets and provide the liquidity that would enable the advocates of free trade to trade freely. In this intellectual milieu, the notion of putting a $700 billion slush fund for failed financial companies at the discretion of the Secretary of the US Treasury seems entirely natural and coherent. It is difficult to exaggerate the sense of entitlement felt – and still felt – in the City of London and on Wall Street.

Britain maintained a more robust stance, pressing businesses that took the taxpayer's cash to give up equity and resisting pressure to lend public funds to large banks on the security of the junk that cluttered their balance sheets. But the determination of a Labour Government to avoid the suggestion of state control of the banking system bordered on the paranoid: that fear not only delayed an appropriate solution to the crisis of Northern Rock for many months but also means that although the taxpayer has an 84% stake in Royal Bank of Scotland, government has little influence over its lending or remuneration policies. Once the acute crisis was over, the subsequent response of British politicians of the centre-left amounted to little more than frequent repetition of the mantra of 'more regulation', with particular emphasis on its global dimension.

Other European countries differ from Britain and the United States in having a long tradition of universal banking. That tradition was a conservative one, to be transformed by the globalisation of financial services from the 1980s onwards. The major institutions would reinvent themselves in imitation of the buccaneering conglomerates emerging in Britain and the United States, linking investment and retail banking with the investment bankers dominating the whole and benefiting from the size of the retail deposit basis. Smaller banks, such as the German Landesbanken or the Spanish Caixa sought to diversify from their local roots by dabbling, with little understanding, in markets for complex securities.

Although the role of the financial sector was smaller in these countries, financial institutions were no less influential, and no less protected when crisis hit. Governments stood behind their universal banks, mostly tacitly – the most explicit support, in Ireland, would prove disastrous as the combination of the extraordinary magnitude of both balance sheets and losses within them, combined with an Anglo-American degree of transparency, led to the transfer of unmanageable obligations to the government balance sheet.

In other countries, however, support was more discreet and the European Central Bank was, from the very beginning of the crisis, ready to put its resources behind the banks of the Euro-zone. The result was a transfer of not only old but new banking obligations to the ECB balance sheet, an outcome which would be handled only so long as the prospect that the potential liabilities would materialise through direct sovereign default or the unwillingness of member states to fund indefinitely the losses of its local banks was remote. By 2010–11, it was no longer certain that these contingencies could be averted, and what had begun as a banking crisis became a European financial crisis.

Postponement had therefore transformed a set of micro-economic problems into a macro-economic one: but European governments would be no better equipped to find a collective solution to this issue than they had been to find local solutions to the earlier issues. Postponement therefore continues: the resolution is ultimately likely to dent the reputation for economic competence of whatever governments are left holding the parcel when the music stops. But the chorus of the music is the same: a refrain of 'more regulation', accompanied by even less willingness in Britain to address the undue political influence of large financial institutions.

Social Markets

Whatever the purpose of more regulation might be, however, it is plainly not the substitution of a planned system of capital allocation for the existing structure of financial markets. The way to deal with the waste and inefficiency of markets and the inequality and exploitation that follows is not to replace the market with bureaucratic process but to address directly the waste and inefficiencies, the inequality and exploitation, which are – along with the goods and services we want and use every day – the inevitable product of a market system.

This is a social market approach. Not just in the financial system, but in the economy as a whole, such a policy involves establishing structures and institutions that emphasise the strengths of markets and attack their weaknesses. The strengths of markets lie in the opportunities they give for pluralism, innovation and choice: their weaknesses are widely rehearsed, and the financial sector has demonstrated in particular the vulnerability of a market economy to rent-seeking behaviour by greedy individuals and organised industry lobbies.

A social market policy requires pragmatic intervention based on analysis and understanding of how particular institutions and markets work. The European centre-left has not been very interested in the mechanics of markets. The view has often seemed to be that if you invest will power in the outcome, the means by which such an outcome is achieved is a purely technical matter. But it is not: in fact it is the central question of economic policy.

The intellectual right, by contrast, had an active interest and understanding of market mechanics even if that understanding was flawed. Market fundamentalism was translated into practical doctrine. More markets were better than fewer markets; and the more trade that occurred in these markets, the more prosperous the economy (at least for the advocates of this philosophy) would be. The policy response was to encourage the proliferation of new financial instruments and financial markets, and to promote, in the name of increasing liquidity, an explosion of trading volumes.

Whether these instruments and frequent trading were of any public benefit is another matter. The assertion that the product of this activity was risk mitigation was simply absurd, as events showed. The end result was the most substantial financial crisis in a century, and everyone agreed that the crisis was caused by excessive and ill-managed risk taking. Asked whether the world he or she experienced had become more or less risky over the last two decades as a result of such financial innovation, the person in the street would assume that the question was humorous. The main impact on the financial uncertainties experienced by ordinary people has been the transfer of much of the risk associated with pension provision from the corporate sector to the individual. The risks which innovation supposedly enabled financial institutions to manage more effectively were, overwhelmingly, risks generated within the financial system itself, and even the claim that such innovations enabled these institutions to manage risks more effectively proved ultimately false.

The Influence of Finance

The same conflation of market fundamentalist ideology with promotion of the interests of large business organisations – and the individuals who ran them – led to the removal of restrictions on the creation of conglomerate, financial institutions. These restrictions had been designed to control the economic power and political influence of financial businesses. The United States and Britain had imposed functional separation between investment and commercial banking, and between market making and banking, by law and regulation. In Continental Europe, financial institutions had always been conglomerate but were conservatively structured and managed. In light of developments in New York and London, many of these businesses reinvented themselves on Anglo-American lines and established substantial presences in the Anglo-American financial centres.

The growth of such conglomerates increased the systemic risks involved in the financial system and enabled the inescapable government guarantee of retail deposits to be leveraged to support speculative activities in other financial markets. The businesses that emerged from this process were largely unmanageable. The risk exposures concealed in increasingly complex, corporate structures and bewilderingly complex instruments were generally beyond the comprehension of their senior management. Organisationally, the businesses resembled collections of unruly barons who would depose any king who imposed restrictions on the aggrandisement of their wealth and power.

If the CEOs and boards of these companies had difficulty in either understanding or controlling what was happening within them, that was *a fortiori* true of external regulators. The issue was not, and is not, that regulators lacked powers. The right to apprehend Bernie Madoff, to block RBS's acquisition of ABN-Amro or to prohibit the establishment of off-balance sheet vehicles with large liabilities and dubious assets has always been there. The issue is that regulators lacked the political authority and the technical competence to intervene. They still do, and always will.

Although poorly structured to manage their own affairs, large financial institutions were, and are, well structured to manage their external relations. Investment bankers are generally politically adroit if not managerially skilled. Smart, selfish and extremely well-remunerated, these investment bankers became the dominant influence in most financial conglomerates. Within investment banks themselves, traders gained influence relative to corporate advisers.

These individuals inspired a degree of awe among politicians. Policymakers recognised the intelligence and the range of contacts of investment bankers, overestimated their importance in business and the economy, and had little appreciation of what they did, beyond the fact that it was very difficult to understand. Financial institutions in general, and investment banks in particular, have become the most powerful industrial lobbies in the Western world.

In the United States, the regulatory process has been corrupted by the method of political funding. In Europe, policies and politicians cannot be bought in the same crude way. Regulatory capture here takes the form of intellectual capture: those who work in regulatory agencies see the industry they regulate through the eyes of established large firms in the industry.

The growing influence of investment banks transformed the relationship between large companies and financial markets. Financial innovation and a more aggressive culture in the City and on Wall Street left all companies in Britain and the United States open to takeover. The effects of this change in removing or galvanising complacent management were initially largely positive. But the outcome was an environment in which merger and acquisition activity became a dominant element in corporate strategy. Chief executives came to see themselves as meta-fund managers, juggling a portfolio of businesses as an asset manager might juggle a portfolio of stocks.

Finance directors became trapped in a dysfunctional cycle of earnings management. Investment managers were judged on quarterly performance figures. Required to contribute to that performance, stock analysts focused not on the fundamental value of a business, but on the relationship between expected and actual quarterly earnings announcements. The primary objective of public companies became the generation of steady and slightly underpredicted growth in earnings. To refrain from 'corporate activity' (mergers and acquisitions) and financial engineering, to resist the expectations of the City or Wall Street and to emphasise organic growth of a business franchise, was to make oneself a potential target of 'corporate activity'.

In other European countries, the corporate sector was more resistant to the adoption of a more financially orientated culture. But financial globalisation meant that the influence of US investment banks was felt there too, and the drive for a single European capital market came, in practice, to mean convergence on American norms. If there were to be a common European standard, it would not in any important respects be a distinctively European one. Many of the most international of large European businesses emphasised the degree to which they had adopted American corporate values, a trend epitomised in the disastrous takeover of Chrysler by Daimler-Benz.

Investment banks have always been controlled by their senior employees and run for their benefit. The traditional business structure was the partnership, and this remains the most appropriate structure for controlling risk and competence in such organisations. The principle that a substantial proportion of revenues goes to executives dates from that era. This bonus culture, which today arouses so much rhetorical denunciation, has survived into a time when investment banks are listed companies, or subsidiaries of listed companies.

But this bonus culture is contagious: it affected not only other divisions of the same financial conglomerates, but all large companies. Since chief executives controlled the process that generated much of the earnings of investment bankers, it seemed to them anomalous that they were paid much less. Moreover, the glamorous process of mergers and acquisitions, and the excitement of apparently transformational changes in business strategies influenced, even dominated, senior management behaviour. It changed the self-perception of the bureaucrats, skilled in corporate politics, who occupied positions at the top of large businesses. They visualised themselves not as managers but as entrepreneurs, discerning and creating new business opportunities. The comparison with rock stars and celebrity footballers was one they made, and the earnings of rock stars and celebrity footballers quickly followed.

The only difference was that chief executives thought, perhaps correctly, that the jobs they did were far more important, and the amounts of money that passed through their hands were certainly much larger. In the United States, many corporate executives paid themselves sums considerably in excess of the earnings of pop stars and celebrity footballers – sums which would begin to be large not just in absolute terms but large in relation to the earnings of the corporation.

The same basic mechanism of boom and bust has been common to successive crises – the Japanese bubble, the emerging market debt crisis of the 1990s, the new economy mania at the turn of the century, the explosion and collapse of the current Euro-zone crisis. Asset mispricing occurs in some market or another. The initial cause is often found in some genuine economic, political or technological trend – the emergence of poor countries within the global economy, the commercialisation of the Internet, or elements of convergence of Euro-zone economies. Consultants and journalists, gurus and financiers, have a common interest in exaggerating the significance and extent of these developments.

Herd behaviour in financial markets leads to cumulative mispricing, and large but substantially illusory profits: the apparent gains are the product of systematic overvaluations which will eventually be corrected. A substantial proportion of the profits which are attributed are paid to individuals associated with the process, and to their bosses.

The mispricing is eventually corrected. The resulting market dislocation imposes collateral losses on investors and institutions swept up in the process. Governments intervene to mitigate the collateral losses, pumping large amounts of money into general support of asset prices. These actions provide fuel for a new crisis in another asset class. The ratchet of state intervention means that successive crises tend to be of increasing magnitude: the financial market junkie needs ever larger fixes of federal funds. Since the 2008 crisis was of a scale that taxed the resources of world governments, the outlook is bleak.

The location of the next dislocation will, as always, be different, because particular lessons from a particular episode are learnt, by both governments and financial institutions – at least for a time. But since attention is entirely focussed on the particular rather than the general, these lessons leave the causal mechanisms that generate crises essentially unchanged.

Looking Forward

The centre-left should formulate a policy programme which reassesses the economic role of the financial sector. The statement 'there should be more regulation' is a hopelessly inadequate response to the problems described in this chapter. The key issue is to define specific objectives of reform. These should include scaling back levels of activity in securities markets to one which reflects the trading requirements of the real economy: reducing interdependencies between and within institutions in order to establish a more robust financial structure; and freeing companies and their managers from the obsession with mergers and disposals and the malign influence of quarterly reporting without diminishing, and if possible increasing, the external accountability of these managers.

At present, the principal objective of regulation appears to be to stabilise the existing structure of financial institutions. This is not surprising, since both nationally and internationally the institutions of financial services regulation are mostly captured. Their goal is the health of the industry, which is in turn interpreted as the health of the particular firms from which the industry is today composed. The purpose is the achievement, not of financial stability, but of industry stability, as if these were the same thing. But the stabilisation of existing organisations and industry structures, far from promoting financial and economic stability more broadly, is a guarantee of further, and potentially more damaging, crises.

Reducing trading volumes requires an increase in the cost of trading: by far the most important initial step is to phase out the government subsidy which arises from implicit guarantees of counter-party obligations (the guarantees provided to creditors by 'too big to fail' policies). Systemic risk must be attacked by simplification of corporate structures, adopting the principles of modularity, loose connectedness, and redundancy that are like well-established mechanisms for protecting complex and interdependent engineering structures against catastrophic failure. Establishing healthier relationships between corporations and financial markets requires a raft of policies aimed at reforming takeover rules, company law and business culture. I doubt whether measures to increase the powers of existing regulatory institutions, national or global, have much to offer.

I have emphasised the financial sector in this chapter because it is by far the most important industrial sector for current policy. But there is a more general point at issue. Effective micro-economic policies can be constructed only on the basis of specific knowledge and analysis of particular markets. Calls for 'more regulation' which are not accompanied by such specifics are essentially empty. If the centre-left is to acquire economic competence in micro-economic matters, it should not be through a strategy of 'planning light'. An appropriate response requires an appreciation of the limits of regulation, and a determination to use the power of markets to achieve social goals, an objective which can only be realised by a readiness to make use of the power of markets in the context of a thoughtful understanding of their deficiencies.

CHAPTER 5

Social Democracy at the End of the Welfare State?

Peter Taylor-Gooby

The European welfare state developed in a specific context: the institutional structure of the nation-state, the politics of representative democracy, the economics of regulated industrial capitalism and the social assumptions of the male bread-winner nuclear family. It became Europe's great gift to the world as a mechanism for managing the conflicts of market capitalism. It was a major element in stable growth for most of the half-century following the Second World War. The defining characteristic of the welfare state settlement is a commitment to social cohesion: the extent to which individuals feel committed to the well-being of others, particularly those in more vulnerable groups. This was expressed politically as an alliance of the mass of the population against the most privileged, between the middle and the bottom against the top.

There are two main variants of this coalition in Europe. Social democracy constrains the free play of the market to promote opportunities and more equal living standards for the mass of the population. Christian democracy has a stronger concern with maintaining status differentials and the established gender order. Both have strong commitments to interventions that make ordinary peoples' lives more secure: pensions and other social benefits, health care, social services and social housing. Both favour regulation to support decent working conditions and employment rights.

The Challenges to the Welfare State Settlement

This settlement now faces distinct challenges from many directions, not least as governments cut back spending in response to the 2008–9 financial crisis. These can be understood in two ways:

- As *technical problems* of development to be managed through a recalibration of the system. Examples are the inter-generational conflicts due to population ageing, the gender struggles due to changes in women's roles in the family, the labour market and civil society and the new patterns of insecurity during working life resulting from the post-industrial transition, changes in production processes and the globalisation of economic competition. These challenges are pressing but can in principle be resolved by shifts within current patterns of welfare state politics. They require a willingness to increase taxation and direct resources towards new and expanding needs (social care for the elderly and for children, adequate benefits – especially pensions – for those with weak employment records, benefits and support programmes to facilitate mobility within the labour market, effective training programmes and the like). They also require regulation of discrimination and an overhaul of education training and labour market law to promote fair access to opportunities. The EU pursues these rights, particularly when national traditions confer advantage in the terms of trade in the Single European Market. There has been considerable progress, more marked in the North and the Centre of the EU, less so in the South and East.
- As *systemic problems* that threaten the viability of the welfare state settlement. The ebbing economic authority of the nation-state, the declining political support for welfare spending and, most importantly, the failure of European countries to sustain consensus support for state welfare are of this kind. The great success of the welfare state rested on its capacity to build alliances between social classes and particularly between the middle and the bottom against the top of the income-distribution. This was possible when individuals shared a common fear of the social risks of unemployment, disability, lack of income in old age, need for health care, education, transport, housing and so on, and when most people were more or less equally unable to meet these needs in the market. Such alliances were reinforced by political experience of the success of welfare states in delivering health care, pensions and other

benefits during the period of sustained growth after the Second World War.

As inequalities grow, the risks that confront routine and more highly skilled workers, those with care responsibilities and those without, and those who can afford private solutions and those who can't, diverge. Globalisation threatens routine workers with competition from those with lower living standards elsewhere, while those with scarce marketable skills can bid up the return across a larger market.[1] Care responsibilities damage those (mostly women) who do earn enough to pay the wages of others to provide the care. Maintaining a strong social democratic coalition becomes more difficult. Patterns of insecurity become more complex and fragmented over time, and more people feel able to meet their needs through market and family provision.

The result is an unstable politics of welfare, gaining support when the economy cycles towards recession, losing it during periods of growth and security. Those areas of social provision directed at commonly felt needs (health care, education) remain strong. Pensions receive ambivalent support as more people understand their provision as financed through their own payments. The most apparently redistributive services (unemployment benefits, last resort welfare, social housing) lose collective endorsement. Such services are seen to benefit a dependent out-group. The alliance between the middle and the bottom becomes increasingly fragile, especially in the more liberal and corporatist areas of Europe where it was least strongly entrenched. The capacity to maintain social provision is now threatened by the current turmoil in the Euro-zone. In this context the resilience of collective support for these services and the search for ways to build a progressive alliance is doubly important.

The Rise of the Extreme Right

The crisis of the social democratic welfare state referred to above is brought out most clearly in the current shifts to the political right and in the backlash against immigration. European countries have traditionally been accepting of immigrants. Many commentators point to the strong case for migration due to populations ageing, as richer countries need to recruit more young people.

During the first decade of the twenty-first century, anti-immigrant sentiment has gathered force in a number of countries. In France the success of the National Front has led the centre-right Government to ban the burkha and to risk conflicts with the EU through discriminatory expulsions of Roma people. In 2010, the far right PVV became the power broker to the minority liberal VVD Government in the Netherlands. In Switzerland, the Government accepted the result of a referendum to ban the building of minarets. In Sweden, the extreme right Swedish Democrats entered the parliament for the first time. In Austria, the Freedom Party came second in the presidential contest and gained 27% of the vote in the general election. In Italy, the Northern League strengthens anti-immigrant pressures. Jobbik has entered the Hungarian parliament. Most significantly, the German Premier repudiated multiculturalism in a speech on 16 October and put the onus on immigrant groups to assimilate to German society. The UK Prime Minister endorsed a similar position in a speech (significantly in the same city, Munich) setting multiculturalism in the context of terrorism on 5 February in 2011.

This shift reflects new conflicts emerging between groups at the bottom: new entrants and the established working class. Anti-migrant groups do not trust welfare states to protect their interests. State welfare is increasingly understood as defending sectional interests rather than providing the basis for a broad alliance between middle and bottom. Both the traditional, more inclusive, social democratic and the more status-centred Christian democratic bases of generous social provision have broken down.

Defending the Welfare State Settlement

Neither the economic globalisation and competition nor the current economic crises are in themselves reasons to abandon the commitment to state welfare. Relatively high-spending welfare states (the most obvious example being Germany but Nordic Europe is also significant) maintain their success in export markets despite their high labour costs even under current circumstances. Most commentators accept that social spending provides a convenient 'automatic' regulator and is essential to maintain demand at times of economic pressure. However, the market logic that represents the state as a burden on a private productive sector is increasingly becoming orthodoxy in the more liberal European countries of Ireland and the UK, and is gaining ground elsewhere. One implication is that the only response to economic crisis is cut-back to contain state borrowing, rather than spending to reflate the economy. Unless social democracy can counter this argument, it will be unable to mobilise serious resistance to cuts.

In the corporatist countries that make up the bulk of Europe, social democracy and Christian democracy had been associated with a tripartite, regulated capitalism. The tradition of social insurance welfare directed primarily at the needs of labour market insiders with access to the secure employment, which is the political foundation of corporatism, is well established. Outsiders in more marginal, less secure jobs are typically managed through weaker and more coercive welfare benefits. This fits the Christian democratic tradition of status-protection across the Centre of Europe and greater Germany, and is influential in France and Italy and surrounding countries. Similar approaches are emerging in the most developed post-socialist countries (Poland, Hungary, Czech Republic and Slovenia).

Social democratic settlements, strongest in the Nordic countries, include a role for social insurance, building on upper-working-class mutual assistance. There is typically much greater emphasis on inclusive provision for more marginal groups, on training and support to help access to jobs, and recognition of the care needs of those with dependants.

In a more globalised post-industrial world, the barrier between insiders and outsiders weakens. The jobs which unions – linked to social democratic governments in Nordic countries – or alliances between labour and Christian democratic parties – in Germany, Austria and Italy, and to some extent France – sought to protect are exposed to the harsh climate of the world market. The resulting conflict between low-skilled workers and immigrant groups competing for a shrinking pool of employment fuels support for the far right. The pressures of the economic crisis simply exacerbate these tensions.

In more liberal countries, the obvious European example being the UK, the wages and employment conditions at the bottom have always been exposed to market competition. Pressure from immigrants has led to conflicts in a number of places, but failed to translate into an organised political movement on anything like the scale of other countries. Whether the stringency of cuts will lead to a resurgence of extreme right politics, as those at the bottom compete more bitterly for fewer and less satisfactory jobs, is at present unclear.

The great virtue of the welfare state is collective commitment to social provision. There are strong arguments for the moral desirability of such commitment in a more unequal and uncertain world in which global shifts intensify migratory pressures. These are reinforced as global warming intensifies the search for radical solutions. The reports of the Inter-Governmental Panel on Climate Change make the case for a reduction in carbon emissions with increasing urgency. International negotiations have so far failed to agree plans for cuts in emissions adequate to contain temperature rises of about 2°C (some 400 parts per million).[2] It has also proved impossible to implement such plans as are agreed.

Optimists see managing climate change as a technical problem and suggest that the introduction of new technology will not only cut emissions but also provide opportunities for profitable investment.[3] Pessimists emphasise the scale of the changes required and point out that these vastly exceed the rate at which new technologies and lifestyle changes have ever taken place in the past. From this perspective, a viable future involves a transition greater even that that envisaged by optimists. The goal of economic growth must be abandoned and with it much of the logic of ineluctable competitiveness and of an international financial system based on investment returns.[4]

Any effective plans will have substantial impact on daily lives and will create winners and losers in access to food, transport, home heating and other needs. These are likely to generate serious social tensions. Social welfare will make regulation of housing, settlement, transport, employment and other energy-intensive activities more acceptable to losers. This adds a practical case to the moral argument for state welfare. However, these arguments, while compelling in themselves, do not explain where the political basis for the re-founding of the social democratic welfare state is to be located.

A New Politics of Welfare?

It is thus much harder to forge alliances between middle and bottom as the incomes and interests of social groups fragment. A more globalised world is perceived primarily as the threat of migrant competition at the bottom, but more as the opportunities of a freer world market at the middle and top. The fact that incomes have diverged sharply in recent years confirms the reality that lies behind these perceptions. European welfare states have developed in a number of directions in response to economic crisis and longer-term pressures. These have in common an attempt to resolve the problem of political alliances by positing a more individualised contract between citizen and government. Below, I outline three approaches which have been combined in different ways in policy programmes; a stress on opportunity, on individual incentives and of decentralisation.

Opportunity-Centred Social Democracy

Here, the key element is a retreat from policies designed to create greater equality of outcomes to equality of opportunity as the basis for common interests in a more unequal society. The approach rests on the idea that the key conflicts in richer societies are less over level of consumption than access to positional goods, such as educational achievement. A common characteristic of such goods is that any one person's enjoyment of them is damaged if others attain them: the value of educational success in opening up desirable jobs depends not so much on absolute level of qualification as on having a better qualification than others. Ulrich Beck's insight that conflicts have shifted from goods to risks (or uncertainties) grasps some aspects of the distinction.

One variant of this approach is forwarded in the EU's *Renewed Social Agenda*,[5] with its emphasis on 'opportunities, access and solidarity'. This links to economic and employment strategies designed to improve job opportunities by making the labour market flexible, while providing support for the least advantaged groups in the market. Another is contained in the third way/*Neue Dritte* claim that widening opportunities will facilitate knowledge-based growth which the state can direct to further expansion of opportunities in a virtuous circle of expanding human and physical capital.

It is unclear how far an opportunities approach can achieve solidarities against those who believe they and their families already have better chances in life and therefore seek to retain positional advantage. This issue has constrained educational reform in a number of countries, most strikingly Sweden – the international exemplar of social democracy – and the most liberal European nation, the UK. Egalitarian systems have been scaled back in favour of more diverse provision. In practice, this allows middle-class groups to exercise their advantage.

From a social democratic perspective, a simple opportunity approach is fatally weakened by its failure to address inequalities of outcome. Mitigating market inequalities requires strong and determined redistributive programmes over and above equal-opportunity measures to broaden access to the most desirable positions. This problem grows more serious as inequalities widen and as labour market risks bear more stringently on those at the bottom. This points to the need for policies which will impose higher taxes on those at the top and insist that collective services provide security across the mass of the population, as well as targeted welfare for those at the bottom and programmes to ensure equal access to opportunities.

Greater Focus on Individual Incentives and Responsibilities

This approach has been applied both in the way benefits are organised and in the provision of services. The shift towards 'make work pay' and 'welfare to work' programmes has been endorsed in both the OECD Jobs Programme and the EU's European Employment Strategy. It is central to the Economic Adjustment packages imposed by the Troika of IMF, ECB and EU in Ireland, Portugal, Greece and Italy. Flexibility and employability are the key directions in labour market policy across Europe. 'Welfare to work' puts greater stress on training, adequate benefits and wage supplements at the bottom than does the incentive-based 'make work pay' approach. Both include restrictions on entitlement, dilution of insurance rights among the unemployed and vigorous promotion of jobs against benefits.

Reforms to pensions and other benefits have followed a parallel direction, cutting back on the redistributive elements in social insurance and strengthening the actuarial links between entitlement and work record, and level of benefit and population age-structure. The sole exception to this direction is the expansion of gender rights, reflecting time spent out of the labour market in childcare and maternity, linked to the promotion of employment for women, especially those with care responsibilities.

The new public management stresses individual incentives among those running services by decentralising budgetary responsibility and fostering competition between clinics, schools and other social agencies. The individualised and competitive logic can be taken further through personalised budgeting. This approach simply shifts (most of) the budget the state would spend on a specific need to the individual, and gives them autonomy on how they spend the money. A recent study of European welfare systems analyses these reforms, especially across corporatist Europe, as a process whereby conservative traditions have gradually responded to the pressures of globalisation and post-industrialism by creating a new and leaner social system which places greater stress on incentives and individual responsibility for outcomes.[6]

This new approach has a number of strengths and weaknesses. It has not been able to deliver the efficiency gains expected, at least according to single-country studies. It has generated improvements in outcomes, in terms of employment, and, where this has been energetically pursued, equality of access. However, it has not been successful in producing greater confidence in government and does not offer the basis for a social democratic class alliance. The reason for this is simple. It focuses directly on individual interests and on competition, not on solidarity nor on commitment to collective well-being. The lesson for social democracy is that technical reforms to management will not deliver effective and valued health care, education and local government services. So that people feel they have more control over provision, the reform of democracy at the local level is also needed.

Decentralising Responsibility to the Level of the Citizen

This is achieved through radical democratisation at the local level. Many experiments in participation, neighbourhood engagement, citizens' juries and similar activities have been carried out, directed mainly at achieving consensus on measures to tackle new problems such as environmental risk. These show that it is possible to achieve democratic agreement, provided that all stakeholders are included, that the process of engagement is perceived to be fair and that the outcomes correspond to the agreement. Such conditions are hard to realise in practice, and demand a high degree of political maturity and collective commitment from participants.

Another approach makes use of the non-state sector and rests on the institutions of organised civil society. While the third sector plays a substantial role, especially in the provision of social care, social housing and some parts of education in a number of countries, it lacks the capacity to provide services that are universal or bridge across substantial citizen groups. As a number of commentators on the vaguely conceived 'Big Society' programme in the UK have noted, the social and educational psychology of groups points to the likelihood that divisions between insiders and outsiders will develop. Civil society approaches may enable individuals to engage with needs in their own communities, but it is hard to see how they can provide a basis for the class alliances necessary to social democracy. One way forward is to strengthen democratic reforms so that they embrace workplace democracy.

Sketched above are some of the approaches that have been pursued by recent governments. These may have the capacity to solve technical problems of cost-efficiency, yet they fail to address the *political* problem of ensuring that people across a range of groups identify their interests as best served by high-quality, common public services, such that they will defend these services when they come under pressure.

This requires two things: an extension of democracy from central government to the welfare state, and a tax and redistributive system that limits the capacity to withdraw from public provision into a world of non-redistributive private health insurance, schools and pensions.

Where Do We Go from Here?

The European welfare state faces an uncertain future. The pressures that assail the welfare settlement of the post-war period have led to reforms that tend to divide individuals and split group interests. This damages the social democratic basis of the welfare state and follows the general trajectory of change in the developed world. The transition to a post-industrial and globalised society similarly erodes the traditional basis of social democracy. This rested on an organised working class in which the interests of the more and less skilled were united, and which was able to forge alliances with groups across the middle class. Social democrats confront the problem of how to construct alliances that will endorse a stable and humane settlement in an increasingly contested, unequal and uncertain world.

The remedies available to social democrats fall into two groups. One stresses the opportunities for a politics of idealism in a better-educated and richer world. Another seeks to identify a material base in economic interests, as cuts and economic pressures bite deep. The challenge for social democracy lies in developing a programme which combines elements from both perspectives and is located within a domestic politics that can sustain it.

An Idealist Politics of Global Welfare?

The key theme of this response is to embrace globalisation in a politics of global internationalism. The real challenges to human welfare and greater equality are no longer national or even continental, but primarily concern the global North–South divide. This leads to proposals on aid and, most importantly, trade. Aid efforts must be redoubled, directed to basic needs and separated from foreign policies or military strategies. It is essential that local citizens gain more control over how aid is used. The chequered history of the UN Development Programme for Poverty Reduction, which has been associated with an advance in local democracy in countries such as Brazil but has had much less success in Bolivia, shows that this is not easy.

Some limited progress in rebalancing the terms of trade in consumption commodities (coffee, cereals, clothing) has been made through the Fair Trade movement. Social democrats should also form alliances with groups in the South to achieve a real voice in the World Trade Organisation and similar bodies. This approach is a departure from the national traditions of social democratic politics. It offers a new approach to developing ways to address the challenges from global competition and immigration which bear directly on working-class groups in the North. It also offers the possibility of alliances with internationalist groups in the middle class.

A further development would be the implementation of a tax on international financial transactions (a 'Tobin tax'). This would be designed to limit some of the grosser inequalities between the returns available in the strongholds of financial capital and those to be had elsewhere. The proceeds would offer a source of support for development in the global South. Social democracy would contribute pressure for greater participation by recipient communities in how this money is to be spent.

The internationalist logic can be linked to arguments for a shift towards a slower growth pathway in national development. On the one hand, the competitive-growth society creates the setting in which the inequalities between winners and losers flourish. On the other, the stresses and pressures of everyday life undermine individual well-being. Again, this approach is unlikely to be sufficiently powerful to furnish the basis for a stable cross-class coalition, but it could broaden the appeal of social democracy beyond an increasingly defensive and decreasingly influential group.

New Alliances based on Material Interests?

This approach rests on the claim that the common interests of various marginalised groups, particularly women, for whom paid employment is now the norm across Europe, offer a cross-class foundation. Provision to facilitate women's employment and to some extent to support social and family care has entered the vocabulary and practice of politics at European and national levels. Success in reducing discrimination and sharing family care burdens more equally varies between countries and is at best partial. While there are real opportunities for a more inclusive social democracy, gender and other issues do not offer the linkages required for the simple reason that gender interests are confounded with class interests. In general, women and men partner within social class groups. Emerging material interests, such as gender, can be no more than one component in a new politics of social democracy.

Much of this is familiar territory. Social democracy pioneered support for gender equality in the workplace and in access to education and training, and was at the forefront of the EU directives and national legislation to promote these rights. Society has become more fragmented. Consequently, the equality approach must be extended across minorities by ethnicity, sexuality, faith, region and age to incorporate the needs of more vulnerable groups.

The experiences of campaigning for community policies, workplace integration, multiculturalism and stronger regional policies and against social exclusion indicate that such an approach leads at best to an unstable political equilibrium. As alliances seek to embrace a wider range of needs they generally become less secure. This implies a headline politics of the 'lowest common denominator', reduced to equality of opportunity and non-discrimination. The challenge for social democrats is to bring home to the full range of groups across our society how market individualism fails to provide a satisfactory route to the realisation of opportunities.

A second material approach suggests that the internationalisation of the working-class movement will offer opportunities as social democracy strengthens in the emerging industrial powers of East Asia, South America and perhaps elsewhere. While political trajectories are uncertain, the logic that the interests of western working-class groups may be best served by international rather than nationally based links may grow more compelling. Such an approach directly confronts the defensive politics of the extreme right for nation and against immigrants. At what stage such an approach might help reconstruct social democracy in Europe is unclear.

Pessimists envisage a third solution – a continuing process of fragmentation and growing inequalities, or the Americanisation of Europe. At some stage this may also lead to circumstances in which class alliances again become attractive. The process could plausibly be helped by a response to climate change that involved an involuntary reduction in economic growth and the necessity for stricter regulation of many aspects of life. As a manifestly shared threat grows closer, collective approaches to well-being may become more attractive.

This brief review fails to identify areas in which there is a clear basis for the kind of interest coalitions that can support stable majorities in government. In some ways this is surprising. The overall trends to inequality and uncertainty in individual lives and the immediate catastrophe of spending cuts and rising unemployment point to common concerns across substantial groups in the population; the politics of the many versus the few. In practice, the variations in skill and opportunity and the decline in opportunities to experience democratic organisation and solidarity damage the viability of the approach.

The above discussion shows how real opportunities exist in internationalism, in building links with social democratic movements in the global South and in seeking to make a common cause with the range of groups who are disadvantaged in globalised post-industrial society. Any emerging social democratic coalition will have to hold together people who differ greatly in culture, life-chances and ideology and who have little sense of shared identity. This is a major and continuing challenge.

An Unattractive Alternative?

The recent experience of the UK in attempting a market-centred response to the crisis is instructive. The UK has occupied a position midway between European social democracy and the liberal market capitalism of the US for much of the post-war period. The centre-left

New Labour Government of Blair and Brown led the way in market responses to the banking collapse and recession, putting most resources into making capital available and supporting bankrupt financial institutions to manage this failure in 2008–9. This action led to a sharp rise in spending in the UK (and in the US) from 2007–9. In France, Germany and Sweden (higher spending countries where recession automatically injected more resources into the economy through mechanisms such as benefits for unemployed people, and where the crisis of finance capital was less severe), the growth in public spending was less abrupt.

European countries in general put very much more resources into maintaining employment, particularly for the core of the working class, compared to the UK. This included such measures as: subsidies for a three-day week through state-financed 'training programmes' at the height of the crisis in France, Germany and Italy; reductions in social insurance contributions; support for new hiring and for the long-term unemployed.[7]

The longer-term response in most European countries takes the level of spending roughly back to the former long-term trajectory or slightly below it (Figure 5.1). In the UK, a Conservative–Liberal Democrat coalition elected in 2010 is pursuing a comprehensive restructuring of the welfare state designed to privatise core services, prioritise work incentives over the reduction of poverty and cut public spending below European levels.[8] The previous government's progress in bringing public spending in areas like health care and education close to the European average is now to be reversed. This programme of spending cuts is cumulative, so that spending in the UK will fall below US and G7 levels for the first time ever, by 2015. The $2 trillion cuts currently being debated in the US may restrain spending there during the next decade so that it is rather longer before the UK cuts bring spending here to transatlantic levels.

Although the cuts in the UK are noticeably more abrupt than those elsewhere in Europe, the coalition's reforms are not simply a matter of a reduction in public spending. More importantly, the cuts are focused particularly on services for lower-income groups, and find their place within a programme of privatisation in virtually all

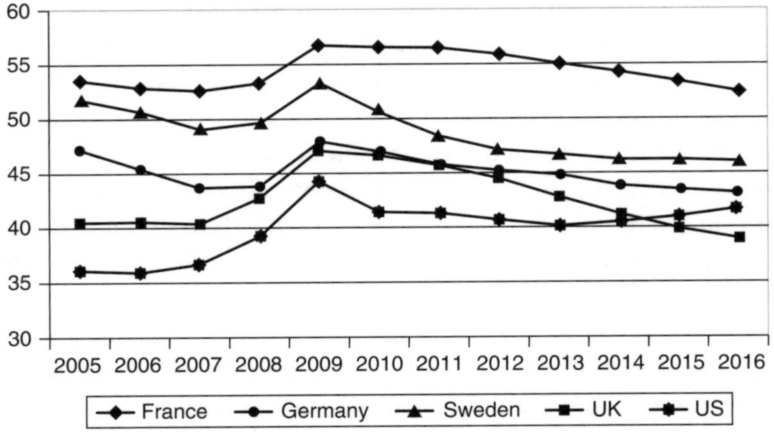

FIGURE 5.1 Public expenditure in major European countries and the US (2005–16) as percentage of GDP ***Source:*** World Economic Outlook Database, http://www.imf.org/external/pubs/ft/weo/2011/02/weodata/index.aspx, consulted 28.11.2011.

local government services, much of the NHS, higher education and universities, a deregulation of employment protection and introduction of a harsher regime for people of working age. This involves cuts to short-term benefits and stricter eligibility tests, designed to reduce the numbers on disability benefit by more than half. The 2010 Government have been enthusiastic in utilising the crisis to decisively alter the emphasis of the UK political economy from one where national policies reflect a European tradition of state welfare, to the US liberal tradition of market competition.

In the past, such programmes have proved difficult to implement; for example, under the 1979–97 Conservative Government. While a tax-cutting agenda can command majority support, any restructuring of services valued by the mass of the population, such as health care and education, is likely to encounter opposition. Unless the economic recovery is unprecedentedly rapid, the 2010 Government will be unable to offer tax cuts. Further, it is pursuing untested reforms of widely used services; and it is a coalition, which means it may experience difficultly in marshalling parliamentary support for the full programme. Even with measures to force unemployed people to take very low-waged jobs, the increase in unemployment is likely to generate further upward pressure on spending. The cuts programme will eliminate at least half a million jobs in the state sector, and rather more in private firms dependent on government contracts. It is unlikely that the private sector will grow rapidly enough to absorb this number in the life of one parliament, as the Government hopes.

The outcome may well be the kind of piecemeal cuts that previous austerity programmes have achieved, tapering off as they encounter opposition from a range of dissatisfied groups. Such a situation would offer social democracy a fresh opportunity, provided it can offer a programme that responds to the changed circumstances of a globally competitive and post-industrial world.

The discussion above indicates that any way forward would need to combine three elements: a way of securing stable economic growth, that was sufficiently regulated to respond to a green agenda and to provide decent working conditions; a combination of outcomes that would appeal to a sufficiently wide range of interests in the fragmented post-industrial electorate; and the capacity to contribute to social justice in a divided and unequal world. Any effective programme must include government investment combined with fairer access to opportunities and internationalism.

New Labour combined these elements to mobilise support against market-centred politics in the late 1990s, but the above discussion suggests a further element, which has received relatively little attention in recent debates: measures to strengthen the democratic side of social democracy. This takes us in two directions: first, institutional – local and regional government, reforms to Westminster and the promotion of a vigorous workplace democracy; second, societal – democracy implies a more equal citizenry. Democratic reforms need to include greater plurality in media ownership and limitations on gross inequalities of power. This implies among other things strongly progressive taxation and the devotion of greater resources to combat tax avoidance. The argument returns us to a social democratic commitment to greater equality, not just because it is an important element in the social side of the equation, but because it is central to any plausible democracy.

Conclusions

This chapter discusses how the social democratic consensus that supported the European welfare state has broken down under the dual pressures of globalisation and post-industrialism. Working-class support for the welfare state has fragmented and proves difficult to reconstruct. The right has grasped the opportunity to exploit these divisions. Middle-class groups are more likely to be attracted by a politics of market opportunities, although that approach cannot deliver to more than a minority. More integrated corporatist societies such as those found in Germany and Sweden strive to resist these pressures, but encounter difficulties in incorporating everyone in a viable welfare state which will sustain political support.

The real problems are less the technical inability to devise solutions to existing challenges than the difficulty of constructing a basis for political consensus that would sustain the welfare state settlement. The political basis of the social welfare impasse is analogous to that underlying responses to climate change after Copenhagen. In this situation, it has not been possible to resolve the conflict between more and less developed nations regarding where the brunt of carbon cuts should fall: on richer nations, to restrain growth in the global North, or across all countries, so that the opportunities for development in the South are curtailed.

Similarly the groups which were able to unite within a vigorous industrial society to support social democracy now find common cause more difficult. They are divided between a (shrinking) industrial sector and (expanding) service sector, between women workers and carers and men, between traditional and newcomer groups, between global North and global South. These divisions do not include those between professionals, technical experts and routine workers in the various sectors, itself divided by the higher value to be added in some areas of the service sector (such as banking, law, cultural, media, IT, education and health care industries), and the lower value accorded to personal care and grooming, childcare, cleaning and similar work.

The policy directions currently being pursued in different countries share a move away from collectivism and social cohesion towards a more individualist politics. The result is further erosion of the potential for social democracy. Whether or not welfare to work and the third way, the new public management, decentralised democracy or organised civil society ('Big Society') policies enable progress in the short term, all weaken the collective political potential for a vigorous welfare state. The lurch towards a minimalist, market-centred programme by the 2010 UK Government may restore growth, but will certainly lead to greater inequality, more poverty, higher unemployment, more homelessness and more unequal social provision. Social democracy must make this an opportunity.

Suggestions from the centre-left on new approaches to make a social democratic settlement more viable range from an emphasis on new social interests, particularly those of women, to a new North–South internationalism of trade and aid, to the revaluing of work and civil life and the building of an international social democratic movement across emerging industrial and post-industrial societies. Such an approach requires domestic support. For social democrats, the problem is finding a way of linking investment, equality, opportunity and internationalism. A key element will be the restoration of a vigorous and thoroughgoing democracy, including genuine local and workplace democracy that engages people directly in collective responsibility for their lives. Without such reforms, it is hard to see how such policies are to be sustained over time.

CHAPTER 6

Equality, Social Trust and the Politics of Institutional Design

Bo Rothstein

In both the rich industrial nations and the less developed countries, it is striking how there are large differences in social, economic and political equality. Measures of political, social and legal rights, as well as respect for human rights vary enormously between countries. The same goes for measures of economic inequality and social well-being such as poverty, literacy and population health. Furthermore, not only is there variation between countries but also huge variation within countries regarding most measures of social, economic and de facto political equality. One example is the variation in the percentage of children who live in poverty, which is much lower in some countries than in others, although they have the same level of general prosperity. In fact, some very rich countries have more children living in poverty than countries that are less prosperous. In addition, in all democracies, possibilities to influence public policy vary systematically with social class.

The overall development within most rich capitalist market-orientated countries is that inequality has increased over the last two or three decades. On top of this, political parties that have increased social and economic equality on their agenda – that is, by and large, social democratic parties – have not fared well in recent elections in many European countries. This is paradoxical, since almost all empirical indicators of human well-being – including economic prosperity and growth – show that countries that have opted for social democratic policies which increase social and economic equality outperform all other countries.[1]

The starting point for this chapter is that for the vast majority of people, human well-being would be improved if social inequality were to decrease.[2] The problem is how to achieve this. This chapter is an effort to summarise the *policy-relevant results* of 20 years research into this topic.[3] The analysis is based primarily on three books that I have published on this topic.[4] Although what is presented here should not be understood as resting on 'proofs' (I think these words are too presumptuous for most of what can count as explanations of how causal relations operate in the social sciences), I limit my pretensions by saying that there are reasonable empirical indicators to support my arguments. This chapter is thus intended to provide direction for those interested in achieving increased equality in their societies.

The first, central message is that *the level of social solidarity in a country is not culturally determined.* That is to say, the Nordic countries are not more egalitarian than Australia, the UK, Kenya, Brazil, Hungary or the US because there is something special about the Nordic culture. Another central message is that *policy measures for increased equality in a society are influenced, but cannot be sustained over longer periods only, by interest-based political mobilisation.* Thus, I reject cultural determinism as well as different interest-based theories such as neo-classical economic theory or the purely interest-based variants of Marxism.

Rather, my argument is that political choices are important, and most important is how central political institutions are designed. In other words: *increased social and economic equality is something that can be manufactured by the design of political institutions.* In political terms, designing institutions is the equivalent of designing policies. This is because institutions (understood as formal and informal rules) have a large impact on what future agents come to understand as being in their interest and/or being in line with their social norms. To be more precise, if one's aim is a more egalitarian society, thinking about how to design institutions is more important than engaging in ideological mobilisation about the virtue of increased equality. Further, I do not argue that solidarity should result in a perfectly equal society (and I don't think such a society is something desirable), but that much more equality, especially in certain instances specified below, is both desirable and possible to achieve through political means.

The Problem of Equality

If we are interested in a more equal society, we need a correct understanding of 'the nature of the problem'. This involves three questions. The first is the 'what is it?' question, namely: What should equality be about? The second is the 'how to get it?' question: What can be expected from (the vast majority of) humans when it comes to their propensity for solidarity? The third question is about strategy, namely: How to make social solidarity sustainable?

The first question – equality of what? – is a complicated one. In an era of 'conspicuous consumption' and increased individualism and social heterogeneity, it is difficult to argue that government has a responsibility to equalise all forms of consumption. That is because consumption cannot be an end in itself and further, ambition should be rewarded. The best answers to the 'equality of what?' question have been forwarded by liberal rights-based philosophers such as John Rawls, Amartya Sen and Martha Nussbaum.

These writers differ in certain important respects, but they agree that *equality should be about guaranteeing access to a specific set of goods and services that are important for people in order for them to be capable of realising their potential as human beings.* Whereas the central term of Rawls's liberalism is 'primary goods', for Sen and Nussbaum it is 'capabilities'.

The terminology implies that the problem is not to equalise economic resources or social status as such, but to ensure all individuals a set of *basic resources* that will equalise their chances to reach their full potential as humans. Standards are access to high-quality education and health care, civil and political rights, equal protection under the law, social services and social insurance systems that support people who cannot generate enough resources from their own work, support for persons with disabilities, etc. The set of such capabilities enhancing goods and services can of course vary,[5] but it is important to realise that equality, as a politically viable concept, has to be about specific things.[6] There is simply no way we, by political means, can equalise the ability to be a skilled musician, to be creative, to be loved, to be an outstanding researcher, a good parent or to be a first-rate ballet dancer.

What *is* possible to do by political means is to increase the possibility for those who happen to have ambitions in these fields and others to realise their talents even if they have not entered this world with huge endowments. This can be done by providing access to specific sets of resources that are likely to enhance their capabilities of reaching their full potential as human beings.

One implication of this thought is that *equality should be about individuals, not collectives* or groups, whether these are based on social class, occupation, kinship, religion, gender, ethnicity, sexual orientations or any other form of collective categorisation. One reason for this is that many of these communities or identities are floating, and branding individuals (especially children and young people) into such collectives by administrative means can result in gross violations of their human rights. A second, more important, argument, is that there is no guarantee that the majority in groups like these will not oppress or exploit individuals who are put under their surveillance or, even worse, jurisdiction. Therefore, *arguments for increased equality should not be based on utilitarian theory but on theories about individual rights.*

Philosophical arguments about 'primary goods' are important, and also inadequate for policy. The reason is that they usually ignore two inter-related problems that have been discovered in empirical research. One is about implementation – more often than not, their suggestions would result in administrative nightmares that would severely damage the political legitimacy for equality and thereby create a political majority against increased equality. For example, many well-known political philosophers (and people on the left in general) have over the years suggested policies for increasing equality that are directed to specific disadvantaged groups. Such policies are very likely to run into a wide range of serious problems of legitimacy when they are implemented. For example, in order to decide who belongs to the disadvantaged group and, if so, how much and what support this person should be entitled to, an army of bureaucrats has to be employed which must engage in investigations that can be very intrusive. Moreover, there will always be a number of 'borderline cases' that either don't get the support they deserve, or do get support they don't deserve. In both cases, political legitimacy is undermined.

Reciprocity and Human Nature

In striving for a more equal society, it is important to start from a correct understanding of 'human nature', especially if these reforms are to have a lasting impact. Ideas about the 'basic human nature' have a long history in the social sciences that has now been resolved, mostly by experimental research. The results from laboratory, fieldwork and survey research that speak against man as a utility-maximising, rational agent is now overwhelming, and refutes the idea of man as 'homo economicus'. Self-interest is an important ingredient in decisions about how to act, but it is far from being as dominant as in neo-classical economics (or for that matter, in many Marxist theories). Moreover, it would be impossible to create solidaristic or co-operative institutions of any kind (including democracy, the rule of law and respect for property rights, not to speak of any social insurance system) if individual utility-maximising self-interest were 'the only game in town', because the temptation to 'free-ride' would undermine the sustainability of such institutions.

However, this new research does not present humans as benevolent altruists either. True, there is altruistic behaviour, but it is usually restricted to very small circles of family and close friends. Or it is simply too rare and also too unpredictable for building sustainable systems advancing solidarity at a societal level. This lesson is important since it tells us that trying to mobilise political support for increased equality by referring to people's altruistic motives is likely to fail.

Instead, what this research suggests is that *reciprocity is the basic human orientation*. The central idea is that people are not so much motivated 'from the back' by utility-based calculations or culturally induced norms. Instead, human behaviour is to a large extent determined by forward-looking strategic thinking in the sense that *what agents do, depends on what they think other agents are going to do*. This idea of reciprocity fundamentally recasts how we should understand and explain human behaviour. Instead of looking backwards to what causes variation in utility-based interests or culturally induced norms, it is important to understand how people's forward-looking perceptions about 'other people' are constructed.

Regarding the prospect for solidarity, results from research show that most people are willing to engage in solidaristic co-operation for common goals, such as a generous set of publicly provided 'primacy goods', even if they will not personally benefit from this. However, for this to happen, three specific conditions have to be in place. First, *people have to be convinced that the policy is morally justified (substantial justice)*. Second, *people have to be convinced that most other agents can be trusted to also co-operate (solidaristic justice)*, that is, that other agents are likely to abstain from 'free-riding'. Third, *people have to be convinced that the policy can be implemented in a fair and even-handed manner (procedural justice)*.

On the first issue, the work of the philosophers mentioned above is useful. The second requirement, which is equally important for generating support for solidarity in the interest of policies for increased equality, has to be resolved by institutional design guided by knowledge from research in policy implementation and public administration. For example, it is not difficult to argue that universal access to high-quality health care and sickness insurance qualifies as a 'primary good' in the above-mentioned sense. However, if a majority cannot be convinced that (a) most people will pay the increased taxes required for producing these goods, or that (b) the good will not be delivered in a manner that is acceptable, fair and respectful, they are not likely to support this policy. If health personnel are known to be corrupt, unprofessional or disrespectful, support for this policy will dwindle. The same goes for sickness insurance.

People are likely to support insurance for people who are ill, but if perceptions of misuse or overuse ('free-riding') become widespread, support will decline. In other words, *solidarity is conditioned on the institutional design of the systems that are supposed to bring about the policies which will enhance equality*. This idea has been formulated by John Rawls:

> A just system must generate its own support. This means that it must be arranged so as to bring about in its members the corresponding sense of justice, an effective desire to act in accordance with its rules for reasons and justice. Thus, the requirements of stability and the criterion of discouraging desires that conflict with the principles of

justice put further constraints on institutions. They must not only be just but framed so as to encourage the virtue of justice in those who take part in them.

The central idea in this quotation is how Rawls specifies that in making a solidaristic system sustainable, we have to be aware of the existence of a 'feedback mechanism' between people's support for just principles and their perceptions of the *quality of the institutions* that are set up to implement these principles.

Of course, history and contemporary events, in addition to experimental evidence, also show that 'ordinary people' are willing to engage in atrocities against other people when they believe these 'others' would otherwise harm them. More generally, distrust in other agents or institutions may lead to a vicious circle that can break any system or policy set up to increase solidarity.

Thus, on the one hand, the idea of reciprocity stands against the cynicism about human nature central to interest-based theories that have dominated most economic approaches in the social sciences. On the other hand, reciprocity is also in conflict with a naïve understanding of human nature as genuinely benevolent, which many equality-enhancing policies have been built on. Instead, reciprocity tells us that if through the design of institutions we can make people trust that most other agents in their society will behave in a trustworthy and solidaristic manner, they will do likewise. If not, they will defect, even if the outcome will be detrimental to their interests.

That reciprocity can go in different directions is also apparent if we look at most of the rankings of countries' performance that are now available. The level of corruption, to take one example, shows staggering differences between countries. This particular 'social bad' also serves as a good example of why reciprocity is a better starting point for understanding human behaviour than its rivals. If we relied on cultural explanations, we would have to say to our sisters and brothers in, for example, Nigeria that the extremely high level of corruption in their country is caused by their corrupt culture. Or if we started from interest-based explanations, we would be unable to explain why the huge variation of corruption exists without relying on either genetic or cultural explanations. However, if we base our explanations on the idea of reciprocity, the explanation for the high level of corruption in, for example, Pakistan is that the institutions in place make it reasonable for most people to believe that most other agents will be engaged in corrupt practices, and thus they have no reason not to engage in these practices themselves.

Solidarity and Social Trust

A central conclusion is thus that reciprocity, as the baseline for human agency, can go in two directions. One direction will result in more solidaristic co-operation for increased equality and thereby increased human well-being. The other is exactly opposite, resulting in negative outcomes such as high levels of corruption, discrimination, civil strife, massive exploitation and ethnic cleansing. Given what is known from the record of human history, it is not advisable to be naïve in these matters.

Most important, then, is knowledge of what it is that makes reciprocity turn bad or good. Theory and research give a reasonably clear answer to what determines the direction in which reciprocity will take society, namely the level of social or generalised interpersonal trust. If most people in a society believe that most other people in that society can be trusted, they have good reasons to support policies that are based on solidarity and thereby will increase equality as it has been specified above. However, if they believe that most people cannot be trusted, the outcome will be the opposite.

As with corruption, research on social trust (and the related concept of social capital) has increased tremendously since the mid-1990s. This is in part because empirical research shows that high levels of social trust at the individual level are connected to a number of important factors such as tolerance towards minorities, participation in public life, education, health and subjective well-being. At the societal level, high-trust societies have more extensive and generous social welfare systems.

How to understand a concept like social trust is not easy, because when asked in surveys most people do not know if most other people in their society can be trusted. One interpretation is that social trust is an expression of optimism about the future. Another interpretation is that when people answer that survey question they are actually making an evaluation of the moral standard of the society in which they live. Both interpretations should be seen as answers to the central question of in which direction reciprocity will turn – what people believe about what other people will do if they try to engage in some collaborative effort with them.

Again, the notion of reciprocity suggests that what people do depends on what they think other people will do, and this is likely to be determined by how they think about other people's trustworthiness, which can be seen as how they interpret the general moral standing of their society. For the case of creating a more equal society, the results are clear. Although not a perfect correlation, societies with more interpersonal trust have more political, economic and social equality, including gender equality. This evidence refers to what is known as generalised trust; that is, trust in people in general about whom there is no way to have anything that comes close to perfect information. This is different from particularistic trust which refers to trust in small groups of friends or clans. Such inward or group-based trust can often lead to severe social conflicts that are detrimental to human well-being.

An important result from recent research is that people from cultures where interpersonal trust is very low do not retain their low social trust when they have moved to a society where interpersonal trust is high. Instead, they update their trust in other people based on new information of how trust relations operate in their new society. Most important for the issue discussed here is how they perceive the trustworthiness of other agents in their new society, and especially of how they perceive the fairness of the public institutions that exist in their new society. This shows that propensity for social solidarity is not culturally determined but can be influenced by institutional design.

Achieving Social Trust Through Institutional Design

How then, can generalised trust be generated? Again, recent research gives a reasonably clear answer to this question. A high level of generalised trust is caused by what has been called high-quality government institutions, especially the institutions that implement public policies. The central basic norm for these institutions is impartiality.

This implies that discrimination (whether based on ethnicity, gender or class), corruption (in its many forms), clientelism, nepotism and political favouritism are very rare or non-existent when public officials or professionals implement public policies. Social trust is thus not generated 'from below' (for example, from civil society or voluntary associations) but 'from above', by how people perceive the fairness and competence of government institutions. Thus, *designing institutions that implement public policy is to create (or destroy) social trust.*

One reason for this effect is that when people make up their minds as to whether most people in their society can be trusted, they make an inference from how they perceive authorities. If the local policeman, schoolteacher, social insurance administrator, judge or doctor cannot be trusted (because they discriminate against people like you, or ask for bribes, or give preferential treatment to some groups), then it is reasonable to assume that neither should you trust 'people in general' in your society. And vice versa, if they are known to be honest, impartial, competent and fair, then it is likely that this will spill over to 'people in general'.

A second reason is that if people think that government institutions are impartial and thus can be trusted, they will infer that most other people think the same and this will make 'people in general' act in a more trustworthy manner. Moreover, if the public authorities are known to be engaged in the type of 'bad' practices mentioned above, then many people will come to think that in order to get what they need in life (immunisation for their children, building permits, employment in the public sector, etc.), most people will have to be engaged in these kinds of bad practices, and thus they should not be trusted.

For social policy and many other policies intended to cater for increased equality in the above-mentioned sense, this has a number of implications for institutional design. The most important is to strive for universal systems and avoid, as much as possible, systems that are directed to supporting specific groups and/or entail bureaucratic discretion. Universal programmes (such as universal child allowances, universal pre-schools and schools, universal pensions, universal health care) are to be favoured over specific programmes directed to specific groups such as 'the poor', to certain minorities, or to women.

The reasons for universalism are fivefold:

1. Universal systems entail a minimum of (if any) bureaucratic discretion. Thereby, not only corruption, but all forms of bureaucratic intrusions connected to needs-testing, are avoided.
2. Since universal programmes in principle cater for 'all', they will include the middle class, thereby almost automatically securing a political majority and making the programme politically sustainable. Programmes built solely on interest-group mobilisation will always be vulnerable to interest-based counter-mobilisation. Universal programmes therefore avoid an us-and-them division of society.
3. Universal programmes eliminate the problem of stigmatisation of specific groups and an individual 'stereotype-threat' mentioned above.
4. Although they also give benefits to 'rich' people, universal programmes tend to be very redistributive, more so than programmes which 'take from the rich and give to the poor'. The reason is that the benefits are usually nominal in money or costs of services, but taxes are either proportional to income or progressive. Even when universal programmes are income-related (e.g. many pension systems in more developed countries), there is usually a cap which makes them redistributive.
5. Universal programmes, especially in services like education or elderly care, will usually be of high quality since the need to keep the more well-to-do people on board will make it difficult for politicians to lower service quality if they want to stay in power. In sum, universal programmes have the capacity to 'generate their own support' as noted by Rawls above.

Admittedly, there are policies for which universal institutions will not work. It is difficult to have a universal policy for active labour market policy since each unemployed person is different and will need different types of support in order to find a new job. The same goes for much of social assistance to dysfunctional families, since each decision on whether or not to take a child into custody must be based on a professional judgement of the specificities of the particular case. In these areas, it is important to try as much as possible to use other means to ensure impartiality and fairness in how decisions are made in the implementation process. High-quality training for professionals and civil servants, systems for accountability and control, possibilities to appeal, are but a few such possibilities. A further proposal would be to single out the very rich (who would not receive benefits) instead of targeting the poor. *In sum, high-quality government institutions will increase the level of social trust, which will make reciprocity translate into solidarity, which in turn will increase the possibilities for establishing policy for increased equality.*

Five Temptations for the Centre-Left to Resist

As this chapter attempts to give practical direction to those who seek more equality in society, it cannot consist only of instructions, but must also suggest things *not* to do or to avoid. As for creating a sustainable, solidaristic society, I identify five such warnings in conclusion. They can, historically, be seen as temptations that politicians and activists who have strived for a more equal society have fallen into, and which have had detrimental effects on the possibility of achieving and sustaining political support for the type of equality-enhancing policies specified above.

First, *do not side with the producers.* Many of the 'primary goods' that need to be made available by the state in order to increase equality are services, and thus entail a great number of employees (teachers, health care workers, and so on). Too often, politicians who have been responsible for equality-enhancing policies have come to side with the service producers rather than citizens. There are various reasons for this, one being that many politicians on the left have a background in, or close connections to, public-sector unions. Of course, public-sector workers' interests are often very legitimate, but in many instances their interests have been set before the citizens they are supposed to serve.

The problem is that many social services have been produced in the form of monopolies where the 'customers' could be taken as given. Such organisations are usually neither service-friendly nor particularly creative or innovative. While financing of the primary goods should be the responsibility of the government, production should in many service areas be left to private and non-governmental organisations. However, it is important to understand that since the services in question are very important for the well-being of citizens, such markets need to be tightly regulated and the producers supervised. Monopolies in service production should be avoided and market-like systems that promote choice and innovation should be supported. Such a transformation requires more, not less, regulation.

Second, *do not fall for the siren calls of special-interest groups.* Politics is admittedly an interest-group battle, but too often politicians have sacrificed universalism for particularlism and launched policies that cater for specific groups. Various groups in the labour market, specific branches of industries or ethnic groups are but a few examples. Multiculturalism is, in many parts of the world, an empirical fact and should be applauded as such. However, this is not the same as saying that we should also have rights-based multiculturalism in the form of specific rights for specific ethnic or religious groups. My recommendation is to avoid what has for a long time been a favourite theme of the intellectual left: namely, identity politics directed at specific minorities.

There are three reasons for this:

1. Such politics is, by definition, anti-majoritarian. Indeed, one could argue that, through its inherent logic, a focus on minorities creates a majority opposed to left-wing politics. It is simply impossible to build a politically effective coalition from a plethora of disparate minority groups, as they often have completely conflicting interests. A political movement with such a focus will reduce itself to a supermarket for specific special-interests and minority groups, rather than building towards a majority. This

has been the case in many European countries with respect to the integration of immigrants and ethnic minorities. Again, support for vulnerable minorities is most effective when universal programmes are designed to include minority needs without singling them out as special rights.

2. Two, identity politics tends to stigmatise the very group it aims to support. Further, as the social psychologist Claude Steele demonstrated, identity politics often creates negative, stereotypical self-images among vulnerable groups. This has been shown to have very negative consequences on the self-esteem of the affected individuals, and on their ability to perform well.
3. Such particularistic politics often breeds a cumbersome bureaucracy which, on a case-by-case basis, is left to decide what type of, and how much, support individuals are entitled to have. This, in turn, feeds criticism of social democracy for an over-reliance on top-down government solutions.

Third, *stay clear of paternalism.* Many activists and many politicians who have strived for a more equal society have in reality often had a paternalistic idea of how ordinary people should lead their lives. This has, with increasing individualism and education, become much more problematic. Especially when it comes to services such as education, childcare, elderly care and health care, the one-size-fits-all syndrome must be seen as outdated. Regulated market-like solutions, where citizens are able to choose from a wide range of different service providers, should be supported. In addition to that mentioned above, there is one more fundamental reason why choice in these areas should be the rule. From implementation research comes an important result: namely, that the operative staff who work face-to-face with the clients – teachers, health care and elderly care staff – must be granted relatively wide freedom of action and discretion in carrying out their work. Accordingly, many decisions of great importance for individual citizens are made by local public organs and individual officials. This, however, creates what we might call *democracy's black hole.* Power is wielded over citizens in what are for them extremely important matters by officials who, for the most part, cannot be held accountable for their actions. The many cases where schoolchildren have been bullied, or when people in elderly care have been seriously mishandled, speak to this problem. Without the possibility to 'go elsewhere' (that is, to allow people to choose between different service providers), violation of basic human rights will be a constant problem for equality-enhancing policies. Again, systems with competing producers need to be tightly regulated since one cannot take for granted that such producers will not try to 'cut corners'.

Fourth, *do not yield to narrow-minded economistic thinking about taxes.* While it is true that universal social policies come with high taxes, for the reason that if 'everyone' is going to be entitled to a reasonable set of publicly funded 'primary goods' then this will be costly for the public coffers, this is not the same as being a burden for the economy at large. It is a misunderstanding that high levels of taxation become a hindrance to economic growth. From a global perspective, rich states have a level of taxation that is almost twice as high as that of poor states. And when the rich Western states are compared over time, the evidence that high public spending is negative for market-driven economic growth is simply not there.

This reveals a misconception regarding what the universal welfare state is about. The large part of this type of welfare state is not benefits to poor people but universal social insurances and social services that benefit the whole or very large segments of the population. These goods are in high demand by almost all citizens, and research shows that in many cases covering these demands by universal systems becomes more cost effective. The economic theory about problems of asymmetric information on markets is well suited to understanding this. Although this theory is quite technical, the logic is very simple. For example, in private health-insurance systems, the costs that such information problems lead to (overtreatment, overbilling, the administrative costs for insurance companies screening out bad risks, the costs for handling legal problems about coverage) can become astronomical, as seems to be the case in the United States. Universal systems are much more cost-effective in handling these problems since risks are spread over the whole population and the incentives for providers to overbill or use costly but unnecessary treatments are minimal. These information problems provide a very good economic justification for universal social insurances. From the standpoint of social equality, this has the advantage of including the segment of the population who, from their 'market wage', never would have had the chance to afford these services.

It should be added that among the OECD countries which today carry the most malignant deficits in their public finances (Greece, Spain, Portugal, the UK, Ireland and the US), one will find none of the countries with relatively high public expenditures; while those with more egalitarian policies (Denmark, Finland, the Netherlands, Norway, Sweden), and thus much higher spending on social services and social insurance systems in general, have their public finances in good order. In other words, the main theme of neo-liberalism – that we need to choose between 'fairness' and 'effectiveness', and that large public expenditures would be damaging for the public economy – proves erroneous.

Fifth, *do not excuse political defeats by blaming structural factors* such as the media, globalisation, international finance or patriarchy. If the pioneers of social welfare policies had done this, they would never have started. Structural conditions may make things difficult but, at the end of the day, I am convinced that they can be defeated by clever forms of institutional design.

CHAPTER 7

Progress and Social Policy: Two-and-a-Half Cheers for Education

Lane Kenworthy

Tony Blair's assertion in 1996 that New Labour's top three priorities would be 'education, education, education' encapsulates a view that schooling and learning should at the core of social democratic economic and social policy.[1] However, the New Labour Governments' subsequent failure to reduce income inequality or increase social mobility in the UK has led to scepticism about education's importance. This feeling has been compounded by the EU's seeming failure to meet the Lisbon Agenda's goal of becoming 'the most dynamic and competitive knowledge-based economy in the world . . . by 2010'.

Sceptics are right to suspect that education is not a cure-all. Yet that should not diminish its centrality to the social democratic project. Good and broadly dispersed schooling is not sufficient to achieve low inequality, high mobility, high employment or rapid economic growth. But it helps. Moreover, schooling is key to achieving other social democratic aims. It ought to be front and centre in a social democratic agenda for the twenty-first century.

Income Inequality

Let's begin with income inequality. Social democrats are right to worry about high inequality. It is objectionable on normative grounds, given the massive impact of luck in determining where each person ends up in the distribution. It may also have ill effects on other social, economic and political outcomes, such as health and democracy. If we compare across individuals in a society, we find that those with more education tend to earn more. This would appear to suggest that increasing the education of others might reduce income inequality.

Unfortunately, while equalising schooling almost certainly would help to reduce income inequality, its influence is likely to be constrained by other factors.[2] One is differences in cognitive abilities and non-cognitive traits produced by genetics, parents, peers, neighbourhoods and so on. Another is structural features of the economy, such as the intensity of product market competition, immigration, trade and the sectoral structure of employment. A third is institutional factors. Wage-setting arrangements – collective or individual, centralised or local – play an important role in determining wage gaps, particularly between the low end and the rest. Corporate governance practices are an important influence on the pay of CEOs and other high-level executives. The development of winner-take-all markets arguably accounts for some, perhaps much, of the skyrocketing pay for those at the top of the labour market. Finally, government regulation of labour markets, of the financial sector, and of other aspects of the economy matters.

The contributing factors noted above compete with education in determining the degree of inequality in earnings across individuals. Further weakening education's impact is the fact that earnings are then pooled in households. Household size and composition therefore play an important role, as does the distribution of employment across households. Some households have no one in the labour market; others have a low-earning full-time worker and a part-timer; still others have two high-earning full-timers, and so on. Last, but certainly not least, there is government redistribution via taxes and transfers.

There are at least two distinct aspects of income inequality. To capture them we are forced to use two different types of data. The standard approach uses income data from country surveys. The degree of inequality is measured by the Gini coefficient (an indicator ranging from zero to one, with larger values indicating greater inequality). But these data include little or no information on the top 1% of the distribution. This is a problem, as an important development in recent decades has been growing separation between the tip-top and the rest of society. To get a handle on this, researchers use data from tax records, with the measure being the share of income going to the top 1%. These data aren't so good on households at the bottom, many of whom don't owe taxes.

The separation between the top 1% and the rest of the population is unlikely to owe much to education. The super-rich include CEOs, financial analysts and traders, entertainers and athletes, entrepreneurs and some people who provide legal and other important services to them. The difference in educational attainment between these people and the upper-middle class tends to be minimal at best.

Combining these considerations, it is no surprise that education cannot be a silver bullet for inequality reduction.[3] If we look across the world's affluent countries, we see little or no relationship between education and income inequality. Figure 7.1 shows these data. Education can be measured in a variety of ways; I use the share of the population aged 25 to 64 that has completed upper secondary education or better.[4] Income inequality is measured as the share of income going to the top 1%.

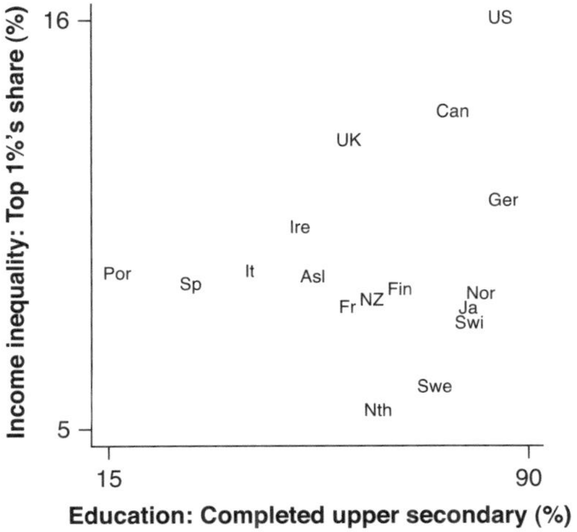

FIGURE 7.1 Income inequality by education
Note: The axes are truncated. Income inequality is the top 1%'s share of pre-tax income excluding capital gains, as of the early 2000s; data are from Atkinson, A. B., Piketty, T. and Saez, E. 'Top Incomes in the Long Run of History,' Working Paper 15408, National Bureau of Economic Research, 2009. Education is the share of the population aged 25–64 having completed upper secondary schooling or more, as of 1997 (the earliest year for which such data are available); data are from OECD, *Education at a Glance*, 2010.

A similar story holds if we examine developments over time. Since the 1970s, educational attainment has risen in most of these countries, yet income inequality has increased in many.[5]

Capabilities and Opportunity

For many, what matters is equality of opportunity rather than of outcomes. But equal opportunity is a chimera; it cannot be achieved. Because parents' resources affect children's capabilities, true equality of opportunity would require something close to equalisation of assets and incomes among households with children. Social democrats should not want such equalisation, as it would sharply reduce incentives. Moreover, truly equal opportunity would not be realised even if assets and incomes were equalised. Individuals' opportunities are influenced by genetic endowments, parents and other adults, peers and a variety of chance occurrences throughout childhood and adolescence. No liberal society – one in which families and other institutions retain a sizeable degree of autonomy – can ensure that its members reach adulthood with equal capacities for success.

Instead of equal opportunity, social democrats should aim to raise the opportunity floor. This is another way of describing Amartya Sen's notion of maximising individuals' capabilities.[6] We want people to be able to make informed choices about life goals and to be able to ably pursue those goals. Ideally, lifting the floor will also reduce inequality of opportunity.

Education is central here. Schooling enhances cognitive skills and non-cognitive traits, it facilitates adaptation to labour market shifts, and it contributes to network ties through which people can better pursue their economic and social goals.

At a minimum, the aim should be to ensure that all young people complete upper secondary education or its equivalent. As Figure 7.2 shows, some rich countries are approaching this goal, but none has yet reached it.

For many people, a university education is key to full development of analytical and communication skills needed to, first, make and pursue truly informed preferences and, second, shift course later in life if need be. Although higher education is not good for everyone,

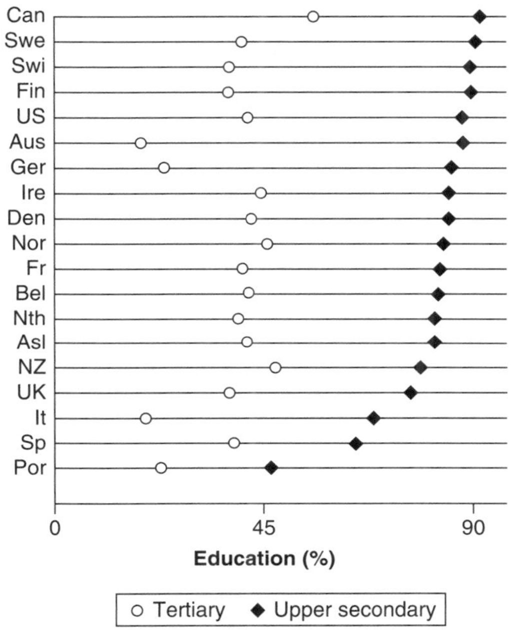

FIGURE 7.2 Education: secondary and tertiary completion among 25–34-year olds (2008)

Note: Share of persons aged 25–34 having competed tertiary schooling or better and upper secondary schooling or better, as of 2008. Data are from OECD, *Education at a Glance*, 2010.

on average it significantly enhances capabilities and opportunity.[7] A number of affluent countries have made considerable progress in boosting the share attending university, but others have not.

From the perspective of capability-enhancement, the most important years of schooling may be the 'preschool' ones. Evidence is still emerging, but James Heckman and his collaborators have made a strong case that years 1–6 are the most critical for the development of both cognitive skills and non-cognitive abilities.[8]

Some home environments are less helpful to children's development than we would like them to be. Evidence on the US summer vacation suggests that during those three months out of school, the cognitive skills of children in lower socio-economic status (SES) households tend to stall or actually regress.[9] Kids in high-SES households fare much better during the summer, as they are more likely to spend it engaged in stimulating activities. Cognitive psychologist Robert Nisbett concludes that 'much, if not most, of the gap in academic achievement between lower- and higher-SES children, in fact, is due to the greater summer slump for lower-SES children.[10]

This is relevant also for inequality of opportunity. Some argue that schools actually worsen inequality, because children from high-income households benefit more than their less advantaged counterparts, thereby widening the disparity. As the evidence from summer breaks attests, that is wrong. Without schools the gap in cognitive and non-cognitive abilities almost certainly would be greater. Though they can't possibly produce full equalisation, schools do *help* to equalise.

Mobility

By social mobility we usually mean the degree to which people's incomes are uncorrelated with those of their parents. Social scientists call this 'intergenerational mobility'. It is not easy to measure, but the data we have suggest non-trivial differences across the affluent countries. Does education affect the degree of mobility?[11] Cross-country comparison is difficult, as we lack education data from a generation ago, when today's adults were in school. Figure 7.3 here uses the share of 25–64-year olds having completed upper secondary education as of the mid-1990s. The pattern may or may not support the hypothesis that education promotes mobility. Overall, there is no association; but if we discount the United States as an exceptional case, the pattern looks more supportive.

Expansion of education and changes in the structure of schooling – for instance, a shift towards later tracking – appear to have contributed to increases in intergenerational mobility in Sweden and Finland.[12] However, in the United States and United Kingdom, mobility seems to have stagnated and possibly decreased in recent decades, despite educational advance.[13] That doesn't mean education makes no contribution, but it does suggest that whatever contribution it makes hasn't been powerful enough to outweigh developments pushing in the other direction.

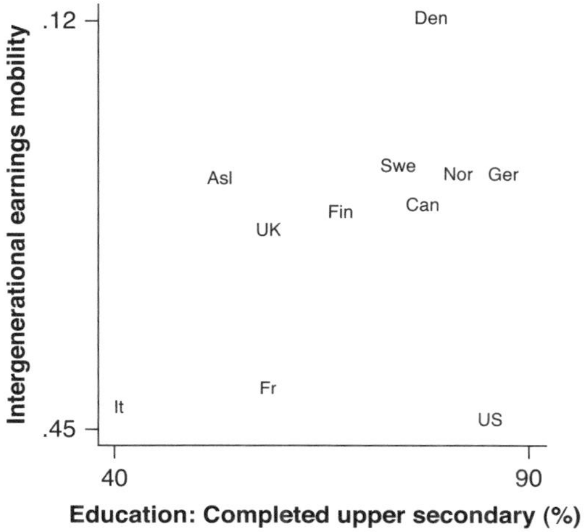

FIGURE 7.3 Intergenerational mobility by education
Note: The axes are truncated. Social mobility is the correlation between fathers' earnings and their sons' earnings, with the axis values reversed so that higher on the vertical axis indicates more mobility; data are from Björklund, A. and Jäntti, M. 'Intergenerational income mobility and the role of family background,' in *The Oxford Handbook of Economic Inequality*, Oxford: Oxford University Press, 2007, Figure 20.1. Education is the share of the population aged 25–64 having completed upper secondary schooling or more, as of 1997 (the earliest year for which such data are available); data are from OECD, *Education at a Glance*, 2010.

One argument sometimes made about the UK is that expansion of university education has hindered intergenerational mobility by enhancing upper- and middle-class families' ability to pass on their human capital advantages.[14] Yet the mobility trend in the US appears to be similar – stagnant or declining – despite only a small increase since the late 1970s in the share of a typical cohort obtaining a college degree. Moreover, university degrees have risen sharply in the Nordic countries, and mobility has increased.

It is important to caution against assuming that more intergenerational mobility is necessarily better. We want a society with sufficient openness and opportunity that people from less advantaged backgrounds are able to move up. But an extremely high level of mobility might well be discouraging. If children's fortunes appeared to be determined by lottery, parents' incentives to invest in their children would surely be weakened.

Nor can we assume that the degree of intergenerational mobility is a straightforward indicator of equality of opportunity. Imagine there were more or less perfect equality of developmental opportunity. Child care centres, schools and other institutions compensate for genetic differences by giving more attention to those with less genetic ability. Children enter Scandinavian-style (high-equality, high-educational content) preschools at a very early age, the school year is lengthened considerably, and other steps are taken to reduce the impact of parents' non-cognitive traits and parenting practices. Thus, everyone reaches their 18th birthday with more or less the same ability. Such a society nevertheless could end up with limited intergenerational mobility if parents pass on preferences for things such as work versus leisure, type of occupation and geographic location.[15]

Employment

An emphasis on the value of employment is one of the things that distinguishes social democracy from other progressive or leftist approaches. Employment has intrinsic benefits for individuals, and it contributes to economic advance, tax revenues and gender equality.

To what degree would increasing skills for those in the bottom half of the distribution increase employment? The story here is similar to that for income inequality. On average, individuals with better skills – as measured by years of schooling completed or literacy – are more likely to be employed. But when we look across countries or over time within countries, we observe only a modest association between education and employment. Figure 7.4 shows employment rates as of 2007 by countries' share with upper secondary education. Overall there is a positive association, but among the nations with more than 60% upper secondary completion the association disappears. Moreover, since the 1970s, employment rates have tended to increase more in countries with less improvement in educational attainment than in those with more improvement. Here, too, the problem is that the impact of education is swamped by that of other factors, such as macro-economic conditions, technological change, global competition, and labour market institutions and regulations.[16]

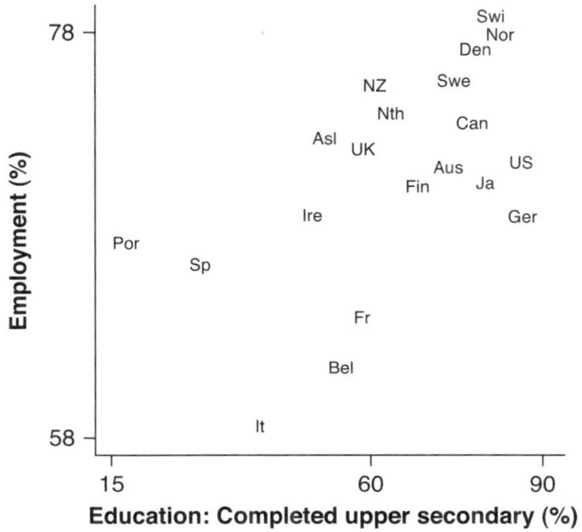

FIGURE 7.4 Employment by education
Note: The axes are truncated. Employment is employed persons aged 15–64 as a share of all persons aged 15–64, as of 2007; data are from OECD.Stat. Education is the share of the population aged 25–64 having completed upper secondary schooling or more, as of 1997 (the earliest year for which such data are available); data are from OECD, *Education at a Glance*, 2010.

And yet, education is critical, in four respects, to a country's ability to get to and sustain the right *type* of high-employment economy. First, as manufacturing jobs increasingly move to developing nations, rich-country economies have become reliant on services for new jobs. Some service jobs will inevitably be low-skill ones; that is particularly true for household and social services. But we want as many service jobs as possible to be the kinds of high-skill, analytical positions that pay better and offer more opportunity for autonomy and fulfilment. A highly educated population doesn't guarantee a skill-orientated employment structure, but it certainly facilitates it.

Second, though the jury is still out on this question, labour markets may function more effectively with modest rather than stiff regulations on employers' ability to hire and fire workers. A successfully flexible labour market requires cushions for those who are dismissed (hence the term 'flexicurity'). One such cushion is generous unemployment benefits and government services to tide people over while out of work and to help them get a new job. Another is workers' adaptability, which is enhanced by a sound basic education.

Third, we want those who begin their work career in a less-skilled job to be able to move to a higher-skilled one. We want, in other words, to facilitate upward mobility over the life course (intragenerational mobility).[17] A solid secondary education plus opportunity for retraining help with this. To be sure, they are not enough. Job ladders – formal structures within and across employers that provide clear routes to upward job movement – are needed. So, too, is individualised advice and assistance, particularly for people with cognitive, psychological or physical disabilities. We also need sources of income support for periods of non-employment. But education, conceived broadly as 'lifelong learning', is fundamental.

Fourth, employment should not come at the expense of children. If most working-age adults are in the labour force, someone must look after the kids. One way to solve this problem is to leave childcare largely unregulated. This is the American way. It allows for a proliferation of private childcare providers, from large firms with centres all over the country to the neighbour down the street. Because competition is intense and quality is unregulated, the price is low, so even adults working in relatively low-paying jobs can afford some version of care for their preschool-age children. However, some of this care, perhaps much of it, is less than ideal from the perspective of child development.[18] A better way is to make childcare part of the schooling system. In Denmark and Sweden, for instance, preschool teachers are required to have similar training and qualifications as elementary school teachers, and their pay is similar.

Economic Growth

A key goal of social democrats is economic prosperity and growth, partly for its own sake and partly because other social democratic aims are more readily achieved in an affluent, growing economy. Education has long been seen as a key contributor to economic growth. At early stages of development, that almost certainly is true. What about in already-rich nations? There is good reason to

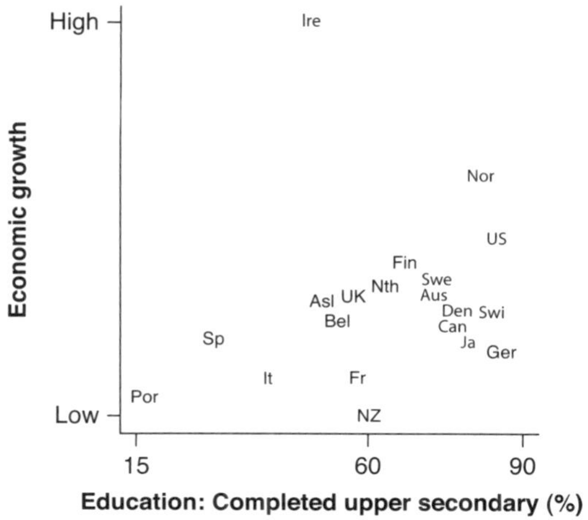

FIGURE 7.5 Economic growth by education
Note: The axes are truncated. Economic growth is the average annual rate of growth of gross domestic product per capita, 1979 to 2007, adjusted for catch-up; Kenworthy calculations using OECD.Stat data. Education is the share of the population aged 25–64 having completed upper secondary schooling or more, as of 1997 (the earliest year for which such data are available); data are from OECD, *Education at a Glance*, 2010.

suspect education will help. After all, growth hinges on technological progress, which should be boosted by education, particularly in the modern knowledge-driven economy.

Yet here, too, the cross-country evidence, shown in Figure 7.5, offers some reason for scepticism. There are many ways for economies to grow, and social scientists have surprisingly little understanding of what accounts for the variation among the rich nations in recent patterns of economic growth.[19] Even technological progress may owe more to the structure of research and development or regulation of product markets than to, say, the share of the population having completed secondary schooling or the literacy level at the low end of the population.[20]

Social Inclusion

We sometimes think of social inclusion in terms of incomes, living standards or access to employment, but the group most at risk of exclusion in contemporary rich nations is likely to be immigrants. Though not the only route to economic success, schooling is the most important source of economic opportunity and cultural assimilation for many immigrants, particularly second-generation ones. If rich countries are to continue to maintain a reasonably generous approach to inward migration, as they should, education will be central to their success in furthering community and social harmony.

Successful incorporation of immigrants has repercussions for other key components of social democratic policy, most notably the welfare state. A large and visible immigrant minority perceived as relying disproportionately on generous social benefits poses perhaps a bigger challenge to sustained welfare state generosity than do tax competition, capital mobility or neo-liberal ideology.

Other Social Outcomes

Across individuals, education tends to be positively associated with health, non-criminal behaviour, civic engagement, political participation, trust and life satisfaction.[21] Once again, these individual-level associations do not necessarily carry over to countries as a whole, because other factors come into play. Yet they offer further reason for societies to ensure that the least-advantaged receive the best possible education.

The importance of schools is not simply instrumental. We spend a good deal of our time from age 6 (or 1) to 21 in schools. In a rich society, they ought to be safe, reasonably orderly, comfortable, attractive and intellectually stimulating places.

Conclusion

Education is not a panacea. But it matters a great deal. It is, arguably, the single most important policy in the social democratic arsenal.

What features of the education system are most valuable in promoting learning and enhancing capabilities, particularly for children from less advantaged circumstances? We have some answers.[22] Teacher quality matters a great deal. High-quality early education pays dividends. Later tracking ('comprehensive' system) is better than early tracking ('dual' system). Curriculum standardisation is good. A lengthy summer break is bad. Financial impediments to university attendance are harmful. On other prominent reform issues – such as school funding, school choice, decentralisation of decision making, the balance between general and vocation-specific skills, and the type of university user fees – the evidence is less conclusive.

Our knowledge about what makes for a good education system is much improved, but we still have a long way to go. Continued progress is vital. Getting education right is as important as anything social democrats can do.

CHAPTER 8

Social Cohesion, Culture Politics and the Impact of Migration

René Cuperus and Mark Elchardus

Europe suffers from immigration trauma. Across the continent, a popular revolt against diversity and the multicultural society is taking hold as anti-immigrant parties successfully peddle a politics of fear and resentment, pitting 'natives' against 'strangers'. Migration supports the economy in many countries and contributes to wealth and welfare, but it also impacts on levels of deprivation and social cohesion. Unemployment, early school leaving, poverty, crime and segregation: these are the symptoms of integration failure. Across Europe, they are provoking fierce reactions and fuelling a cycle of estrangement, distrust and social malaise, the fertile ground on which right-wing populists and anti-immigrant and anti-Muslim movements flourish.

The response of social democratic parties to both the problems of integration and the sentiments of social malaise has clearly been insufficient, and as a consequence some of social democracy's historic social and cultural achievements are now under significant threat.

The authors of this chapter are respectively from the Netherlands and the Flemish region of Belgium; both are areas which perform rather poorly as far as migrant integration is concerned. It is therefore no coincidence that they are confronted with successful right-wing, populist and anti-Muslim parties and movements. Both countries can be considered instructive examples of bad practice. They can be viewed as a heightened prism for what is happening in many European societies, and offer a starting point for an urgent reflection on how social democracy should deal with the long-term impact of migration and growing diversity.

Integration Failure in Europe

In this chapter we refer to integration as defined in the European *Common Basic Principles for Immigrant Integration Policy*, where it is measured in terms of social, economic and political participation. The most crucial aspect of integration is indeed participation: joining mainstream society by attaining an adequate level of education and employability. A particular group of people can be considered insufficiently integrated when their school performance, labour market participation, life expectancy and imprisonment rate deviate negatively and disproportionately from the averages of the population as a whole.

In most contemporary European societies, immigrant groups and their second and third generation descendants all too often fall on the precarious side of this divide. Some European societies perform better on this score than others, but overall the record lies somewhere between poor and very poor. While integration is a complex and multifaceted process, two institutions play a crucial role in the process of integrating 'newcomers' into modern societies: education and the labour market. These institutions, more than others, can and should deliver full citizenship.

Overstretched Education Systems

In many of Europe's post-industrial societies, education systems have failed to adequately integrate the children of immigrants and provide them with the means to access the benefits of citizenship. The systems and institutions of many countries have been challenged with equipping young people with the knowledge, skills and attitudes to succeed under very difficult circumstances. Yet a survey of the relevant indicators underlines the magnitude of this shortcoming: the children and grandchildren of immigrants are massively overrepresented among early school leavers, and in the weakest educational tracks; they are more likely to live in precarious socio-economic conditions, to have very low levels of education and to be unemployed; they are underrepresented in post-secondary education, and more often than not have parents who are unfamiliar with the education system and often with the language used in schools.

Looking at the PISA's standardised tests of secondary school pupils for reading and maths in the OECD countries, the average score of natives (520) is much higher than that of non-natives (481) – though within the latter category, there is a wide variety of attainment, with students of Chinese and Indian origin scoring high averages, well above those of the natives (563 and 561 respectively), and pupils of Turkish origin scoring well below those of non-natives in general (448).[1] Pupils who are Muslim or come from a Muslim background tend to perform less well. In the Netherlands and in Belgium, for instance, it was observed that pupils of Turkish or Moroccan origin perform less well in school than other immigrant groups,[2] and in Sweden it was observed that pupils of African descent perform less well than pupils of Asian descent.[3]

Poor performance leads to early school leaving. For the Flemish educational system the overall drop-out rate of pupils of Moroccan and Turkish origin is more than four times higher than that of natives.[4] The poor educational performance can partly be explained by poor knowledge of the language in which education is provided. In cities with a diverse population, such as Brussels, where about 50% of the population is born without Belgian nationality or to parents without Belgian nationality, many pupils attend school in a different language from the one spoken at home. In the Dutch-speaking Brussels secondary schools, only 15% of the pupils usually speak Dutch with both parents. No less than 28% of the young adults, aged 20 to 24, have no secondary-level diploma and must be considered a drop-out or early school leaver.

On top of this, educational systems characterised by a greater degree of parental choice of school tend to create higher levels of segregation between the schools, greater inequality between the schools, and hence greater inequality between the pupils. This strongly contributes to the lack of integration of minority groups in education, and fosters negative attitudes towards the educationally segregated and poorly achieving minorities and immigrants.[5] Both the Dutch and the Flemish dual school system of public schools and 'faith schools' are characterised by a very high degree of parental school choice. This is a big obstacle for optimal integration results.

Closed Labour Markets

The failure to integrate immigrants and their descendants into the education system impacts on unemployment and poverty levels. Returning to the case of Brussels, of the young people under 24 who left school, 35% are unemployed (compared to 12.5% in the Flemish region). The diversity of the city expresses itself in high levels of poverty: Brussels has a poverty rate of 28% (compared to Flanders's 6%) and about 27% of the young people under the age of 18 grow up in a family with at least one unemployed parent.[6] Brussels, as a consequence of its international role, increasingly displays many of the characteristics of the new polarising global city with its painful and glaring divide between a well-to-do, cosmopolitan expatriate community and a precarious underclass of poor migrants.[7] The cited figures are therefore even more dramatic when looking, not at the city as a whole, but at the poorer townships where the migrants are concentrated and youth unemployment hits 40%.

The general problems of educational failure, unemployment and poverty experienced by migrants and their descendants can be observed in many European countries, but they seem to vary in intensity depending on specific welfare state characteristics and policies. Strong welfare states, which tend to attract disproportionate numbers of immigrants and asylum seekers, also tend to have well-protected labour markets. Such protection alleviates the problem of 'the working poor', but at the same time tends to make entry into the labour market more complicated for newcomers and for people with elementary skills. It creates a split between 'insiders' and 'outsiders'. In this way welfare states with well-protected workers' rights tend to increase the number of unemployed and long-term unemployed migrants, over and above the exclusionary barrier already in place due to weak educational credentials.

Welfare states also strongly affect integration in other ways. According to Ruud Koopmans: 'In countries with a limited welfare state such as the UK and the classical immigration countries, immigrants are, by and large, forced by the discipline of the market to make it on their own ... However, in the Netherlands, Sweden and Belgium, immigrants were able to survive on welfare support without making such adjustments'.[8] Easy access to welfare provisions such as benefits is held responsible for destroying first the need, then the motivation to work, and in the long run also the self-respect of immigrants and their children.[9]

Koopmans maintains that the variation of tolerance in regard to immigrants across European welfare states must be understood in this context. Germany and Austria have done a better job of integrating immigrants because 'their restrictive aliens legislation has made naturalisation and residence rights dependent on performance. Immigrants who become long-term dependent on social welfare risk expulsion ... these welfare states have replaced the discipline that the market exerts on immigrants in countries such as the UK or the US with the discipline of the state'.

The combination of overburdened and segregated educational systems, closed labour markets and open welfare states has turned out to be a recipe for social disaster. While the problems of integration are present everywhere, they are likely to be exacerbated in strong welfare states with a history of pacification democracy. This includes countries where parents, as a means of pacification, have been given far-reaching freedoms over the schools they choose for their children; where special measures were not taken to restrict access to nationality and/or social security; where the political landscape is fragmented and the party system open, allowing new anti-immigrant parties to easily establish an electoral bridgehead; and where the immigrant population comprises a high proportion of Muslims.

Social Malaise – Separating Myths and Reality

Taken together, these two pillars of integration failure have given rise to new forms of vulnerability and resentment. They have created extra opportunities for political parties to exploit the closely interrelated feelings of malaise, vulnerability and xenophobia, particularly in countries with proportional representation and fragmented political landscapes. A dangerous vacuum has emerged whereby 'cultural' explanations are employed to stoke up social tensions between the immigrant population and their descendants and the native population.

Threatening Minorities and Strangers in a Strange Land

The gulf separating the different populations that have come to coexist within national boundaries is clearly illustrated by a qualitative study of natives in mixed neighbourhoods in the Netherlands. It shows that the natives differentiate between themselves and the non-natives by calling themselves the 'hosts' and the latter the 'guests'. They express anxiety and discontent, and feel they are under threat. Much of their anger is explained by the feeling that 'the guests' do not behave properly according to expectations and common sense: 'the guest should behave in terms of language, norms and values according to the core mores of the host society: act normally and appropriately'. According to the respondents the people of foreign extraction are unwilling to adapt: 'they do not play by the rules'. Their unwillingness to integrate is, according to the analysed perception in the study, illustrated by their refusal to (learn to) speak the Dutch language, by the irresponsible way they raise their children, the absence of a work ethic, the ostentatious way in which they manifest their religious adherence, their isolation, and by their claim to special treatment.[10]

The over-representation of immigrant groups and non-natives among the prison population is a telling example of the integration failure which drives such divisive attitudes. It is quite striking that in the countries that perform poorly in labour market integration (the Netherlands, Belgium and Sweden) one also observes the highest disproportion of foreigners in prison. In those countries they are five to eight times more likely to be in prison that non-foreigners, while in Austria and Germany they are three-and-a-half times more likely.

Failed integration also creates associations between being non-native, being poor and being chronically welfare-dependent. This, in turn, tempts members of the native population to define failed integration, deprivation and inequality not as socio-economic issues – even less as questions of interpersonal solidarity – but as problems brought on by the migrant cultures themselves, as culturally or religiously induced social fraud. In this sense, welfare states and well-protected labour markets tend to foster a supposed 'cultural explanation' for low educational achievement, low labour market participation and high rates of poverty.[11]

Furthermore, research in Belgium has revealed that 'the strangers' are perceived as heavily involved in crime, profiteering from welfare provisions but nevertheless privileged by the elites and the politicians. Levels of xenophobia and ethnic prejudice were particularly high among people with a high fear of crime, among those with feelings of relative deprivation and among those who considered the social security system to be vulnerable to fraud.[12]

These 'cultural explanations' fuel a cycle of mutual estrangement which heightens the socio-economic marginalisation and poor integration of immigrant communities. For example, in the Netherlands many people of Moroccan and Turkish origin do not really identify with their new country, but rather continue to consider themselves as foreign to their new nation. They are therefore more likely to be susceptible to radical forms of belief and to the rejection of the core Enlightenment values which underpin Western societies.

These developments have led to a broadening of the meaning of integration to include, besides indicators of participation, the extent to which the non-natives share the values and lifestyle of their new countries. Such a shift in the meaning of integration was already evident in several European societies around 2005, when the Netherlands Institute for Social Research (SCP) started collecting data on cultural identification. The findings show that ethnic minorities vary considerably in the extent to which they identify themselves as members of Dutch society. Some 58% of the Turkish community in the Netherlands identify themselves as Turks and only 12% regard themselves as being part of Dutch society. Moroccans are more inclined to identify themselves as simultaneously Moroccan and Dutch. In contrast, Surinamese and Antilleans are far more inclined to regard themselves in whole or in part as Dutch.

While the variations in educational achievement according to national origin indicate that cultural factors are involved, blaming welfare dependency on culture clearly confuses the effects of a wrongheaded approach to integration, education and labour market policy with the cultural specificity of a group. This confusion, combined with the indicators of failed integration – educational failure, poverty, welfare dependence, high crime rates, perceived lack of loyalty and rejection of core Western liberal-democratic values – give rise to the problematic perception of 'threatening' minorities. This perception is exploited by right-wing populism.

The Winners and Losers of Globalisation

The problems associated with diversity are also a consequence of tragic timing. They correspond with the ageing of the native population and the shift towards a more knowledge-intensive economy. The old and the less educated members of native societies feel increasingly vulnerable and are therefore particularly susceptible to the related feelings of discontent, resentment, insecurity, estrangement, fear of crime and xenophobia.

The vulnerability of native people with elementary levels of education and skills is not so much a side effect of globalisation as it is a problem of 'meritocratic homogamy'. When a number of generations pass through a system of schooling that is relatively open, most of the people equipped with the talent, opportunity and background to succeed have enjoyed the full benefits of education. They have become highly educated, academically trained professionals and have married other highly educated professionals, creating families with ample resources to give their children a head start.

This development cannot be considered a zero-sum game, yet it does imply that there is a growing number of two-parent families with low levels of education who have dropped out of education, and have very little to offer in the way of resources, motivation and social relations to support the education of their children. The chances of their children moving up in society are slim, and look even less likely than those of the children of immigrants.

While one can raise many questions about the theories explaining prejudice as a rational reaction to perceived competition,[13] it is very likely that these people, as they experience social demotion and relative deprivation, will feel squeezed between what they consider as strangers and guests on the one hand, and 'meritocratic elites' on the other hand. Opinion poll research in the UK has revealed a (lower) middle class that feels squeezed between (bankers') bonuses and (migrants') benefits, as Patrick Diamond and Giles Radice formulate it in *Southern Discomfort Again.*[14]

Nostalgia and Real Loss

While phenomena such as racism, xenophobia and ethnic prejudice are real, they should not be allowed to cloud a correct interpretation of the social dynamics that create them. Failed integration does pose a real threat to good citizenship, decent neighbourliness, mutual trust and social cohesion. As alluded to above, research shows that many native people complain that a substantial proportion of immigrants do not support and espouse the values and practices upon which the European welfare state and Western liberal democracy were built.

Such charges are, without doubt, fuelled to some extent by prejudice and xenophobia; but they should not be dismissed solely on such grounds. To many people they are painfully real and correspond to their everyday, not imagined, experience. Many of the people who express negative attitudes towards foreigners or vote for right-wing populist parties are motivated by disagreeable experiences, by disillusion about the ideals and practices of the so-called multicultural society, and by the sense that a society precious to them is falling away.

The report by the Dutch Institute for Multicultural Affairs aptly expresses this feeling of loss in its title *Een vreemde in eigen land* ('Becoming a stranger in one's own country').[15] This sentiment indicates that the process of estrangement has not only separated the natives from the migrants, but has created a feeling of autochthonous homesickness – the painful experience of suddenly feeling like a stranger in the city and the neighbourhood where your family has lived for generations.[16] This creates fertile ground for a politics of nostalgia, exploiting a longing for a time when there were no strangers. It lays the foundations for the dangerous populist notion of a 'lost heartland'.

Yet, when such feelings of nostalgia are analysed in more detail they turn out to be related to the feeling that the social security system, the welfare state as it was developed in the post-war period, is being ruined and that the role of national governments, which once made democracy and political engagement meaningful, has become trivial.[17] This implies that this form of nostalgia touches the core of social democratic principles and policy. Many people seem to think that the achievements of the welfare state are in jeopardy because the problem of rising diversity has not been handled adequately. The longing for a return to a time without diversity can be dismissed, but the longing for effective politics, a more potent state, and a vigorous defence of the welfare state certainly cannot be. These are crucial social democratic responsibilities.

The Social Democratic Encounter with Diversity

Social democracy's core achievements and values are threatened by inadequate integration, dissolving social cohesion and a sense that the 'good society' is on the way out. Across Europe the severe erosion of the centre-left's electoral position, due in large measure to the loss of its traditional voters to populist right-wing parties, reflects the struggle to respond to the related problems of estrangement and homesickness, and to answer the challenge that diversity threatens social security, equity and safety.

These acute problems – both social and electoral – have divided and still divide many European centre-left parties. This is exacerbated by an internal split in the social democratic constituency between groups with markedly different attitudes and lifestyles. On the one hand, there is the well-known socio-economic split separating supporters of a self-regulating free market who are indifferent to issues of equality from supporters of more equality and state regulation. On the other hand, there is a new split which is socio-cultural rather that socio-economic (sometimes labelled as authoritarianism versus libertarianism or as national communitarism versus cosmopolitanism), and concerned with issues of identity, membership of society and community, and the maintenance of social order.[18] This new cultural cleavage runs right through the heart of the social democratic electorate.

The traditional, working-class electorate of the social democratic parties often combines leftist positions on the socio-economic cleavage with what many consider as rightist positions on the socio-cultural cleavage. The more highly educated supporters claim that their own combination of a centre-left/social-liberal position on the socio-economic cleavage and a multicultural-cosmopolitan-libertarian stand on the socio-cultural cleavage is reasonable, consistent and leftist.

Within social democratic parties this has led to a sharp and sometimes acrimonious split between the two constituencies of the left. On one side of the divide, there is a politically correct, cosmopolitan element, often highly educated and in favour of broad and easy access to full membership in the societal community with few, if any, demands for integration in terms of values and lifestyle. The cosmopolitans are in favour of a multicultural model of society and easy access to welfare provisions. They are against restrictions on immigration, tough law-and-order measures for crime fighting and a more hard-line approach to youth delinquency. They are also often opposed to discourses which try to balance rights, responsibilities and duties, deeming this to be paternalistic or even authoritarian and repressive.

On the other side of the line, there is the more traditional social democratic electorate composed of workers, the less educated members of the middle class and the socially vulnerable. Many of them are in favour of conditional access to social security and community membership, contingent on the acceptance of responsibilities. They are in favour of restrictions on immigration. They sometimes show a fair amount of welfare chauvinism and tend to be in favour of a tough approach to crime and social fraud.

Over the last few decades, most social democratic parties have resolutely followed their more highly educated electorate and thus lost a large section of their traditional constituency. Parts of their traditional electorate apparently felt closer to the populist and even right-wing parties in terms of the problems of citizenship, crime, access and identity. Such issues were for them not necessarily more important than the socio-economic ones, but were in their minds closely intertwined with such issues. As a consequence, social democratic parties have become, electorally speaking, to a large extent parties for the more highly educated professionals working in the public sector, turning historical workers' parties into parties without workers. Dutch and Flemish sociologists summed this phenomenon up in the phrase 'farewell to the leftist working class'.[19]

A Cocoon of Misplaced Political Correctness

It is tempting to assign exclusive responsibility for the cumulative processes of failed integration, estrangement and polarisation to the progressive or social democratic elites, but it would be historically wrong to do so. As historians of European immigration have demonstrated, all the established political parties have played their part in this unfolding 'multicultural migration drama'.[20]

In the early stages of migration, guest worker programmes in countries such as Germany, Austria and the Netherlands were favoured by business interests, employers' organisations and right-wing conservative parties, and disputed by trade unions and social democratic parties who opposed labour and wage competition.[21] Later on, it was the Christian democratic pro-family parties (CDU in Germany and CDA in the Netherlands) that promoted the large-scale family reunification of guest workers,[22] based upon a belief that families always act as a strong control measure and are positive for integration. In doing so they created the most important avenue for continued, massive and uncontrolled legal immigration.

When the problematic aspects of mass migration and diversity became apparent, and the difficult nature of integration became clear, many politicians and representatives of government – social democrats foremost amongst them – mobilised to fight the racism and prejudice which came to the surface by way of the xenophobic parties. They did so, no doubt, driven by the traumatic European legacy of colonialism and the Holocaust, and afraid of a resurgence of fascism. However, many of them unfortunately underestimated or even denied the reality of the problems and social pains in emerging European immigration societies. They dismissed the feelings of homesickness, and put a cordon sanitaire around the problems and tensions of failed integration. Therefore they were perceived as members of an aloof and privileged class, totally disconnected from ordinary day-to-day life, unable to see a reality that to everybody not blinded by political correctness was plain to see.

Particularly since the 1980s, the progressive parties have taken up positions in the frontline fight against xenophobic and far-right parties, such as the Vlaams Blok in Flanders, the FPÖ of Haider, the Front National of Le Pen and the Centrumdemocraten of Hans Janmaat in the Netherlands. Unfortunately and counterproductively, this worthy fight has ended up in a cocoon of political correctness, a disturbing form of selective blindness manifested in the denial of the failures of integration, the inability to see the glaring intellectual shortcomings of the concept of multiculturalism, and, as a consequence, the loss of large parts of the traditional social democratic constituencies.[23] Once the process of immigration was underway, the main concerns of social democratic parties seem to have been to accord basic rights to immigrants, to implement a policy consistent with the goals of substantive freedom and equality, to avoid prejudice and intolerance and to combat the rise of racist and xenophobic parties. But, however, lofty the intentions and principles were, the outcome has been close to disastrous.

Looking back, it is now clear that the signals sent out by the traditional social democratic electorate have been ignored, and also that the guiding values of social democracy have been either forgotten or unimaginatively applied. The result: a segregated society with migrant ghettos of poverty, deprivation and welfare dependency, as well as mutual distrust between newcomers and the autochthonous population. This can only be viewed as social democratic progress by the most blinkered optimists.

Towards Vibrant Diversity

It is clear that social democracy needs a comprehensive answer to the challenges of failed integration and declining social cohesion. The principles that can guide us in the search for such an answer are clear. We want all people to be free, to be able to fully realise their potential and live according to the values and insights of a given culture, society or community. It is not in the value we attach to freedom that we differ from conservative liberals. Our fundamental difference concerns the extent to which we consider freedom to be equally distributed. Conservative liberals assume that everybody is equally free, and so markets can regulate most of our economic, social and cultural life. For social democrats, freedom is very unequally distributed, and therefore the role of markets is real but limited and the state should be used to increase the equality of freedom.

The different forms of inequality that block access to full freedom for many people are still essentially collective, linked to class, gender and ethnic origin. They are not individualised. That is why the fight for equality and freedom cannot be limited to offering individual opportunities – however important and crucial these are – but must address the economic, social, cultural and political factors that systematically block the road to freedom of different groups. The lack of opportunities for migrants, their children and grandchildren is due to factors that systematically inhibit their educational achievement and their access to the labour market, consequently undermining their motivation to work and creating estrangement and anomy.

These factors must be collectively addressed in order to promote integration, and by doing so to increase welfare and well-being for everybody. Synergy between freedom and equality implies that everybody is given the opportunity to realise his or her potential, but that everybody is also held responsible for the essentially collective conditions under which such opportunities can be offered. That is why individualism cannot provide an ethical foundation for social democracy. The congruence of freedom and equality implies an inseparable link between rights and duties, advantage and responsibility, individual fulfilment and collectively created opportunities.

A fair society and active, participatory citizenship presuppose each other.

Other crucial and perennial dynamics in the social democratic heritage are realism and pragmatism: the willingness to revise the habitual ways of doing things in the light of experience and evidence. Three conditions are required to achieve this: borders, laws and the capacity to enforce them. Freedom and respect for individual rights have only been achieved in situations where a state of law could be created within boundaries and effectively enforced. For social democrats aspiring to universalise rights, freedom and equality, this implies a triple mission: increase the number of states in which our vision of rights, freedom and equality can be realised and enforced; expand the boundaries of the networks of states and supranational organisations in which this is possible; maintain the boundaries within which these rights can be enforced.

More freedom, more equality and maintenance of the boundaries that make freedom and equality possible – these are the goals a social democratic answer to failed integration should aim for. Part of the electorate has left social democratic parties because they hold them responsible for ineffectively maintaining the boundaries, for losing control over immigration, for allowing the emergence of new forms of inequality, and for allowing the emergence of a new segregated and deprived underclass. In short: for allowing the undoing of half a century of social progress.

Growing diversity poses particular problems for strong welfare states. It is no accident that Europe's most successful welfare states were created in homogeneous Scandinavia. Strong welfare states need high levels of social cohesion and trust and a strong sense of community, but the outcomes of failed integration have strongly eroded those conditions in several societies. Social democracy has never been very sensitive to the less material issues of community and identity, and these have not played an important role in the development of the social security systems and the welfare state.

Yet today they have to be faced up to. For better or for worse they have been put on the societal agenda in the form of questions about identity. Two opposing models for dealing with identity have shown their limits. The French model of *laïcité* has apparently not been able to avoid strong feelings of estrangement, nor the rise of strong anti-Muslim sentiment and the violent revolt of Muslim youth in the *banlieues*. The other model of almost unopposed multiculturalism has also been largely abandoned because the use of cultural difference to legitimise divergence from core values is not compatible with the state of law, nor is it consistent with the need for a strong sense of reciprocal welfare communitarianism as the foundation of solidarity, freedom and equality for everybody.

Social democracy should engage much more with identity and cultural values and develop its own project as a meeting ground of open, non-ethnic identities. Never pursue a politics that denies or violates identity, never allow identity to constitute itself as a basis for particularistic legislation. Therefore the ruthless force of extreme Islamophobia, the attempt to reduce Islam to solely extremist positions, and even the eradication of religious freedom with a ban on the Koran, should be as actively resisted as should be political Islam and the creation of a fundamentalist Islamic identity that is incompatible with the core values of Western liberal democracy.

Policy Consequences

It seems quite clear which policies should be aimed for. The way in which these should be carried out will necessarily vary from one society to the other, because they must be adapted to the specificities of each educational system, labour market and welfare state, to the nature of the immigrant population, the fragmentation of the electorate, the strength of anti-migrant, anti-Muslim parties, and many other relevant conditions and circumstances. One can therefore only announce policy goals and invite a discussion on how these goals can be optimally achieved under the different national conditions.

The educational opportunities of migrants, their children and grandchildren should be drastically increased. This implies that inequality within educational systems be reduced. Crucial features of the education system – such as the degree of public guidance in the choice of schools, the degree of parental guidance and the age and extent of tracking – should be adapted to reduce the inequality between schools, between the educational outcomes of different groups, and to improve the educational achievement of minorities. Their drop-out rate should be reduced, their participation in post-secondary education increased.

Labour market policies should be revised so as to allow a greater participation of minority groups and particularly their young members with elementary qualifications. This supposes an intensified fight against discrimination, and also, in several labour markets, a change of policy and probably a weakening of the protection of the well-established workforce in order to facilitate the entry of minorities, the young, and people with elementary qualifications.

In implementing those policies, an equilibrium between rights and duties should be aimed for. By way of more intensive parental guidance, parents should be made responsible partners in the educational careers of their children. Policies should be devised that offer more opportunities, but that also increase the motivation to seize those opportunities. The rewards for working as compared to living off welfare should be increased. For people able to work, unemployment benefits should after a while be made conditional on meeting a duty to work. Increased efforts should be made to involve the members of minority groups in political and cultural life.

International comparisons tend to suggest that strong welfare state provisions are only compatible with integration of new groups when access to welfare is made conditional. In a number of societies this requires more limited access to nationality and the broadening of the circumstances under which the residence permit can be rescinded, for instance after long periods of unemployment.

Integration cannot succeed when immigration itself is not brought under control. The easy access to welfare which makes countries attractive to abusive and illegal asylum should be eliminated. The correct use of asylum should be restored, and it should not be used as a conduit for economically motivated immigration and, worse, human trafficking. Immigration should be controlled so that the challenge of integration through participation becomes feasible. In several societies this will no doubt imply restrictions on family reunion. Within

Europe, national border control should be restored. This means that the Schengen agreements should be reviewed.

Racism, ethnic prejudice, anti-Semitism and Islamophobia should be vigorously combated, in particular through effective forms of education for democratic citizenship. The high crime rates within young migrant groups should be brought down substantially so as to get rid of one of the key sources of estrangement, negative stigmatisation and multi-ethnic distrust. And finally, the means should be developed to better monitor and combat the spread of radical forms of Islam that deliberately obstruct integration, deepen estrangement and threaten Western liberal democracy.

In the long run, successful migrant integration and the end of mutual estrangement are preconditions for the vitality of our liberal democracy and social solidarity, as well as for the continuity of social democracy in Europe.

CHAPTER 9

Identity, Community and the Politics of Recognition

Michael Kenny

As social democrats continue to ponder the damage done to left-of-centre parties in Europe by rising concerns about immigration, they would be well advised to drill into the historical and cultural roots of current anxieties. There are good reasons to think that these concerns represent the tip of a bigger socio-cultural iceberg, rather than themselves being the sole or main cause of the European left's current woes.

In the British General Election of May 2010, for example, while immigration was undoubtedly a high-profile and difficult issue for the governing Labour Party (and was at the heart of the most spectacular media event of the campaign),[1] it was not central to the campaigning of either of the main opposition parties as the Conservatives opted not to make it one of the major themes of the campaign. This is not to deny the political potency of migration as an issue in its own right, in either the UK or elsewhere. But it may well be more pertinent to regard it as a symbol, as much as a cause, of the weakening of the emotional and cultural rapport between indigenous (both 'white' and 'non-white') working-class communities and parties of the left.

The fraying of this relationship is of considerable significance. As Michael Lind has recently argued:

> In both Europe and America the centre-left has been crippled by the defection of the native white working class. In Britain, the per cent of the working class that voted Labour dropped from 56 per cent in 1970 to 33 per cent in 2010. In the US, the Democrats lost the House of Representatives in the 2010 mid-terms in part because the Republican advantage over the Democrats among the men and women of the white working class, which includes four out of ten Americans, widened to 29 per cent.[2]

The decline in the proportion of the working class supporting left parties is itself a long-standing phenomenon. And it represents only one half of a difficult pincer for European leftists – the other being the steady decline of the manual working class as a portion of the electorate.

Social democrats are having to face up to these changes in the context of their current political downturn. But to grasp fully their underlying causes and current implications, it is important that they consider these trends in historical terms. Specifically, they need to understand how an interlocking set of changes has eaten away at the emotional bedrock of support enjoyed by parties of the left in the last half century. While the historical sketch offered below relates primarily to the UK, many aspects of this account, and my subsequent argument for the imperative for social democrats to consider a new politics of 'recognition' (to complement their established preferences for redistribution and rights), are pertinent to developments in other European countries. Indeed, rather than seeing itself as being entirely on the defensive on questions relating to migration and identity, I want to suggest that a considered focus upon questions of recognition and identity may point the way towards a wider, much needed revitalisation of centre-left thinking.

Changes in Working-Class Community

While it appears that voters from different social classes exhibit broadly similar levels of cultural anxiety and concern about immigration, these issues assume a particular importance in relation to working-class communities, where the evaporation of a sense of allegiance to the political left is most marked. Today's resentments need above all to be understood against the backdrop of long-term changes in the character of these communities.

As far back as the 1950s, leading sociologists began to consider the implications of a number of inter-related social trends – including the explosion of consumer goods, changes in popular leisure habits, the decline of religious belief, falling support for other 'traditional' institutions (such as the Church of England), a growing propensity among young people to identify with new sub-cultural styles, and important changes in the pattern of family life (including the rising number of women joining the labour force) for working-class communities.

These developments were accentuated by the rapid demise of manufacturing industries and the shift towards a post-industrial economy in later decades. The decline in manual working-class occupations contributed to a significant fracturing within the working classes, with greater concentrations of deprivation, immobility and insecurity for some, and new opportunities associated with skilled employment, higher incomes and the acquisition of assets (notably through rising home ownership) for others. In addition, over the course of the last three decades, successive waves of inward migration have contributed significantly to a growing (and, for some, destabilising) sense of ethnic, cultural and religious diversity, not least in many of Britain's cities and towns.

The experience of rapid ethnic and cultural diversification is undoubtedly an important factor in explaining a growing mood of resentment and disenfranchisement among many working-class communities. But the less dramatic, longer-term changes signalled above need also to be given their due. Sociologists writing 40–50 years ago detected two contrary, yet interlinked, forces changing the nature of working-class relationships. Some focused upon the impact of the relative 'affluence' associated with rising living standards and consumer spending, arguing that these changes, and the slow decline of the labour ethos, signalled a new process of *embourgeoisement*. These grand claims were significantly dented by the work of figures such as John Goldthorpe,[3] but an emerging sense of aspirational individualism and a desire to escape the boundaries of working-class life became widely recognised features of social life in the 1950s and 1960s.

What the cultural theorist Stuart Hall termed a growing sense of 'classlessness'[4] was for a long while dismissed by many on the left as a form of ideological manipulation, or even self-delusion. During the 1980s, this current was powerfully harnessed to a proliferation of consumerist opportunities. These helped generate a rising set of expectations about the quality and nature of public, as well as private, services, and engendered a significant decline in deferential attitudes towards elites and institutions.

Other commentators (for instance Richard Sennett and Jonathan Cobb)[5] began to explore the emergence of a different mood from the late 1960s among many working-class men, characterised by the emotions of nostalgia, fear and resentment that were sparked by a growing sense of culturally transmitted humiliation and exclusion. These authors noted the growing desire for 'recognition' welling up within these communities.

These two cross-cutting trends laid down some important attitudinal patterns that have been accentuated (rather than invented) in the form of contemporary reactions to mass immigration. Both of these forces have continued to hollow out the mid-century communities fondly described by social democratic writers like Richard Hoggart.[6] And they have helped contribute to the decline of the collectivist institutions of working-class life (such as trade unions, labour clubs, working men's clubs and Workers Education Associations) through which a firm political and emotional bond between Labour and many British workers was forged.[7]

By the 1980s and 1990s, this connection was growing significantly weaker, a development symbolised by the defection of many working-class voters to the Conservatives in 1979. This process was in key respects masked by the political success of 'New Labour' after 1997. Central to the ethos of New Labour was its desire to demarcate itself culturally from the supposedly parochial and workerist culture of 'labourism' (which it associated with its caricatured predecessor – Old Labour).

It proposed instead a new political economy. This involved celebration of the imperative of adaptation to external economic forces, support for flexible labour markets and a liberal economic policy, which generated the wealth to sustain a period of increased investment in public services and resource transfer to those on the lowest incomes. Moreover, '[t]he state – powerful, centrally directed, technocratically managed but using market forces, too – was the instrument for both public-service reform and social change'.[8] Labour's overarching vision of 'the good' was a preponderantly individualistic and consumerist one, served up with occasional side orders of communitarian rhetoric. Parts of this framework undoubtedly chimed with the experiences and aspirations of many, and also created a sense of alienation among those for whom the new economy meant insecurity, low wages, and a sense of political disenfranchisement.

More generally, New Labour's approach consummated a major (and rapid) about-turn in the representation of indigenous working-class communities on the political left. While the manual trade unionist was an iconic figure within the party's political culture (though only occasionally part of its leadership) for much of the twentieth century, as the century closed this figure was suddenly relegated to the margins of its imagination, supplanted both due to the liberal multiculturalism favoured by the party's metropolitan leadership and its relentless economic modernism.

This growing distance between parts of its social base and the party's leadership was for a while offset by the economic and social benefits which New Labour delivered. Once the rise in living standards which his government oversaw began to stall, from about 2003, it became increasingly clear that the party's support had become much shallower. It was now ousted from control of local government in a number of its former strongholds. And in some areas it began to receive a potent new challenge as the far-right British National Party fought a number of successful battles to win council seats and slowly increased its vote at General Elections.

Nor were these trends confined to Labour's heartlands in the North of England, Scotland and Wales. In many other places where there were sizeable pockets of Labour support, and where the party had broken through in 1997 – suburbs, commuter towns in the Home Counties, semi-rural towns and small towns in the Midlands, East and South East – Labour's lack of cultural roots and inability to connect with the aspirations and experiences of ordinary people were also increasingly apparent.

There is no single explanation for the fraying of these relationships, though it is clear that Labour's inability to sustain rising living standards for many middle-class and low-income voters played an important part. But culture and vision, as well as economics and redistribution, were central to this story. It is this aspect of their current woes that social democrats have been slowest to accept, a vestige of the preference the left has for the language of resources, living standards and redistribution.

Yet in a period when the most contentious issues and political challenges have arisen from tensions and arguments focusing upon identity and culture (most obviously in the case of migration),[9] this mind-set has become an inhibition. The notion that the proliferation of divisive cultural and ethical questions within political life can be countered solely through strategies for redistribution is far from persuasive. The evidence supplied by recent research into the shifting patterns of attitude and identity in 'white working-class' communities suggests that the recourse to such forms of identification has become a much more entrenched pattern in some parts of the UK, and elsewhere.[10]

The lexicons of redistribution and rights do not speak to the growing tendency for citizens to engage in public debate and develop forms of political reasoning that are rooted in the language of identity, culture and belonging. Rights-based thinking has been central to the argument of those commentators who have called for greater procedural fairness in the allocation of contested public goods in order to head off 'white' grievances about the supposed favouring of migrant families and other ethnic minorities.[11] But this approach appears unlikely to make a significant dent in these problems. The idea of establishing a process that enjoys legitimacy irrespective of the cultural background of participants rests upon an assumption about the neutrality of the relevant public authority which is exactly what is under challenge from the contention that indigenous community interests are endemically marginalised by the political mainstream.

By contrast, a response that speaks from a position within the wider culture, and sets out the vision of the common good which it aspires to create – rather than defending a rationalistic position that claims, implausibly, to be above the political and cultural fray – may fare better. This may mean working to convince people that they are all members of neighbourhoods that should pull together around their shared interests, and actively promoting civic enterprises and spaces where mixing and integration are likely to prosper. And it could mean considering whether there are forms of provision that would lead to a greater sense of cultural empowerment and recognition without damaging inter-ethnic relations in neighbourhoods and communities (an argument which is currently being aired, for instance, in relation to an emerging debate about whether specifically English identities and symbols should be given greater public acknowledgement).

It is, then, only by opening up to and engaging with these issues, and contemplating what a progressive form of identity politics might comprise, that the centre-left may be able to remake its relationship with some of the communities from which it has become most estranged. Against such a view, some argue instead that the left needs to reassure its 'core' voters by adopting more hard-edged, populist positions on immigration or crime, closing down a flank where it has become vulnerable over the last decade. The analysis offered here suggests scepticism about whether such a move could on its own address the long-term changes that are reshaping the relationship between fractured and diverse working-class communities and parties of the left.

What, then, would a social democratic politics of identity look like? Here I sketch three different foci which such a sensibility would usefully introduce to this tradition's political thinking.

Shaping a New Politics of Identity

Social democracy has tended to be most politically successful when its leaders have confidently expressed a sense of national purpose, and its parties have been attuned to the cultural identities and social experiences of a majority of workers. But following the decline of the forms of community life and their shared historical memories, which emerged from the era of mass industry, the wellsprings of support for the left have been significantly eroded.

A tough but increasingly imperative question which social democrats need to face is whether the decline in the quantity and depth of working-class support available to parties that are simultaneously trying to pitch themselves on the centre ground of political debate represents a terminus for the social democracy of the collectivist age. Can centre-left politics respond coherently to the continuing impact of the two forces shaping the working-class community – the desire of many for protection from the uncertainties of the global economy, on the one hand, and the impulse to pursue an independent and fulfilled life, at arms length from the dictates of the market and state, on the other? Is it still possible to imagine a coherent national vision that speaks to both of these values?

Only a project that sets out to (re)create a progressive sense of identity and belonging across a range of geographic and cultural communities looks adequate for this highly challenging endeavour. This involves several distinct but inter-related steps. It necessitates, first, the sociological enterprise of updating the left's appreciation of the forms of belonging that matter to people in the conditions of the twenty-first century. It suggests, second, the need for greater ethical reflection upon the values inherent in different kinds of community (from local to national, religious to voluntary) and the ways in which these can be encompassed within a newly constituted politics of the common good. It means, third, enriching the increasingly technocratic and statist identity which Labour assumed during its years of government. And it requires, fourth, that the party, its political representatives and local bodies be returned to and reconnected with the communities from which their mandate originates.

Reviving social democratic parties as outcrops of a diverse civil society, rather than vehicles for competition over state control, is an arduous, yet necessary, precondition for a wider revival. Left parties need to bear the character of, and be in dialogue with, a wide range of different communities of support. But the imperative towards diversity of reach places an even greater premium upon the ability of leaders to speak across, as well as to, social and cultural differences, and to rediscover a sense of national purpose and common ambition.

Develop a New 'National-Popular'

While the defence of indigenous traditions and ways of living can take chauvinistic forms which the centre-left should challenge, it is mistaken to see only prejudice and bigotry within the defensive and anxious responses to change that characterise working-class communities. Such a knee-jerk liberal response underestimates the conservatism and pride in local places that flows through many of Britain's urban, semi-urban and rural communities, and all of its national cultures.

The left's favoured languages of redistribution and rights are found increasingly wanting in the face of these dimensions of popular reasoning. Neither of them allows progressives to appreciate or harness those facets of contemporary consciousness that may not strictly comply with liberal precepts, but reflect an abiding emphasis upon the values of tradition or established ways of living. These often feed into powerful senses of local pride and scepticism towards the imperatives and values of the free market and bureaucratic state.

The persistence of such sentiments represents the continuation of an age-old dilemma for the rationalistic left: how should it relate to the folk traditions and contradictory consciousness of ordinary people? Do the 'masses' still need to be led towards the philosophical principles of Enlightenment? Or do some features of popular common sense provide resources and ingredients for a progressive politics, and thus need to be engaged, nurtured and re-worked by centre-left parties? And what to do in the face of those forms of broadly conservative reasoning – customary ways of thinking and sharing, established patterns of living and a burgeoning sense of environmental preservationism – which can appear backward and parochial to the outlook of modern metropolitan liberals?

Earlier generations of socialist and social democrat were divided deeply in response to these issues. Despite streaks of populist authoritarianism, New Labour's relentless support for the imperatives of global economic change and upbeat modernism positioned it on the side of the rationalistic version of Enlightenment. One of the most fundamental challenges facing social democrats now is whether they can once again come to encompass the other side of this argument. There are dangers, certainly, in a wholesale lurch into communitarian traditionalism which results in the abandonment of conceptual commitments to equality, freedom and tolerance. But there are equally profound limitations to a political culture that is indifferent, and sometimes actively antithetical, to, the moral and cultural practices of civil society (as in the case of some forms of secularist liberalism which find favour on the political left).

In government, Labour found itself on the wrong side of a large number of groups who felt that practices or institutions they valued were of no matter in the face of a political economy that gave considerable sway to both the free market and the overbearing state. Hence, the recurrent complaints that Labour allowed retail giants like Tesco's to reshape the centres of many towns and villages, driving local shops out of business, and that government seemed willing to stand by while some of the key institutions of local communities – post offices or community pubs – were shut down.

Had Labour perceived the many different complaints emerging from some of these and other communities as cries for recognition of communal identities, rather than forms of parochial special pleading, it is possible that it might well have developed a different political response. It certainly should have thought more carefully about banning fox hunting, a totemic move which played to metropolitan sensibilities but came to symbolise the party's lack of feel for rural communities and their traditions. More generally, progressives need to think much harder about how to combine support for the expansion of choice and plurality within public service provision, with policies that address the preservationist and anti-commercial instincts of significant parts of the population – for instance, in terms of protecting children from TV advertising, or placing limits upon working hours in order to preserve the quality of family life.

The thinker who, perhaps more than any other in the twentieth century, made the case for a politics that was embedded in the complex and contradictory currents of popular-conservative sensibilities was the Italian communist Antonio Gramsci. His emphasis upon the construction of an alternative 'national-popular' does not translate easily into the terms of contemporary politics. But his thinking provides some important clues for today's beleaguered centre-left. Gramsci understood the 'national-popular' to signal a political project that involved socialists speaking simultaneously to a diverse range of social groups in terms that arise from and reflect back their daily experiences, and also seeking to provide an overarching vision of an alternative social future.

Gramsci chided his fellow socialists for their lofty and overly rationalistic approach to the 'folk wisdom' that emerged from within the interstices of everyday life. These sensibilities, he argued, provided the forms of common sense through which social groups made sense of the world they inhabited, and provided crucial resources that needed to be engaged, harnessed and sometimes transformed by leftist parties seeking to construct alternative visions of the social order.

Languishing in a fascist prison from 1926–37, Gramsci was all too aware that rival political forces were often more adept at harnessing the frustrations and discontents that coursed through popular common sense. Should the gap that has grown in today's Europe between many popular sentiments and the parties and institutions of liberal society widen, there is every chance that the quests for recognition and protection will harden into greater resentment and ethno-cultural rivalry.

More generally, Labour and other parties of the centre-left need to ask themselves how they have come to project forms of political reasoning, often based upon their adherence to individualistic models of the self, or rationalistic theories of justice, which are cut adrift from popular wisdom about, for instance, the value of landscapes, the importance of established ways of living, and the multiplicity of ideas of 'the good' that are ignored or disapproved of by the left. Questions of place, belonging and culture need to be much higher on the agenda of social democrats.

Engage More Carefully with the Needs and Position of 'White, Working-Class' Communities

The left needs to think hard about how to repair its fractured relationship with working-class communities. This means both that it has to come to terms with the growing inclination of many of their countrymen and women to think of themselves in ethno-cultural terms, and that it needs to acquire a sense of proportion about the phenomenon of white, working-class alienation; refusing the temptation to see only bigotry and resentment within these communities (a trap into which some current sociological research also falls).[12]

Recent research commissioned by the UK government's Department for Communities and Local Government[13] indicates a marked geographic variability in terms of anti-migrant sentiments, identifying a number of regional 'hot-spots' of prejudice and hostility. It suggests, too, that in many communities that have experienced high rates of migration there has been no significant shift in terms of resistance to migrants and ethnic minorities. But in areas where tensions and resentments are most acute, there is much to worry about. A study commissioned by the UK government's National Communities Forum in 2009 reported a deeply established sense of communal grievance,[14] and a widely held belief that the needs and traditions of the indigenous community were under threat in some of these places.

Equally, a progressive politics of recognition has to mean challenging some of the problems in the area of political representation that fuel the frustrations and disaffection of working-class citizens. The question of how to return a sense of voice and agency to individuals from these social backgrounds ought to be one of the starting points for social democratic reflections on how to renew and improve representative political systems. This means prioritising such issues as counter-acting recent patterns of political 'professionalisation' that have significantly narrowed access to the legislature, further reducing the numbers of working-class people going into politics.

More generally, the sense that the Labour Party came to take for granted many of its own voters in constituencies where it enjoys huge electoral majorities has helped generate a profound sense of political disenfranchisement. For this reason alone, the left should throw its weight behind any reform of the voting system that introduces overdue competitiveness into more constituencies. More generally, social democrats are going to have to learn to live in a world where working-class voters, like their social counterparts, are more independent and plural in their voting intentions; and where many will have to be persuaded to use their vote at all. Rather than clinging on to the assumptions that guided politics in the collectivist era, the centre-left should signal its embrace of a new, more uncertain period in the history of working-class allegiances.

Conclusions

These three injunctions are bound to generate challenges for parties that are trying simultaneously to reach beyond their core constituencies and secure the allegiance of voters from different social classes. A progressive politics of identity needs to be both outward-facing and framed around the importance of creating diverse social coalitions of support, and also sufficiently engaged with poorer communities to have depth and durability. Whether such a combination can be achieved over the medium and long terms remains to be seen.

Above all, the centre-left needs to consider the dynamics and growing importance of what Canadian political theorist Charles Taylor has termed the yearning for 'recognition' in contemporary society. The notion that groups and individuals deserve respect from each other and the democratic state is one of the most important, long-term legacies of the identity-based movements that have arisen within Western democratic politics since the 1970s. But while these demands were previously articulated by groups and communities that were orientated predominantly to the political left, the rhetoric of culturally based grievance has migrated across the political and social spectrums, stretching from the Tea Party to the EDL. The politics of identity may currently be most developed and apparent within the United States. But it has in important respects come to characterise European political culture as well. Here, too, people's need for belonging, security and identity increasingly shape their relationships to, and expectations of, politics and politicians.

CHAPTER 10

The Power of European Integration: Choice and Purpose for Centre-Left Politics

Olaf Cramme

For most of its past, the European Union has struggled to evoke political emotions or ideological contention. Too complex, too technocratic, too remote and too irrelevant – the image of Brussels has not easily lent itself to the stories, arguments and narratives with which politicians seek to court their national electorates. Many have argued that only such a hidden and impenetrable role would allow EU integration to proceed, carefully managed by Europe's ruling classes who have quietly developed an exceptional mode of transnational governance. Indeed, the unique design of this mode of governance now accommodates a continent-wide parliament with genuine law-making powers, a sophisticated rules-based system for open borders guarded by a single judicial authority, and even a common currency. Despite many hiccups over recent years, progress on integration has gone by and large according to plan.

This quiet convention was dramatically interrupted, however, by the ramifications of the global financial crisis of 2007–8, which started as a US sub-prime mortgage crisis, was followed by a severe credit squeeze on the real economy, and turned into a crisis of sovereign indebtedness in the Euro-zone, which – at the time of writing – continues to threaten the very existence of the Euro itself. All of a sudden, the EU became a very emotive subject.

In the streets of Athens, Madrid and other European capitals, demonstrators have directed their anger against what they perceived to be a ruthless bureaucracy which is about to decide on the fate of their nation. Others, in turn, have rallied against the looming spectre of a 'transfer union', in which cautious housekeepers have to bail out their profligate family members. The fight for the Euro is markedly exacerbating the divisions between the fiscally prudent northern countries and their less conservative southern partners. It is shaking the power balance between the EU's institutions, prompting both inter-governmentalists and federalists to demand further revisions to the Lisbon Treaty, whose accomplishment had proved such a nerve-racking task not long before. Not least, the effects of the crisis have sparked a new debate about the possibility of a multi-speed or two-tier Europe – not so much out of choice but out of sheer necessity.

In essence, the thread connecting these disputes is how to reconcile reinforced supranational governance, deemed indispensable for safeguarding Economic and Monetary Union (EMU), with democratic legitimacy and national self-determination. The tensions and trade-offs surrounding deeper political and economic integration are now firmly back on the table, only this time they have been further exacerbated by the reluctance of political parties to acknowledge the significance of constitutional politics: how should we govern – and be governed – in a world where borders count less and less? Needless to say, this question is proving to be highly controversial among policy-makers of all political stripes. European governments are faced with far-reaching choices on accepting tough benchmarks and common standards, setting up strict mutual supervision and pooling competences in sensitive policy areas, such as fiscal policy and taxation, which hitherto constituted the sovereign and unreserved rights of proud and independent nation-states. If the struggle for democracy in Westphalian Europe took decades or even centuries, its redefinition in the EU polity is currently being fast-tracked.

At such a fundamental moment in the process of EU integration, the centre-left cannot simply hide behind the façade of opposition politics, shifting the responsibility onto the incumbent centre-right governments that currently rule across Europe. There is much more at stake than just contributing to the debate about how to fix the EU's immediate problems. Devoid of a clear governing purpose in the aftermath of the financial crash, and stuck in the midst of a profound identity crisis, social democracy is struggling to come to terms with unbridled market forces in an age of rapid global change. In this context, the EU has turned out to be an amplifier and a promise – yet the left seems largely oblivious of both.

The purpose of this chapter is therefore to shed light on the existing weakness of social democratic politics vis-à-vis the EU, and to offer some direction for how the left can use the power of European integration for its own objectives. To be sure, such ambitions make for a tall order. Today, social democratic pro-Europeanism is increasingly questioned from within while also enjoying little public recognition. Instead, it is the parties of the centre-right which are recognised as the more competent problem solvers at the European level.[1] How has this come about?

The Weakness of Social Democratic Pro-Europeanism

To find the answer, it is worth briefly exploring the relationship between social democracy as an ideology and the motivations behind European integration. This relationship matters because in political and public debate it tends to be overshadowed by the excessive focus on personalities and individual achievements. For instance, much has been written about the fact that the majority of the EU's founding fathers – from Robert Schuman and Konrad Adenauer to Alcide De Gasperi and Jean Monnet – were of a conservative creed. It is also often pointed out that it was the likes of Helmut Kohl and Margaret Thatcher who ultimately defined the balance between 'deepening' and 'widening' in their very own ideological battle over the future of the EU. But social democrats, too, demonstrated visionary leadership in the interest of Europe: Aristide Briand's speech, as early as 1929, calling for a union of European nations; Paul-Henri Spaak's masterminding of the report which paved the way for the creation of the European Economic Community (EEC) in 1957; or Willy Brandt's *Ostpolitik* that made re-unification conceivable in the long run – to name but a few.

What primarily distinguishes the left from the right is not so much the political merit which has (or has not) been attributed to individuals in the course of history, but rather social democracy's internal conflict with the basic idea of transcending national politics and pooling sovereignty in the pursuit of collective interests. The European idea was as ingenious as it was simple: only a state of dependency between the different nations' key industries, as well as other economic activities such as farming, would secure long-lasting peace on a continent where the quest for hegemony and resource dominance had caused so much misery and devastation. The steel and coal industries, traditional strongholds of social democratic and trade union support, thus became the first targets. What followed was a determined drive by leading policymakers throughout the 1960s and 1970s to use the power of integrated markets to cement the vision of an interdependent Europe. The left, for its part, remained by and large a passive bystander, occasionally voicing criticism yet without challenging the project at its core. The cause of friction was less about the objective itself but more the 'market' as the principle means. Social democratic ambivalence was the inevitable result.[2]

The turning point came in the 1980s. Elected on a platform of traditional left-wing ideas, including far-reaching re-nationalisation, Keynesian spending programmes and punitive taxation, François Mitterrand conceded, less than two years into the first term of his presidency, that 'socialism in one country' essentially had no future alongside the development of a European community in which the aim of economic convergence was gradually becoming more central. Capital flight in response to Mitterand's early announcements just proved how vulnerable individual nation-states had become in the customs union of the EEC.

The appointment of Jacques Delors, a pro-market socialist, to the helm of the European Commission in 1985 only accelerated the awakening of the social democratic family. The shift in thinking was significant: confronted with the dominance of monetarism and supply-side economics – brought home by a series of electoral defeats in the 1980s – the centre-left increasingly regarded European integration as a suitable vehicle for its own process of doctrinal modernisation. In this process, the focus on constraints and obstacles was replaced by a belief in the transformative capacity of the community approach. Europe became the new hope.

Scholars have put forward two main explanations for this turn towards positive engagement with the EU.[3] First, social democrats began to recognise the significant implications of globalisation and subsequently accepted the view that only co-ordinated policy making could deliver on the left's traditional promise of taming capitalism. Retaining a commitment to the ends while changing the means, this revisionist strand of social democracy led the way from the early 1990s onwards, as more and more centre-left parties embraced the dynamism of open markets while championing a cosmopolitan vision of international co-operation.

Second, support for EU integration served as a way to disguise and correct a perceived failure of social democratic policy output at the national level. The unfolding rationale was that unhealthy competition between labour based on wages, hours worked and the level of social spending and security had gradually reached a degree of Europeanisation at which the defence of acquired rights seemed to demand joint as opposed to individual member state action. In other words, the breaking down of barriers between EU countries (negative integration) had as far as possible to be balanced by common rules, standards and regulations and the provision of social goods (positive integration).

In the final decade before the millennium, the social democratic family had at last adopted an unequivocally positive stance on European integration. The old doubts about using the market for a higher political and even social purpose had faded. Yet the main centre-left parties went down very different paths to reach this conclusion, with some regarding the EU as a 'protector against globalisation' and others expecting Brussels to support the difficult reform processes of Europe's social models. The diverse reasoning, in turn, resulted in widely diverging preferences not only about the policy areas to be covered by integration, but also about the ultimate political goals and the institutions that could be entrusted to meet them. Social democracy's internal heterogeneity manifestly weakened the broad consensus for 'more Europe', leaving the centre-left deprived of a coherent European agenda at a time when it dominated the political landscape in the EU15. This painful lesson had far-reaching implications, inasmuch as a serious debate about Europe's socio-economic governance was largely avoided. Instead, 'market failure', from climate change to global poverty and financial speculation to rising inequality became the new prevailing motive, shifting the focus steadily from internal to external concerns. Neo-liberal globalisation was the designated enemy.

When the global financial crisis broke, the dominant picture, however, was that of a significant gap which had emerged between the political rhetoric and the prospect of real change. Social democracy got stuck in a lonely fight against global developments whose actual implications were often ill-understood or not appreciated by the European public, let alone shared by other global players. To many, the processes of Europeanisation and globalisation looked almost identical, making the task of pitching the former against the latter all the more difficult. Moreover, the policy solutions presented by the centre-left, from a 'Robin Hood tax' to a 'Green New Deal', meant little to citizens concerned about stagnant wages, job insecurity and migration.

As a result, national politicians rushed to conclude that the EU does not lend itself easily to positive campaign themes and largely abstained from putting Europe at the heart of the social democratic offer. Centre-left support for European integration developed an empty meaning.

EU Predicaments in Social Democratic Politics

What are the underlying causes of the weakness in social democratic pro-Europeanism? The historical abstract illustrates how the centre-left failed to develop its own compelling narrative of how the EU could serve the goals of a more equal and prosperous society. While the direction of travel seemed to be moving unequivocally towards greater integration, the political dividends remained firmly hidden. For sure, sceptics argue that the EU has become a major electoral and political liability, as more and more people question the actual impact of European policymaking on their lives and their countries. This scepticism is, however, predominantly voiced by those who challenge the EU on *democratic* grounds. Their core argument is that democratic representation and popular influence have been seriously perverted in the European polity, undermining the nation-state as the only possible guarantor of self-governing legitimacy.

What has been given far less attention is the *policy* deficit which engulfs social democratic politics vis-à-vis EU integration. This is not to suggest that the democratic challenge is secondary or less relevant, but that in the 'living constitution' of the EU both dimensions are mutually reinforcing and hence absolutely pivotal in securing popular acceptance.[4] From a centre-left perspective, this means coming to terms with at least three specific predicaments which have so far impeded a stronger social democratic imprint on the European project: first, the overwhelmingly economic logic of EU integration; second, new political cleavages within European electorates; and third, the EU's institutional architecture.

The Economic Logic of European Integration

To begin with, there is the ideational challenge of a market-driven Europe. Although social ambitions were enshrined in the Treaty of Rome, it was successive waves of economic liberalisation, in particular after the Single European Act in 1986, which developed into self-fulfilling prophecies and came to define the competences of, and the relationship between, the various levels of EU governance.

The fundamental freedoms of the internal market – of goods, capital, services and people – came to form the legal backbone to which, in theory at least, all other concerns and policy ambitions ought to be subordinated. Consequently, the role of EU jurisdiction was increasingly defined by defending the constitutionalised free-trade regime against all forms of protectionism and favouritism, giving precedence to Community over national law. While in practice its application is less rigid and dogmatic, so that political sensitivities can be respected – for instance, with regard to housing, health, the media and (nuclear) energy – European law has pushed EU integration further in the direction of economic liberalism. It is for this reason that trade and competition policy are the two areas in which the authority of Brussels is greatest.

Europeanisation must therefore be considered in a very different way to globalisation, inasmuch as the former, far more than the latter, is subject to a suprastatist principle enshrined in the Union's formal treaties. Critics, such as Colin Hay, have long deplored the centre-left's lack of imagination when it comes to alternatives to neo-liberal economics in the international order.[5] Hay challenges the notion that the so-called 'Washington consensus' meant a mere accommodation of preferences as opposed to shaping them in the first place. In the case of the EU, however, breaking the overriding logic is all the more daunting given the degree to which economic integration has deepened. It is not only that open markets have created a favourable environment for a particular kind of liberal ideology, but also that Europe's strongly intertwined economies have become powerful sources in the defence of economic liberalisation. Social policy, however (often presented as the antidote by the centre-left), does not have as much punching power and its advocates have struggled to present a coherent intellectual case for its advancement. Two countervailing aspects of EU social policy illustrate this point.

On the one hand, there is the argument that the liberalisation of the Single Market and its four freedoms has led to a downward convergence in social security spending, in particular after the intake of the Eastern European countries. The evidence, nevertheless, suggests that fears over a cumulative 'race to the bottom', brought on by policy competition and migration, remain largely exaggerated or unfounded, even though opening-up has contributed to new domestic disparities. A number of rulings by the European Court of Justice with regard to the Posted Workers Directive a few years ago – conceding primacy to the freedom of service provision over national collective agreements – briefly managed to generate genuine social outrage, but ultimately failed to resolve the chief underlying tensions: namely, how to establish common ground on the level of social protection between countries at different stages of economic development.

On the other hand, it has been contended that the EU is well placed to shield its citizens from the harsh effects of international economic competition. Adherents of this view tend to frame the Union's new twenty-first century rationale along these very lines: if the market has become truly global, 'market-correcting' must now be increasingly European. Such reasoning demands centralised co-ordination in those social policy areas where positive scale effects can be identified – that is, where policy is more effective if implemented jointly; for instance, thanks to lower implementation costs or better insurance. Yet, the extent to which globalisation actually contributes to negative developments remains highly contested in the EU27, not least in relation to the labour market. Furthermore, convincing proposals about where the EU can genuinely add value in the social realm have been few and far between. Consequently, limited initiatives such as the Globalisation Adjustment Fund represent the best possible outcome.

Against this background, the European centre-left looks somewhat bereft of an identity which can be linked to recognisable policy achievements. In the past, 'peace', 'reconciliation' and 'unification' offered crucial cynosures for positive social democratic engagement with EU integration. Today, no such equivalent exists. After Jacques Delors's push for 'social Europe' at the end of the 1980s, the Lisbon Agenda – an ambitious policy framework for economic and social modernisation – can be considered the last major initiative for which the left can claim true ownership.

Yet not only has the Lisbon Agenda failed to live up to expectations, social democrats have also quickly retreated from it as they are overcome with growing self-doubts about the purpose of centre-left governance in the global age. Indeed, it seems that the left is almost ashamed of its past achievements.

Europe's Political Fragmentation

The second major predicament relates to the new political and electoral cleavages which the processes of integration, at both European and global levels, have created. Structural and ideological voting along traditional left–right lines is in steady decline. This has been brought about by the emergence of an additional value-based dimension which stretches along an authoritarian–libertarian axis.[6] Along these lines, the current open economic and political order can be supported, or indeed rejected, on at least two different levels: on the one hand, when it comes to the life chances and economic opportunities that individuals enjoy in a society transformed by increased competition; and on the other hand, with regard to normative visions of the self, the good life, the nation, societal justice or even religion.

The current political alignment of the EU is influenced by the fact that these economic and cultural dimensions cannot be captured by consistent orientations vis-à-vis European integration. In a transnational context, Stefano Bartolini has shown that views on 'boundary control *versus* boundary transcendence' have as much of an impact as views on 'integration *versus* independence', while market preferences do not necessarily coincide with cultural ones even when both dimensions are aligned.[7] In other words, someone who favours stronger national sovereignty and independence could either be characterised as an 'economic protectionist' or a 'cultural nationalist', but not necessarily both. Conversely, someone who argues for deeper EU integration and greater openness to the world could be a (neo-)liberal Europeanist and/or a cultural cosmopolitan. In turn, those who sympathise with renewed independence and an open world, are either economic liberals who tend to resist control from a new administrative centre, or globalists who prefer a loosely defined international culture to a more closed European one. Finally, a person who advocates reinforced national control and continued integration may be either a 'social-market Europeanist' who wants the EU to carry out strict supervision of the market, or a Europhile who sees European culture as a distinct counterpart to US-driven globalisation.

As a matter of fact, this new polarisation and fragmentation affects the political system as a whole, not only social democracy. Mainstream parties have long since lost their hegemonic role and ability to channel and represent widely divergent interests. In liberal democracies with electoral systems based on proportional representation, fringe, populist and 'single-issue' parties have vigorously stirred up the political establishment, creating new dynamics for coalition building and political bargaining. Although 'Europe' has largely remained a non-salient issue for the public-at-large, and hence had only a limited impact on the outcomes of national elections, this may no longer remain the case in a post-sovereign-debt-crisis EU – as the emergence of the 'True Finns' has glaringly demonstrated.

In fact, it can be considered surprising that anti-EU populism has not spread further. The Union remains a high-profile target for all those who want to challenge it on either cultural or economic grounds. For instance, sustained opposition to the European project can be framed around a dispute between the centre and the periphery, in which it is argued that integration is undermining the exceptionalism of certain groups and territories. It can also be framed around a functional divide between the economic winners and losers of market openness.

What exacerbates this challenge for the centre-left, however, is the idiosyncratic sociological composition of its support base, which originated in working-class communities but nowadays seeks to transcend traditional class structures. Recent studies have shown that EU scepticism is far more pronounced among the less well educated, the less skilled and the poor than among their opposites – for both economic and cultural reasons.[8] This exposes social democracy, like no other ideology, to strong polarising political viewpoints, rendering it almost impossible to settle on a 'catch-all' position. If the left's policy identification is weak in the EU context, its political identity is even more under siege.

Idiosyncrasies of the EU's Institutional Architecture

The third predicament is institutional and thus directly impacts on the other two. The situation is well known: the EU has developed a system of governance which exhibits a unique division of responsibilities between its institutions and member states, often described under the heading of 'subsidiarity'. Since its inception, the EU has gradually expanded its regulatory authority, evolving from a customs union and a free-trade area to the Single Market and a common currency. The pooling of sovereignty is obviously strongest in the case of EMU. Here, monetary policy and exchange-rate instruments of macro-economic management have been passed to the independent European Central

Bank (ECB); fiscal policy is subject to strict supervision within the framework of the Stability and Growth Pact; and supply-side reforms are now closely monitored, if not co-ordinated, through programmes seeking to foster greater economic convergence.

In terms of the individual institutions, conflicting views with regard to the degree of federalisation have required careful management and balance. Although the European Council, with its heads of state and government, clings to its prerogative to set the principal course of action, the European Commission remains endowed with wide-ranging supervisory and policymaking powers, while the European Parliament has steadily acquired more authority to take forward initiatives and carry out substantial legislative scrutiny. As such, the 'community method' sits alongside 'inter-governmentalism', and – depending on the political climate, the policy issue at stake or indeed exceptional (external) events – one can trump the other. In short, the EU is neither a loose confederation nor a genuine supranational entity.

Social democratic critics of this particular order lament two related aspects. On the one hand it is argued that the EU is a profoundly 'conservative' system, inasmuch as it does not allow for far-reaching institutional change due to its consensual character and complex procedures. Instead it is said to protect the status quo and thus serve the economic logic outlined above.[9] In effect, the multiple EU power centres and their adherent processes of checks and balances do not lend themselves easily to political reformism, let alone decisive leadership. The relative weakness of the Euro-parties, including the Party of European Socialists (PES), is not only representative of an inability to gain support for EU ideals, but also of the impediments to exerting real influence in a system made up of numerous independent actors – from the nation-states and EU institutions to the various political parties, interest groups and populations (in the case of elections to the European Parliament and/or national referenda).

Hence, there is an 'institutional trap': if social democrats want to pursue a pro-European policy, they are left with little choice but to adopt a politics which largely respects the prevailing settlement, before seeking its gradual modification. A full-blown attack on the

EU's institutions or policies inevitably risks undermining the system as a whole.

On the other hand, centre-left politics is said to be squeezed between encumbering influence, if not unwelcome interference, from the top (the EU level) and insufficient room for manoeuvre at the bottom (the national level).[10] From this critical perspective, half-way federalisation has brought the worst of both worlds to the fore. Whereas, in the past, nation-state social democracy could deploy the full range of macro- and micro-economic instruments to tame rampant capitalism, it is nowadays limited to prioritising supply-side reforms and fighting a rather defensive struggle to maintain existing levels of social security and welfare. The EU institutions, by contrast, lack the mandate and competences to be a more forceful corrective to the injustices created by open markets. Some, like Fritz Scharpf, have taken this argument even further, asserting that EMU makes member states suffer from uniform policies – such as one-size-fits-all ECB interest rates – which do not correspond with individual member state needs.[11] At the same time, the EU does not possess a suitably large budget to address the adverse effects of market integration.

The litmus test for the sustainability of this complex institutional architecture is thus whether it is capable of addressing both the destabilising imbalances *between* EU member states and the increasing disparities *within* them. By all accounts, defining this complex space is a significant challenge for social democratic practices and policies.

Choice and Purpose in EU Politics

In view of these formidable predicaments, social democracy is facing an existential choice. Will it seek to use the power of European integration for the pursuit of its own policy agenda, or will it gradually turn its back on the idea of an 'ever closer union' and the aspiration of regional solidarity in a world where size matters? The choice is stark indeed because the centre-left currently occupies an uneasy, if not untenable, position in the context of EU politics: its constituency is bitterly divided along the 'demarcation *versus* integration' axis; its capacity to be a driving force of the European project and exert political influence is hardly recognised by the public; its habitual policy tool box has been severely scaled down by the particularities of the EU's institutional design; and its promise of a fairer and more equal society has to some extent been eclipsed by widening inequalities across almost all of Europe.

Unsurprisingly, the temptation to question and challenge social democratic pro-Europeanism is growing fast. Widespread dissatisfaction with Europe's ruling classes and the state of democracy more generally is taken as a convenient pretext to elevate the left's localist and communitarian traditions, which emphasise an unfulfilled desire for self-governance over any form of macro-democratic engagement – as if a partial return to 'socialism in one country' could ever present a plausible alternative to taking on the destructive forces, and undemocratic nature, of global capitalism.[12] The EU's 'democratic deficit' should be of real concern to centre-left politics but it must not give way to a defeatist, or indeed parochial, view that transnational policy making must always and inevitably be less responsive to popular demands and needs than more traditional modes of representative democracy. Social democracy that is defensive and reactionary will struggle to capture the future.

Yet if parochialism is a serious danger for a European left racked by profound self-doubt, unwarranted despair vis-à-vis integration is another. Far from being a simple impediment, the EU's social-model framework has proven highly resilient and adaptive to the deep societal transformations that have been brought about not only by open commodity and capital markets but in particular by technological advances and changes in family relations and lifestyle patterns. Social spending as a proportion of GDP has not declined since the 1980s but increased both in absolute and relative terms – at least in a majority of member states.[13]

Indeed, the economic benefits of the Single Market have significantly added to European GDP and as a result of this growth dividend, national welfare states are generally better funded, to the benefit of the low-skilled and less educated working people. Importantly, the EU legal order for the creation of the common market is underpinned by much 'progressive' flanking legislation and court action in the realms of the environment, consumer rights, health and safety rules and anti-discrimination. Then there are the achievements of the European social agenda itself, which range from focusing member states on labour market modernisation, to establishing common objectives in the field of social inclusion and social protection, to redistribution in favour of weaker member states and regions through instruments such as the structural and cohesion policy. As a result, in some countries like the UK, the EU's constitutionalised socio-economic settlement is actually viewed with great concern by the free-market and libertarian right which strongly opposes any entrenchment of social rights.

None of this is to suggest that the predicaments for social democratic politics can easily be overcome. But they do suggest that the EU after the global financial *cum* sovereign debt crisis requires a very different approach from the futile antagonism between 'Market Europe' and 'Social Europe'. This is to say that the dominant agenda of 'market making' or 'market enabling' is gradually being replaced by a process in which the creation of a democratically, economically and socially sustainable European polity is taking centre stage. Standards, objectives, targets and regulatory frameworks will become at least as important as directives that break down trade barriers and favour one-sided economic liberalisation. Integrated proposals of the kind that former Commissioner Mario Monti presented with regard to Single Market reform are likely to offer the most promising balance between divergent socio-economic interests in a heterogeneous EU27.[14]

For the centre-left, this offers an important new perspective in terms of influencing Europe's policy agenda. Yet beyond this, it could also help to define a new social democratic governing purpose for the twenty-first century, one which is not only about winning back power but also about delivering against expectations, coping with external constraints, pursuing sustainable development and building trust in the practice of democratic politics, which is challenged above all else by the powerlessness of national politicians in the face of global developments. If social democracy is to rediscover its mission of marrying economic efficiency with social justice, it needs new means and vehicles for change. In this process, the EU could be its best ally.

The Quest for a More Assertive and Relevant Policy Agenda

How can the left become a more dominant agenda-setter and claim stronger ownership of the EU project? For a start, social democrats need to better identify the policy space in which Europe can make a qualitative difference to the objective of creating a more cohesive and solidaristic society. Investing the proceeds of growth from increased global market competition into the welfare state and public services did not prevent widespread wage stagnation and rising income inequalities which post-hoc redistribution could not contain. The scholars Jacob Hacker and Paul Pierson therefore speak of the need to rebuild the 'institutional foundations of middle-class democracy' in order to reign in the polarisation of 'pre-distributed' wealth in capitalist societies[15] – a challenge which middle- or small-sized nation-states can hardly overcome on their own in an open and interdependent Europe.

But above all, social democrats must ensure that the programme they offer strongly reflects Europe's most pressing structural dilemmas, including: the untapped potential of millions of socially disadvantaged and economically inactive people; the destabilising divergences in the competitive position of member states as a result of poor adjustment of wages in response to a slowdown or increase in productivity; or the fragile and shrinking tax base of governments in an era of tight fiscal constraints and spending cuts. In this context, the following three, broad policy ideas seek to provide an illustration of what a more assertive and relevant EU agenda for the centre-left might look like.

First, an 'EU Social Investment Pact' could provide an attractive conceptual answer to the overly narrow focus on competitiveness in the debate about EU economic governance and current-account imbalances.[16] While the notion of social investment is not new *per se* and has been successfully adopted by some pioneering member states over the past two decades, today its operationalisation and implementation have been severely hampered – on the one hand by the prevailing emphasis on austerity politics, and on the other by a surge in populist welfare chauvinism, brought about by anxieties over immigration and the effectiveness of public spending.

A Social Investment Pact could break this logic and offer a compelling alternative vision which combines short-term fiscal consolidation with long-term policies that seek to empower individuals and contribute to societal cohesion. It would also be capable of providing a more intelligent balance between budgetary discipline and social assistance, between strict conditionality and an emphasis on progress, thus creating a real sense of reciprocity. The EU can lead from the front by setting common targets and objectives, sorting out definitional ambiguity and ensuring compatibility with other reform programmes. Much is to be gained by such a co-ordinated and integrated approach.

Second, unsustainable imbalances and slow adjustment processes inside EMU, and possibly across the entire EU, could be countered by a strengthened European macro-economic co-ordination mechanism to ensure that nominal wage and labour cost developments are more consistent with price stability and trends in productivity. The conditions of monetary union with a single interest rate have clearly exacerbated the divergences in inflationary pressures and price competitiveness across the Euro area, thereby undermining its stability. For the left, this poses a particularly challenging problem as both subdued wage developments in surplus countries and above-average inflation rates in deficit countries tend to hurt the poorest in society. Meanwhile, national trade unions will be extremely reluctant to accept any infringement of their autonomy over collective bargaining. But the constraints of EMU and the ramifications of the financial crisis have basically shown that such autonomy is actually rather limited and subject to fiscal and monetary decision making, over which member states have restricted or no control. In this respect, a macro-economic co-ordination mechanism at the EU level could be for wage-setting and inflation surveillance what the Stability and Growth Pact is for fiscal policy.[17]

Third, social democrats must elaborate a much clearer conception and vision of where tax competition in the EU is a legitimate means for economic catch-up, in particular by less developed and wealthy member states, and where it primarily undermines the national tax base while providing few or no benefits for ordinary citizens. So far, calls for any kind of tax co-ordination, let alone harmonisation, have been routinely dismissed as an outright assault on national sovereignty and each member state's freedom to compete for foreign direct investment. The left's often dogmatic reasoning on the dangers of tax competition simply did not cut through into the public debate.

Yet in a deepened Single Market, taxation also increasingly constitutes an obstacle to the development of cross-border economic activities, while tax competition has led to a shift of the tax burden from capital to labour and consumption – to the detriment of low-income earners. The European Commission's proposals for a 'Common Consolidated Corporate Tax Base' certainly point in the right direction, but they merely seek to reduce cross-border profit shifting. What is required is a more compelling account of why formal sovereignty in an integrated EU actually undermines legitimate democratic control over the design of national tax systems, and how limited or partial Europeanisation of tax policy can be a suitable and progressive corrective against the background of fiscal and budgetary constraints.[18]

To some, the realisation of these and similarly ambitious ideas might appear inconceivable, or even utopian. But at least they are not defeatist. Social democracy must not underestimate the power of European integration at a time when the phenomenal pressures of globalisation and far-reaching societal transformations are asking profound questions of all traditional political ideologies. At some point, a movement, initiative or policy idea will capture the attention of the wider European public. The centre-left ought to make sure that it is part of it.

CHAPTER 11

Back to the Future: Towards a Red-Green Politics

John McTernan

Parties of the centre-left win elections on the twin issues of future and fairness, and when they cannot articulate a vision of the future and show how that future can be fair for all they lose. After a decade in the 1990s when it seemed as though a new progressive paradigm – New Democrat, Neue Mitte, New Labour – was successfully establishing a popular centre-left political project, the new century has been bleak. The energy in politics has been anywhere but the centre-left: in a new generation of 'compassionate' conservatives who turned the progressive playbook against incumbent centre-left governments in insurgent populist movements of the right; and, in the long-term perhaps most threatening, in new entrants to the left of traditional social democratic parties, in particular green parties. The threat of these last is not simply electoral. They appear to set out a radical politics that stakes a greater claim on embodying fairness and future than the programmes of centre-left parties.

Tactical responses to this latter challenge have been intermittently successful, but they will only be a temporary solution because of the fact that green politics contests the core competence of social democratic politics – the ability to frame the problems of individuals today and to set out a transformative vision of how collective action can resolve them in the future. At its core this is a politics of hope that was not afraid to be utopian, and however wrongheaded some leftist and green policies are, in some ways they are colonising this territory; in particular through their willingness to describe the world as it should be, not simply accounting for the world as it is and proposing modest amelioration.

There is a route back to electoral success for the centre-left but it demands a clear-sighted analysis of the current challenges, an honest return to the roots of social democracy, and taking a series of practical and policy steps which would build a red-green politics.

Reframing the Political Challenge

For a hundred years, social democracy has shaped our politics. Parties of the centre-left are responsible, directly when in power, and indirectly when parties of the centre-right responded to them, for the shape of the world in which we live and work. Health and safety, the welfare state, anti-discrimination legislation and the fabric of our societies reflect a series of victories for progressive politics. Policy change was hard won and had to be constantly defended, and sustaining electoral victory was not easy, yet viewed from the second decade of the twenty-first century, it already looks so much easier back then. Rather than nostalgia, this sense of crisis is real. Despite moments of exhilaration – the election of Australian Labor in 2007, Obama's victory the following year and the election of Dilma Rousseff to succeed Lula in Brazil last year – the sound of 'the melancholy, long withdrawing roar' of a receding tide of electoral support has been most prominent in recent years. Successive progressive parties have fallen out of government, and few have a convincing route map back to power.

There has been a great deal of agonised discussion about the nature of the electoral coalition that supports the centre-left which has focused on the decline of working-class support for centre-left parties. Much of this has produced a melancholy mood of declinism, rather than practical impact. One bright spot has been the observation that as the working class decline, the – typically university-educated – progressive middle class grows. Thus, what economic and demographic change takes with one hand it gives with another. However, it seems now that those middle-class voters are themselves becoming less reliable supporters, and are increasingly attracted to alternative parties of the left and to green parties. In Helsinki, the inner-city workers' housing which was once uniformly red, now occupied by 'black-collar' workers – creative industry types who wear a T-shirt to work – votes solidly green. Balmain in Sydney, birthplace of the Australian Labor Party, has elected a Green MP to the state parliament.

The classic social democratic coalition of the liberal middle class and the organised working class is being eroded at both ends. Worse, leaning one way to appease one group risks alienating the other: a harsher line on crime and immigration can shore up the core vote – and is arguably good policy – but it risks alienating more liberal voters who value cultural diversity and civil liberties. Tilt environmentally towards them and you begin to lose the core vote for whom green taxes are a straightforward cost-of-living pressure.

Sketched in this way, it can seem an insuperable challenge. How can both ends of the coalition be satisfied at the same time, particularly if 'values' issues divide them more profoundly than common economic concerns and policy demands can unite them? However, the fundamental problem is in fact this way of framing the political challenge. Triangulation and the other tactics that worked so well for nearly 20 years are now a cul-de-sac precisely because they are just that, tactics. To persist with them now simply because they once worked so well is to risk being trapped in a contour of history.

The problem is not one of better tactics or cleverer campaigns, but one of purpose, and this is where the centre-left currently fall down. In many respects, the global financial crisis was a godsend for Brown's Government, providing a purpose and definition to a drifting administration following an initial attempt to define itself as 'not Tony Blair'. Similarly, the crisis gave an equivalent boost to Kevin Rudd's Labor Government in Australia. Without this external crisis there was no burning project for either of these governments, which were reduced to being what Jaroslav Havek satirised as parties of 'Moderate Progress Within the Bounds of the Law'. This is not to deride the achievements of the 1990s, but there is no way forward without a renewed purpose. To identify what that should be social democrats must return to their roots.

Explaining the World to People

Labour parties have their origins in solidarity, epitomised in the radical, mobilising claim that 'an injury to one is an injury to all'. Over time, social democrats convinced the majority of working people that there were fundamental issues that affected them as individuals which could only be addressed through collective action. This language may sound old-fashioned, but it won pensions, socialised medicine, health and safety at work and the other rights conservatives now defend as their own. Rather than simply defending these gains, social democrats need new causes. Today, the most obvious candidate for this cause is the environment. It meets all the tests. This threat affects the individual and their families and communities but cannot be met except through collective action. It requires not just national but international action; but successful, co-ordinated, global action which relies on rules that intervene in, shape and manage markets. Social democrats are well qualified on both of these measures.

But there is a political contest going on. There is a perfectly plausible centre-right approach to climate change which tackles it with little care for equity, redistribution or development issues. Indeed, green politics has a special place in the arsenal of moderate, modernising conservatives. It is used to demonstrate that they 'get it', acknowledging that they have to change to get back into office. David Cameron even travelled to the Arctic to see the ice cap melting for himself. Of course, the right are doing this in part because they face a similar erosion of their electoral coalition. David Frum, the revisionist Republican thinker, has said that victory in US politics used to be about holding on to your base and then adding enough swing voters to get yourself over the line. Now, he observes, you have to aggregate many groups of voters, some of whom are antithetical to each other, and hold them together however you can while you run to the finishing line.

In the terms we currently conduct our politics, this is not easy to sell. The tactic of triangulation is now much derided, but it was effective in its time. The problem is that the trade-offs leave the centre-left looking like an apologist and not a change agent. This has been especially difficult in debates over globalisation and its concomitant, immigration. A pragmatic, realistic and correct position embraced the opening of markets and the lowering of trade barriers. Trade has lifted more out of poverty than aid alone. But a footloose, cosmopolitan liberal elite did too little to address the pain of those dislocated by global shifts in production and population. As a result, the global financial crash caught the left out – a crisis of deregulated financial capitalism did not lead to a swing to the left because there had been no sustained critique while the crisis was brewing, and outrage and passion were left to the fringes of politics. To be popular again requires rediscovering a populist instinct, and replacing desiccated rationalism with energy and morality. Again this is a true return to our roots.

One of the reasons the centre-left failed on globalisation is that it failed the basic test of politics – explaining the world to people. While the old left had many failings, its one great strength was that when a voter, constituent or citizen raised a specific problem, party activists and elected members combined a promise to address the issue with a pledge that such problems would not arise in a socialist society. Naïve at times, sinister at others, but this was an evangelising movement – we were constantly transmitting, not simply receiving. In the absence of ideology, the centre-left has drowned in minute particularism. MPs become social workers, upward transmitters of grievance instead of proselytisers. After living standards were boosted by an increase in credit, the public now feels that this was a conjuring trick – where did the wealth actually come from? What do our economies actually produce any more? While they see and feel a huge economic movement from the North to the South and from the West to the East, the political classes don't have anything to say in explanation of what is actually going on, nor a plausible account of what a practical response might be.

Added to this is the pressure of the consumption of resources; not simply the rising world population, but the industrialisation of India, China, South East Asia and the rise of the new middle classes. Sit in a focus group anywhere in a developed economy and you will be struck by the sophisticated economic analysis of centre-ground voters – middle-class and working-class. 'Peak oil' is a contested concept, still on the margins of political discourse, but the notion that things are running out is common sense and increasingly mainstream. But again, the political classes do not seem to want to level with their electorates. Finally, there is the question of morality. For an increasing number of people, something is simply wrong with the world as it now is: 'We buy things we don't need, with money we don't have, to impress people we don't like'.

Returning to Our Roots – a Red-Green Politics

The centre-left should be clear that this unease is an opportunity. A period of politics that bookends with Thatcher and Blair in Britain, and Reagan and Clinton in the US, is ending. The central point is that a pressing set of economic questions was settled on broadly liberal terms, and that an equally pressing set of social questions was settled on similarly liberal lines. Politicians who could simultaneously support privatisation and gay marriage were those who triumphed in this phase, but it is now over. Though the dominant questions of the coming period have not yet been framed, it is clear that they will have at their core a response to climate change. Changes are happening already that we must mitigate, but they also represent an existential threat to our economy, standard of living and our way of life.

It requires a transformative response, and is therefore the foundation of a renewed purpose for parties of the centre-left. It answers a question that these parties have been struggling with for much of the last decade: What is the point of the centre-left? It cannot be to celebrate our past successes, nor can it merely be to be better managers of the status quo, particularly the welfare state, than the right. If the pattern is that progressives will only win power sporadically, then they require a project and a purpose, not merely a programme, such that when they take office they make changes on the scale of a Gonzales, a Keating or a Clinton.

Addressing the challenge of climate change provides just such a purpose. It provides a frame for domestic and international policy, provides a metric for success and it inspires. The greatest purposes are those in which every part of the country from a household recycling food waste to a business eliminating paper packaging makes a contribution to delivering a vision.

How does this play out in practical politics? Former Leader of the Dutch Labour Party and Deputy Prime Minister of the Dutch government Wouter Bos has identified three key areas for progressives looking at the next stage of modernisation. First, social democrats must empathise more with popular anxieties. An approach of this kind will underscore the concepts of identity, trust and security, and place them at the centre of political discourse. Second, social democrats must recognise the flaws of a strong statist approach and in doing so create the political space for moralism. As Bos argues, 'insecure citizens want politicians to take a moral stand' as well as to propose policy. This means articulating a politics of 'morality, values and symbols' to a greater extent than the centre-left has done. Third, social democrats must rediscover their roots. Modernisation is only intelligible if people understand where social democracy has come from.

This tripartite strategy applies to forging a red-green politics. It starts with putting empathy and trust back at the heart of centre-left politics. In response to difficult policy questions, newly elected progressive politicians always start with an acknowledgement of the human reality of an issue and of how people feel and talk about problems. Too often, what is lost in government is that empathy. It is often absent as well in the way in which green politics is conducted. Green parties share one of the abiding sins of the left – a streak of puritanical disdain, with its implication that failure to support green politics equates to profound selfishness.

In this current form, green politics offers a binary choice between selfless (and good) and selfishness (and bad), but we are both selfish and selfless at the same time. Any discussion with a group of parents reveals these contradictions immediately. Mothers and fathers readily admit that they will do anything to defend their own children: there is selfishness in the contest for scarce goods, whether public or positional, alongside a generosity in the willingness to sacrifice something today for a better tomorrow. Even the hard-hearted opponent of doing anything about the environment if it costs something changes their view when they think of the way this will affect their grandchildren.

This ability to throw forward into the future is central to being human, and is a powerful potential energy. Harnessing the spirit of deferred gratification should be at the core of a progressive response to climate change. It starts with refusing to make people choose between being selfish and selfless and celebrates the ability to change – praise, not criticism, prompts behavioural change, so the centre-left should use a language of generosity itself. Furthermore, this response has to be local and micro-local, such as feed-in tariffs for renewable energy that incentivise neighbourhoods and localities to develop schemes from wind-farms to hydro. Worldwide prices for recycled paper are rising rapidly – why shouldn't councils make rebates, even micro-rebates, to those who successfully recycle? This is about the collective recognition and reinforcement of individual action.

Second is the return to morality. The centre-left should do this because it is the right thing. Achieving consent and support will not be easy, but ease of victory is not the only measure – nor were decent housing, free health care, universal suffrage including women, union recognition and rights at work. The centre-left must rediscover its confidence. It humanised the last century, and it must green the coming one, standing up for its values.

Finally, social democrats must return to their roots – back to the future. Many of the first concerns of the labour movement were environmental in their focus – whether the work environment or the home. The fights for sanitation, for slum clearance, for social housing, were allied to social activities that promoted healthy living. Socialist cycling clubs and walking groups liberated people from smoggy cities and gave them access to the countryside. From that came mass trespasses and a challenge to the traditional forms of land ownership, which resulted in the establishment of national parks.

In the UK, figures like Octavia Hill drove the housing movement and the creation of the National Trust which now has stewardship for so much of the British landscape. That drive for self-improvement remains, but it has been privatised into gym membership and the hardy individualists who are urban cyclists. But the bike may be the key; it may literally be the vehicle for restoring a collectivist approach. Mayors across the world, from Paris to London to Adelaide, are providing bikes in central city areas for commuting and for leisure, but this should go further. This survival from the nineteenth century is the most efficient way to convert human energy into transport, it reduces our carbon footprint, is healthy and liberating. But our cities require more and more cycle-friendly roads. The threshold at which bicycle travel becomes an equal partner in road space with cars is relatively low in terms of journeys, at around 15%. As Copenhagen and university cities and quarters demonstrate, when this threshold is satisfied cycling rapidly becomes one of the dominant modes of transport. Nor should this progressive response neglect the role of public transport.

One demographer noted that the flight in the US to the exurbs first created communities that trended Republican, but that over the last 10 or 15 years as those exurbs have densified they have moved Democrat. His observation was that when enough people live in a community next to each other they stop caring about the right to bear arms and start worrying about the need for mass transit. This suggests a whole urban agenda – cities are a great machine for green living, but they are also places that make social democrats of us all.

No sense of fairness and future can be sustained without the inspiration of putting utopianism and hope back at the heart of what we do. May Day represents the struggle for the eight-hour day, and today we should reflect on the radicalism of the claim for eight hours to work, eight hours to learn and eight hours to rest. It asserted the right to control over our time. Through the last century gains were made – paid holidays, shorter working weeks – but the fundamental shape of our lives is still imposed by work on us, not by us on work. That is being challenged by a new utopian claim – the campaign for a 21 hour week. Their vision is bold:

> Moving towards much shorter hours of paid work offers a new route out of the multiple crises we face today. Many of us are consuming well beyond our economic means and well beyond the limits of the natural environment, yet in ways that fail to improve our well being – and meanwhile many others suffer poverty and hunger. Continuing economic growth in high income countries will make it impossible to achieve urgent carbon reduction targets. Widening inequalities, a failing global economy, critically depleted natural resources and accelerating climate change pose grave threats to the future of human civilisation.
>
> A 'normal' working week of 21 hours could help to address a range of urgent, interlinked problems: overwork, unemployment, overconsumption, high carbon emissions, low well-being, entrenched inequalities, and the lack of time to live sustainably, to care for each other, and simply to enjoy life.[1]

Unrealistic? Unaffordable? A dream? It is all of those things, yet once read, the argument sticks. Should we really live to work? There is a human and environmental cost. It is not the answer, but it is part of the question that a renewed centre-left politics, a red-green project, must pose.

Persuaders for Change

None of this is intended to suggest that we should neglect or ignore the traditional strengths of social democratic parties. The intimate relationship with trade unions is seen sometimes by modernisers as a drag anchor preventing progress, yet it also roots us. The world of work is still one of the major places in which people make and find meaning. 'What do you do?' remains one of the most commonly used opening remarks for good reason.

Though unions are a product of an industrial age and reflect – particularly in their hierarchical structure – their nineteenth-century origin as organisations, they also have some of the characteristics of successful twenty-first-century organisations. They are, at base, affinity groups – networks of individuals with overlapping social and economic interests. They are in large part enablers – from reforming factory conditions to negotiating family-friendly work conditions. They are in the business of transforming the context in which people make their own lives. They are trusted interlocutors. And this is profoundly important because we are in the business of behaviour change.

In all of public policy there is no weaker area than the language and thought devoted to lasting cultural transformation – assertion ends up substituting for analysis. Because a law has been passed, things will happen. Or, more sophisticatedly, because there has been a publicity campaign change will happen. But when was the last time you changed your mind, let alone your behaviour, because of what a stranger said to you? Exactly. Our friends, family and close colleagues are the biggest influence on us – and our shifts in opinion and behaviour are slow and socially rooted. Again, this is where the breadth of the labour movement matters to us.

Unions are persuaders for change. At their best, those like the Union of Shop, Distributive and Allied Workers in the UK, the Service

Employees International Union in the US, the United Voice (formerly the LMHU) in Australia have adopted modern organising principles and have drawn traditionally hard-to-organise workers into membership. What if those techniques were used to sell a new red-green agenda? Not just the abstract policy, nor even the jobs and growth agenda – but the hopes and the meaning of a new way of living. Again, this is about bringing new forms of meaning to what was once our greatest strength – our reach; not just the fact that we were connected to the majority of families through workplace membership, but that we knew and channelled their hopes and their fears – and we used their language.

Mario Cuomo said that we campaign in poetry, but we govern in prose. The real problem is that we fail – in campaigning, in governing, in operating – to find a language that connects. This is not about visions, or inspiration, it's about habits of life and ways of being. We knew that once when we built first the mutual welfare organisations that stood outside the state, and then when we constructed the modern welfare state that has liberated so many. It is time to relearn what we have lost, time to go back to the future.

CHAPTER 12

Globalisation Challenges to Centre-Left Internationalism

John Lloyd

Social democrats in Europe, out of power in most states, struggle to understand how to become popular again because they struggle to speak to the majority. Indeed, they also struggle to speak to minorities.

In the high summer of social democratic electoral success – the second half of the 1990s and much of the 2000s – social democratic parties were able to take advantage of generally strong growth in the countries they governed. That growth came mainly from the success of lightly restrained capitalist success in most parts of the world – in Europe itself, in the US, in China and in India. In many countries, social democrats in government took advantage of the tax benefits of that growth by expanding social spending and introducing liberal reforms, popular or at least accepted in easy times.

In the course of that period, the European centre-left pursued strongly cosmopolitan aims and policies. These included a strong belief, with largely rhetorical reservations, in globalisation, in growing global trade and in increased financial flows. It meant, also, strong support for increased power to and integration of the European Union. It meant support for rapidly increasing immigration, as opportunities for low-skilled labour increased. For many countries, such as the Scandinavian states, Italy and Spain, mass immigration was a substantially new phenomenon.

Support for globalisation had its limits. The most obvious in the 2000s, which caused a major rift in social democratic ranks, was the support of the British Labour Government for intervention in Iraq in March, 2003, following the attack on the Twin Towers on 11 September 2001. The argument, among others, advanced by the then British Prime Minister, Tony Blair, that the people of Iraq should be liberated from a genocidally inclined tyrant failed to find support in most quarters of the left. The strong view against that was that no action of this magnitude should be undertaken without the assent of the UN Security Council; that Iraq was not a threat to the world or the region which could not be contained by sanctions and no-fly-zones; and that the agenda of the major state to intervene, the United States, was one composed of revenge for 9/11, desire to secure oil supplies and a quasi-imperialist mindset which could not accept rival centres of power.

Social democrats will have to deal with these issues, as they seek to develop policies which reflect their commitment to freedom and democracy, increased social equality and security, and continued policies for a reduction of poverty and marginalisation throughout the globe. At the international level, these can be presented as four large issues, central to the social democratic polity, which apply particularly to the UK, but to other centre-left parties also.

The Politics of Globalisation

It is true, as Pascal Lamy, Director General of the World Trade Organisation, argued at a Progressive Governance seminar last year that social democracy is not exhausted, because 'the contradictions of market capitalism are still with us, and a significant portion of humanity continues to suffer its side effects. The 'social question' is as burning an issue at the beginning of the twenty-first century as it was in the middle of the nineteenth century'.

But if the objects of social democracy remain, its relevance to active politics has declined, and needs to be reconstructed. Globalisation and its effects are at the heart of that decline. The bases on which social democracy has stood – in particular the organised labour movement, as well as the recent alliance between this group and a significant part of the middle class – has declined sharply. More, the aims of social democratic labour movements to secure higher incomes and an ever more comprehensive welfare state irrespective of income, are now unsustainable. The state we are in is likely to be a high water mark, at least for a time. The entrance into the global labour market of the millions from China, India and the other rapidly modernising states means that our commodities will cost more and our labour is increasingly less competitive in more spheres.

Every social democratic party must, in different ways, recognise and come to terms with these facts. That these parties have often not done so helps to account for the fact that in nearly every European state, the centre-left has been expelled from, or not managed to attain, power. Right-of-centre parties, sometimes in alliance with parties further to the right, now command: they seem to have better expressed the will of diverse European electorates. Part of the reason may be what Patrick Diamond has written about the Labour Party's misunderstanding of Thatcherite Conservatism. Though opinion surveys in the 1980s and 1990s pointed to a large sympathy among the electorate for traditional social democratic values of welfare, redistribution and fairness, still the Conservative Party of the time, Diamond argued, 'had a much stronger sense of the epochal changes sweeping the world than the left'.[1] That may be true again, and not just in the UK.

A contemporary example illustrates an important point about the present condition of the European labour movement. As this is written, Sergio Marchionne, the Chief Executive of FIAT, has succeeded in signing a new labour contract for the company's two largest Italian plants with the majority of the unions there, following a referendum in which the majority of the workers – with the exception of Federazione Ipiegati Operai Metallurgici (FIOM), traditionally the most militant of the major union groupings – voted in favour.

Marchionne has for the past year conducted a high-profile campaign for more flexible and efficient working, pointing out constantly that the level of productivity in FIAT's Polish and Brazilian plants greatly outstrips that of the Italian factories, and arguing that continued FIAT production in Italy depends on the new labour contracts. Alone among the union confederations, CGIL-FIOM refused to accept the company's logic – arguing that the new contracts heralded the end of Italy's version of codetermination at least on work-related issues among state, capital and labour. In this they are correct: the question is whether or not it can be avoided.

Within the Democratic Party itself, there is more or less open dissension: some have expressed support for the FIOM stance, while others have remained silent, or criticised it. Both the divisions within the Italian labour movement and those within the main (if now weakened) party of the left illuminate the strains which the effects of globalisation press upon the centre-left everywhere: and which split what is left of the labour movement into factions which must calculate how far it is wise to accept new (and relatively disadvantageous) terms of work, how far the trends which produce these new contracts can be withstood.

Dilemmas of this kind are not new, and will increasingly arise. The protests of students against higher fees; the determination of workers in the public sector to resist cuts to jobs and pay; the defence of public service provision – such struggles will replicate themselves across the wealthy economies of Europe: and nearly all of them will strike a chord, in the heart or at least the conscience, of those who define themselves as of the left. (It is the violent striking of such chords which is visiting a prolonged torture on the British Liberal Democratic Party, at ease for its oppositionist decades as a party of vaguely pro-public-sector radicalism, now facing a season in a hell of too-well-defined public-sector reductionism.) The largest questions facing the leaderships of the social democratic parties of the continent concern how they will react to these pressures, and whether they are able to understand, and at least in some measure master, 'the epochal changes sweeping the world'.

Two main tendencies remain visible on the left, in response to globalisation. One is to argue that it is exaggerated, and that the shifts in national economic and social arrangements required to deal with it are often overdone. The other is to view it as a truly transformative force, different in scale and velocity to that which has gone before. The second perspective is correct. Globalisation refers to 'the expanding scale, growing magnitude, speeding up and deepening impact of transcontinental flows and patterns of social interaction . . . a shift or transformation in the scale of human organisation that links distant communities and expands the reach of power relations across the world's regions and continents'.[2]

It is, however, highly uneven and 'far from a universal process experienced uniformly across the entire planet'. The words used in this process – expanding, growing, speeding up, deepening impact, shift and above all transformation – convey the revolutionary nature of the rubric of globalisation. Marx's respect in the Communist Manifesto for capitalism and the bourgeoisie – who 'during its rule of scarce one hundred years, has created more massive and more colossal productive forces than have all preceding generations together' – is faintly audible.

Not only does social democracy need to find and master governing strategies within the national confines of global transformations, it also needs to find collective responses to these transformations in societies which have been encouraged to seek both individual enrichment and individual freedom. As the French political scientist Dominique Schnapper puts it:

> . . . most likely limits are necessary . . . to the expansion of (social) rights. If they become too far-reaching, they become not merely financially unrealisable but also create a client mentality in people, which makes them indifferent to democracy . . . the risk is that this destroys the real ambition of democracy, namely the common participation in political life.[3]

Social democracy, which in many countries (most obviously in the UK in the New Labour period) has presided over large expansions in welfare and social rights, now faces the need to develop a politics of more modest and more collective aspirations.

For the foreseeable future, state spending will not be available to solve, or at least disguise, social problems. There will be no other choice to be made than one which emphasises personal responsibility, longer and more productive working lives, less reliance on the state and continual adjustment to change. For those on lower and middle-incomes, the relative looseness of the past decade-and-a-half – in which credit was easy, employment high and income differences, though widening, tolerable – is ending.

In all societies that will have, and is having, two consequences. First, the gross inequalities of income – especially those in a financial sector seen as having visited a large number of the current problems on

Western economies within which many of the largest institutions are supported by state money – will be no longer grumblingly tolerable. No government of any stripe can, or should, ignore the issue. It may be economically true that banks have created an environment in which, in its highest reaches, Medicean incomes are the norm and thus must be paid to attract or retain the most able talent. It may also be true that, in the larger scheme of things, the incomes of the super rich are neither here nor there; but it is not socially true.

As Adair Turner, Chairman of the UK's Financial Services Authority has noted, the rewards and penalties of global capitalism have produced a class of super rich whose salaries are measured against world standards, while leaving a much larger class of relatively poor and insecure workers whose prospects are limited. Those in between, the majority in the wealthy states, have varying fortunes at varying times – being sometimes squeezed, sometimes comfortable or better.

When the tide was coming in, all boats rose. As it goes out, only those in the highest end of the income and property ladders remain securely afloat. The measures required to deal with this are now under active consideration. The most effective would come from those paying, and being paid, hyper-salaries – the bankers, executives, sportsmen and women, entertainers and others – as they discovered what Will Hutton, in his *Them and Us*, calls the 'indispensable value' of fairness. Stating it in this way underscores what appears to be the fantasy of such a possibility, since we have become accustomed to these groups taking as much as they can get.

But what has been in better times an inconvenient by-product of globalisation is now likely to become a major threat to social cohesion and even social peace. Governments have no choice but to attempt to find some means of moderating it: social democratic governments would have a larger interest in creating the conditions and exerting pressure which might bring a slow change of heart and culture, or put pressure on those parts which would cause the heart and culture to follow.

Social democrats have traditionally looked to the state to moderate inequalities, and should continue to do so. Activism in regulation, in setting labour norms, in promoting social partner dialogue and agreements is best developed in the Scandinavian states and Germany, also the current winners in growth among the European states. The argument that states will be less able to provide but more able (necessarily) to regulate both domestically or internationally is too sharp a dichotomy: successful states will need to continue to do both. A more cosmopolitan world will only be possible if the majority can be brought to accept it, and for this acceptance, a sense of a social and economic stake in one's own country will be necessary for as far ahead as one can see, or any politician or government can plan.

Tensions Over Immigration and Integration

Immigration, which has attended globalisation in the wealthy world, continues to cause increasing resentment from natives (including descendants of immigrants) towards immigrants. Tony Barber has noted that the most recent European Social Survey shows 'a steady deterioration in Europeans' view of immigrants over the past eight years, driven by the perception that the newcomers – who tend to be relatively youthful – are a financial burden on society, intensifying competition for jobs and benefits'.[4] He quotes research by the Norwegian political scientist Elizabeth Ivarsflaten to the effect that 'no populist right party managed to receive more than 5% of the vote . . . without mobilising grievances over immigration better than all major parties'.

In some European countries, such as Germany and the UK, the support for the far right is small, in both cases under 2% of the electorate (paradoxically, the Eurobarometer data show that the UK registers by far the highest concern about immigration – with 28% of the survey naming immigration as one of the top two issues facing the country). In other countries, however, such as in Switzerland (for the Peoples' Party), Norway (for the Progress Party) and the Netherlands (for the Freedom Party), it is high. In Italy, the fastest growing party remains the Northern League, which among the major parties has most insistently pressed opposition to immigration, at times in overtly racist fashion. Sweden, which had thought itself largely immune to a recoil against rapid immigration, found that the Swedish Democrats polled enough votes (5.7%) in the last election to become a significant parliamentary presence (20 seats).

No party can ignore this, and especially not social democrats since, as Tito Boeri of Milan's Bocconi University notes, it is the people who have been used, through generations, to vote for the left who feel the immigration pinch (pressure on wages, competition for jobs and public services) most:

> ... rightwing coalitions and xenophobic movements are more credible than social democrats in restricting migration flows and welfare access by immigrants. The reassuring face of social democrats is turning into a nightmare precisely for those European citizens who represent their traditional constituency – blue-collar workers, low income households and persons living on social welfare.[5]

Two routes out of this dilemma are demonstrably useless. One is seeking to beat the parties of the right, or even far right, on their own ground of opposition to immigration as a matter of principle. The other is proclaiming the benign effects of immigration and regarding all opposition as deluded or racist. What is left is a threefold strategy, now beginning to take shape.

First, where immigrants or communities descended from recent immigrants are Muslim, the choice must be made by them to dissociate themselves from Islamist terrorism. Many are now doing this – recognising that while fears of non-Muslims may be exaggerated and result in absurdities as the banning of the burkha, they are not baseless. This is the more so, as plans to cause death and damage in European states continue to be uncovered, and as Islamist attacks on Jewish and Christian communities in majority Muslim states proliferate (as this is written, more than 20 have been killed after a suicide bomber detonated himself outside a Coptic church in Alexandria, Egypt). The work, in the UK, of such bodies as the Quilliam Foundation, created and run by former fundamentalist Islamists, does much to counter the corrosive effects of ambiguity within the Muslim communities towards Islamism, and there remains much more to do.

Second, immigrants need to be integrated, and to integrate themselves. There is no necessary dichotomy between retention of religious and other customs, dress and languages, and the enthusiastic adoption of the culture and political and social order and habits of the host community: a range of distinct communities, such as the Jews, Hindus and West Indians, do so in differing ways but with general success. As David Goodhart has written, the problem is not the retention of differing traditions but the insistence on a separate cultural and social life which distances itself from the host community, and even sees that community as inimical.

Third, where immigration is the result of poverty and lack of opportunity in the immigrants' countries, the better solution is not immigration to relatively wealthy states but assistance on the part of the latter to raise the standard of living in the former. The argument that the rich states of Europe, where birth rates are declining to below reproduction rates, require constant infusions of immigrants to meet present and future labour needs may be true in the short term but is a self-indulgent policy in the medium and long term. It perpetuates unreformed labour markets, low pay, low security and low productivity where the labour force, whether immigrant or indigenous, is largely trapped in employment which offers no prospects or opportunities for betterment. The decision by the UK Coalition Government to retain the level of spending on international development – doubled in real terms by the previous Labour Governments – is right, and should be seen in that light.

Globalisation imposes on the wealthy European countries responses which can no longer be neatly divided between domestic and foreign policies. The rage of Islamists against non- and 'bad' Muslims; the refusal on the part of some communities to integrate because integration is seen as a betrayal of their culture, or the opening of that culture to degraded Western social norms; the use of immigrant labour to fill low-paid jobs – all these are global in their application, and require responses at home and abroad.

The Future of the European Union

The construction of the European Union was the outcome of a great ideal, or rather, a succession of ideals. For the core states of the first community led by France, Germany and Italy, the aim of Monnet, Schumann, Adenauer, Spinelli and de Gasperi was to obviate future slaughter of the kind all had lived through. For that generation, now in its 80s or older, securing peace was a goal for which they thought their countries should pay any price. For a later entrant, Spain, and to a lesser degree Greece, the acceptance by the Union of their applications underpinned democratic turns following years of dictatorship and/or instability. For those countries once in the Soviet bloc, their entrance after 1989 was seen, by their new leaders (often former dissidents) and others as a 'completion' of Europe. In his *Reflections on the Revolution in Europe*, Ralph Dahrendorf wrote of three unifications: that of Germany; that of East and Western Europe; and that of language, the last being the end of the hollow exchanges at every level between Soviet bloc and Western representatives and their replacement by discussions, where at least the reference points were common.

The first two, however, are largely forgotten and the third, while still an active mechanism for modernisation and democratisation in Central Europe, has suffered inevitable disappointment and delay. The ideals which provided the imperative for greater integration have, in both new and old members, collided with the probably increasing reluctance of the member countries' electorates to cede more power to the Union's institutions. This, in addition to the rise of parties – often those described above in the context of anti-immigration stances, but in this case of the left as well as the right – which express a visceral hostility to the Union.

For the early idealists, the peace and democracy imperatives, and the political will which flowed from them, had to prevail over the obstacles that were bound to arise. But political will is now lacking, and problems mount. Most obviously, the Euro, heralded in 2000 as a step towards common political as well as economic governance, is now in deep trouble. While some such as the Prudential's Sir Martin Jacomb have argued that exiting the Euro-zone would be a price worth paying if it were 'the only way to prevent the national economies of the peripheral countries becoming mired in failure, (saving) millions from falling into long-term unemployment'[6], others, such as Martin Wolf of the Financial Times, argue that the political commitment and the scale of the disruption consequent on one or more European members leaving the Euro-zone would be so great that such an eventuality is unlikely unless matters get much worse. More likely is a default on the debt by the worst affected states. This was the case with Russia in 1999 and Argentina in 2001, both states which have survived and, in quite different ways, prospered since.

For social democrats, attachment to the principle of a common monetary unit which visits such a fate on already poorer states will be a hard policy to maintain, unless there is a credible strategy for relieving their burden at least in the medium term. The left-of-centre parties and movements need to have the development of such a strategy at the heart of their policies in this new year: lacking it, they can only decline further in popular esteem, and cede more ground to those parties which put the Euro and its effects in the same box as a Europe swamped by Muslim and other immigration and the ravages of global capitalism.

There is a still deeper issue for social democrats when facing the future of the European Union. It is the old one, which now stands out even more starkly than in the past: that is, that the EU is not a democracy in any other than a formal sense. Laws and regulations central to the public life of EU members are debated and decided in Brussels and Strasbourg by officials, commissioners and members of the European Parliament, nearly all of whom mean nothing to nearly all the citizens of Europe – a deficit in democratic control which would grow much worse if, as the new Constitution foreshadows, political integration is further pursued. As Dominique Schnapper has noted, 'To create democracy at the European level – there is no reason to think it is impossible – will take a long time. It took centuries to build the nations'.

This is the perspective which the centre-left should take – recognising that democracy cannot be constructed only by elite manoeuvring (necessary as that usually is) but must be underpinned and supported and co-constructed by popular involvement and engagement. It will be counter-productive for social democrats to call for greater integration, in the face of obvious popular recoil from, at best wary indifference to, the institutions themselves. The cause will be to launch a long-term strategy of seeking a popular base, using both national and European fora to focus discussion and action on that goal.

This is not advocated only because it accords with an abstract social democratic aim of strengthening democratic involvement. Strengthened democratic involvement is necessary for the further development of pan-European politics. The stalemate reached in further change in Europe, and potentially insurmountable difficulties faced in finding a base for a European foreign and defence policy, rests in the end on the refusal of citizens to countenance further integration, or to see the EU and its institutions take more powers. The privileges enjoyed by members of the European Parliament and other senior officials, as well as the not-infrequent abuse of these privileges, increase the strength of popular distaste.

Social democracy in Europe can no longer afford simply to be 'for' Europe. As a movement which has long claimed a popular mandate, its greatest task is to attain a popular base.

Global Security in a Dangerous World

On its widest definition, discussion of global security would include the complex of issues surrounding national and global security, intervention, and the part the UK and Europe should play in it. That debate within the left-of-centre movements is often rather a residual one, but is nevertheless of great importance in the UK, a country more committed than any other after the US to operations in Afghanistan and other theatres.

The EU has stressed its soft power, and there is much to stress. The protection against Russia and the example offered by the EU to the former Communist states of Central and Eastern Europe has been transformative. Its insistence on measures taken by the new eastern member countries to democratise, promote civil society, free journalism and tackle large defects in their provision of human and civil rights has been a large element in their modernisation and democratisation. To be sure, the European ideals, however defined, are often seen to be disappointing, but such a view usually underestimates what has happened in these states since the end of the Comecon pact, and of the Soviet Union. What had been a totalitarian polity enforced on all is now a series of democratic developments. Where, as presently in Hungary, these show signs of authoritarianism, the influence of the EU in conjunction with democratic opinion in the country limits the drift. In the end, the European Union is not a wholly secure prophylactic against a descent by one of more countries into authoritarian rule, but a considerable barrier which shows no sign of being breached yet.

However, hard power remains a necessary companion. The United States now shows strong signs of military overstretch: its insistence that European powers take the lead in the intervention in Libya (which won a mixed response in Europe, with only France and the UK willing to give full-throated assent to taking the proffered role) is both pointed and necessary. Though both countries stressed their action was taken under the aegis of the UN and with the assent of the Arab League, the hard facts of intervention presently see the interveners drawn deeper and deeper into a developing civil war, with both further intervention and withdrawal being bad choices. UK Prime Minister David Cameron made much of the differences in his intervention from the approach of Tony Blair in Iraq, but – as he is learning – he is likely to be faced with the same dilemmas, if with hopefully less murderous outcomes.

The interventions undertaken by the Labour Governments of 1997–2010 – in Kosovo, Bosnia, Sierra Leone, Afghanistan and Iraq – were part of a common approach both to particular crises, usually including humanitarian crises, and to long-term global trends which continue to present major threats. In his first speech as Leader to the Labour conference last September, Ed Miliband said that 'many sincerely believed that we faced a real threat . . . but I do believe we were wrong. Wrong to take Britain to war . . . because war was not a last resort, because we did not build sufficient alliances and because we undermined the United Nations'. However, he was wrong to argue that we did not face 'a real threat'. The threat – of a Saddam-led Iraq with weapons of mass destruction – was real, but like most of the threats of the modern world unpredictable.

It was real – even if the stores of chemical and biological weaponry had been destroyed and Saddam's regime had not succeeded in acquiring the necessary ingredients and technology to make atomic weapons – because he intended to do so, and would have resumed the quest once sanctions decayed and the world's attention moved on. It was real because Saddam was the most aggressive and ruthless leader in the Middle East, responsible for two invasions into neighbouring countries (Iran and Kuwait) and massacres of his own people (both the Kurds and the Marsh Arabs). It was real because Saddam was among the largest sponsors of terror in the area, especially against Israel, which he wished to destroy. It was real because he had as complete a grip on the military and the security services of his country as had Stalin (his main role model) in his time, and had in his sons heirs to his power as ruthless and probably even more unpredictable than he.

It is of course arguable that intervention was a mistake, but it is impossible to know. To present the issue as though the civil war into which Iraq descended after the invasion is incontrovertible evidence that the project was wholly misconceived is a misunderstanding of the nature of modern armed conflict. For leaders like Slobodan Milošević, and much more Saddam Hussein, tyranny backed by terror is their preferred system of ruling, and their regimes require a constant identification of new enemies and a permanent effort to extend their power and possessions. In Saddam's case, he was willing to be allied – in spite of the secular nature of his regime – with Islamist terrorist groups, whose sponsor he would increasingly have become.

Islamist terror is growing. The targets now no longer have any obvious connection to a given country's participation in the invasion of Iraq, or its position on the Middle East. Recent attempts show a determination by the individuals or groups who engage in them to avenge perceived insults to Mohammed, or (as noted above) to cleanse the Muslim world of non-Muslims through terror. As Philip Bobbitt has written, modern terrorism works through various forms of 'contracting out' or 'franchising', with lone or small groups of operators who have imbibed the general line of hatred of the West, of the 'Jews and Crusaders' and of democratic rule encouraged to identify targets and maximise victims.[7]

The response to this complex of issues will be the major part of the agenda for the police and security services, and for the military, for years to come. The UK Coalition Government's Strategic Defence and Security Review of October 2010 proposes to integrate, under the purview of the new National Security Council, the analysis of all threats to national and global security including cyber attacks and natural disasters. The management of risks, of which terrorism is the most immediately threatening, remains at the core of the security effort of the present Government, as it will for a future Government of the centre-left.

Social democrats urgently need to develop their thinking on these issues. It is tempting to regard Blair's efforts to give flesh to the UN-developed concept of the 'responsibility to protect' – the ultimately failed effort to get agreement that those leaders who made war on their own people would lose the immunity of sovereign government – as the actions of a misguided idealist. That view, often in a less charitable form, is popular in the British left, including in the membership of the Labour Party. In his speech in Chicago in 2009, some 10 years after his speech in the same city which outlined the underpinning philosophy for humanitarian intervention, Blair refused to accept the criticism, arguing instead that while he was wrong in 1999 to assume that deposing one tyrant was sufficient to address a particular programme, the struggle against a fast-spreading terrorism had to continue and deepen. The difference now, he argued, is that the present battle cannot so easily be won:

> Because it is based on an ideology and because its roots are deep, so our strategy for victory has to be broader, more comprehensive but also more sharply defined. It is important to recognise that it is not going to be won except over a prolonged period. In this sense it is more akin to fighting revolutionary communism than a discrete campaign such as the one which changed the Balkans a decade ago.[8]

Many on the centre-left now claim to regard Blair, and indeed New Labour, as of an at least partly discredited past. Ed Miliband himself emphasised that a 'new generation' had taken over. But the new generation faces the same problem faced by the preceding one: a militant, strongly supported and ruthless ideology which seeks power wherever it can get it, and which proclaims a deep hatred of democratic governance, pluralism and other religions.

Conclusion

European social democracy has not yet succeeded in confronting the key issues in these areas: in globalisation and the immigration which is seen as its accompaniment; in the distance 'Europe' is from most people; in the dilemmas of a world in which rulers are still able to make war on their own and neighbouring populations. In the easy past two decades, in which the centre-left did well in many European countries, these questions were largely avoided.

Today they cannot be. Winning back the trust of those who have observed an indifference to, even a betrayal of, their personal and collective values in social democratic policy dictates a re-engagement with what life is now believed to offer people, and how they mean to maintain their living and ethical standards. In this, the policies we adopt towards the rest of the world have ceased to be the preserve of diplomacy, and have become local and personal.

CHAPTER 13

The Squeezed Middle and the New Inequality

Liam Byrne

Analyses of electoral defeat and political disaffection too often resort to personality, style and presentation. They have tended to ignore the structural trends unfolding across the West, and the way the 'statecraft' of the third way began to fail. This more significant development, which in both the UK and US was labelled the rise of the 'squeezed middle', created insecurity and distrust among a key group of voters who were increasingly bypassed by the economic growth of the last decade.

Over the past 10 years, members of these income groups – especially 'C2s' or those earning between £20,000 and £30,000 a year, typically employed in construction, manufacturing and the service sector – have been disproportionately affected by three harmful trends in our economy: stagnating living standards, extreme differences in wealth and wages, and the repercussions of the financial crisis. These problems have manifested themselves amongst voters in many different ways, but most acutely in rising concern about welfare reform, immigration and behaviour of corporate and financial services' elites.

These phenomena are strongly linked to the promise of opportunity and reward articulated by centre-left governments in recent years, as well as questions of aspiration, fairness and identity. Centre-left parties set out a contract with this electoral constituency which held that 'playing by the rules will allow you to get on'. But as the decade went on, it became clearer and clearer that the deal had stopped being honoured. Many families found themselves working just as hard as ever – but without the commensurate rise in living standards that was promised.

The intersection of these problems is threatening to undermine the progress and optimism associated with parties of the centre-left in the

1990s. Using the UK as an illustration, this chapter explores the origins and growth of these issues, and relates them to the development and speed of globalisation after the 1980s. It argues that although a particular form of economic development contributed to the phenomenon of the 'squeezed middle' and the rise of a new form of inequality, the solution lies not in 'more of the same'. On the contrary, the only way to address these problems is by revisiting the underlying assumptions of the Anglo-American economic model, while embracing globalisation over the next decade.

What Do We Mean by the Squeezed Middle?

During the 1970s and 1980s, decisions on four continents established a global market place creating the conditions for the long, prosperous boom in world trade in the US, China, India and Europe. During this period the UK grew faster than either Continental Europe or Japan for the first time in a century: productivity rose, wages rose and wealth per head rose faster than anywhere in the G7.

However, while for many this continued to be a prosperous period, research undertaken by the UK Treasury in 2009 on incomes and living standards suggests that beneath the happy arc of rising average incomes, something else was going on, especially for those families on 'median incomes'. Treasury analysis of 'real disposable income' (adjusted for tax, inflation and household composition) suggests that from around 2005 this group experienced a barely noticeable 0.14% increase each year – well behind the national average. Between 2005 and 2006, and 2007 and 2008, the final incomes of social group D (semi- and unskilled manual workers) actually stagnated.

As there was no growth, the gap between this group and those at the top of society widened. Yet because the hours people were working had remained constant, they were working as hard just to stand still. This was exacerbated by rising fuel, food and housing costs, such that these groups felt badly squeezed. This represents a new form of inequality between those on median incomes and the very rich.

In the British case, although between 1997 and 2001 workers' share of national earnings rose from 68% to around its post-war average of 73.5%, the trend then went into reverse. Between 2001 and 2009, productivity rose by over 9% while workers' share of national earnings fell from 73.5% to 69.6%. At the same time, the corporate rate of return in Britain soared from 11.8% to 14% (2001–8). In 2009, workers' share of national earnings stood at around £768 billion. Had this share matched post-war averages, an extra £23.4 billion would have been added to people's pay packets.

These issues were compounded because for the millions of people employed as sales assistants, cashiers, construction, factory and routine workers, Treasury research calculated that around a third could expect to feel labour market competition from unskilled migrants. Thus, while the UK economy grew during the emergence of what President Clinton called a 'world without walls',[1] UK net migration also surged to historic levels.

Between 2006 and 2008, Britain experienced wide-ranging changes to its immigration and border control system, resulting in tougher immigration policing at home and new laws to ensure people 'earned' their citizenship. Yet across Britain the frustration with immigration reform was playing into a much deeper and complicated concern about the decline of traditional feelings of community and belonging, the mass workplace, and changes to family life. This 'New Anxiety' was not reducible to emotional insecurity, but was also an economic insecurity, and was compounded by the global financial crash which destroyed 1m jobs, and £400 billion of UK net wealth.[2]

These trends are not unique to the UK, but have been observed in the US by authors such as Paul Krugman,[3] Robert Reich,[4] and formar Chief Economist to Vice President Joe Biden, Jared Bernstein. Bernstein's book *Crunch*,[5] for instance, attempts to explain what *Time* Magazine recently called 'the death of the American Dream'.

These writers have illustrated how the gigantic growth in American productivity since the early-1970s has barely produced any improvement in the real incomes of the average American family. The emergence of what Reich calls 'super capitalism' has effectively destroyed stable payoffs to workers in a context where consumers no longer enjoy ever cheaper goods, but compete for fuel and food in a demanding global marketplace. Wages have not risen to compensate for this, but have flattened. Again, as the financial prizes are carried off by a rich elite, the gap between the top on one hand and the middle and bottom on the other has widened.

What is now clear is that the same risks confronted new Labour's statecraft because of the nature and balance of the jobs it created.

Although the UK invested in tax credits, childcare, education and skills, inequality was not fundamentally reversed.The reason for this is clear if we assume that the trend rate of growth is 2% a year. Yet Treasury work, referenced above discovered that 'squeezed middle' earners could only foresee an average rise in household income of 1.3%. If that continued, it implied this group of workers will fall behind the trend rate of growth by 0.7% every year. Or alternatively, their incomes must grow at 0.7% a year above their long-term average performance to keep pace with the average growth in wealth. For an average 'C2 worker' that is £330 a year above normal income growth, and £230 a year extra on top of normal income growth for an average 'DE worker'. This amounts to around £2 billion a year.

Especially in an age of fiscal austerity, it is now clear that this old model will not work. We simply cannot generate enough in tax from the global leaders to redistribute to the bottom third of workers to help them keep pace.

Things Fall Apart

This slowly unfolding crisis of living standards then ran into the hard shock of the financial crisis, which ultimately exposed the shortcomings of a fiscal strategy that relied too much on tax receipts from sectors prone to asset bubbles.

Between 1997 and 2010, the UK Labour Party advanced a successful national strategy in which an extra £587 billion was invested in repairing and renewing Britain's health, education and police services. A further £130 billion was transferred through tax credits to help ensure that work paid. The economic model designed to achieve this combined low personal and business taxes and an open economy to generate tax surpluses and domestic growth to fund public service investment and tax transfers to alleviate inequality.

In many respects this public reinvestment approach to tackling inequality was funded by getting more people into employment. The employment rate in the UK during Labour's tenure was among the highest in the world. In the years before the financial crisis we see that tax receipts rose by around £129 billion,[6] nearly two-thirds of which came from income tax and national insurance contributions.

Economic success in Britain, then, did not *just* rely on financial services. By 2006–7, business services and education, for example, were paying more in taxes. This is shown in Tables 13.1 and 13.2 below.

However, while it is possible to overstate Britain's reliance on financial services, new Labour's statecraft was still *too* vulnerable to structural changes in the domestic and global economy. New Labour's fiscal policy was not *wholly* reliant on financial services – but it was too exposed to asset bubbles in the construction and financial services sector.

Between 1999 and 2000, and 2007 and 2008, HM Revenue and Customs's receipts grew by some 40%. Yet, financial and housing sector tax receipts had grown from £30.4 billion to £59.8 billion,[8] or 3.2% to 4.24% of GDP. Such a rise suggests that the Treasury accounted for half of the increase in total receipts across the period.[9]

This vulnerability of this model becomes all the more stark when one recalls the scale of fiscal shock that tends to come with a banking crisis, as Tables 13.3 and 13.4 show. The costs of any banking crisis

TABLE 13.1 Rise in UK tax receipts

	2002–8 £m	% of increase
Cumulative increase in tax receipts	129,295	
Cumulative increase in personal tax	80,986	63
Cumulative increase in CGT	2,234	2
Cumulative increase in Corp Tax	14,342	11
Cumulative increase in VAT	19,573	15
Other	12,160	9

2006/07 Tax Burdens by Sector – Effective Incidence[7]
(controls for where the burden of taxes has been passed on to consumers or other sectors)

TABLE 13.2 Breakdown of UK tax receipts

	Tax burden by broad tax category, £m						
Sector	Personal	Direct business	Consumption	Property	Environmental	Total	% of taxes
Business services	34,328	8,056	2,362	1,757	46	46,549	16.1
Education, health and social work	36,172	416	1,671	168	88	38,515	13.3
Financial intermediation	22,869	6,986	2,589	3,970	21	36,435	12.6
Manufacturing	27,528	4,172	1,906	2,052	369	36,026	12.4
Wholesale and retail trade	22,807	5,099	871	5,741	257	34,776	12.0
Transport services	8,808	818	5,361	739	20	15,746	5.4
Construction	10,624	2,666	63	567	328	14,249	4.9
Real estate and renting	4,004	2,927	2,308	3,961	32	13,231	4.6
Public admin	11,427	55	24	0	28	11,534	4.0
Oil and gas extraction	672	7,238	11	185	0	8,107	2.8
Insurance and pension funding	2,079	2,583	2,637	321	5	7,625	2.6
Hotels and restaurants	4,258	465	92	1,579	95	6,489	2.2
Recreational and social activities	4,336	710	202	469	35	5,752	2.0
Postal and telecoms	3,603	428	671	500	12	5,215	1.8
Other services	2,997	769	294	389	19	4,468	1.5
Energy, gas and water supply	1,336	1,019	156	1,051	63	3,624	1.2
Agriculture, forestry and fishing	905	171	32	7	22	1,136	0.4
Mining and quarrying except oil and gas	381	45	5	53	6	490	0.2
Total	199,132	44,623	21,257	23,509	1,445	289,966	
	69%	15%	7%	8%	0%		

TABLE 13.3 Overall fall in tax revenues

£M	Total HMRC receipts	Fall £ (m)	%
2007–08	451,063		
2008–09	439,103	−11,960	−2.7
2009–10	408,496	−30,607	−7.0

TABLE 13.4 The collapse of tax revenues

	Fall in receipts £m	Decline from peak (%)	Fall as % of total fall in receipts
Fall in tax receipts, 2008/9–2009–10	−42,567		
Fall in personal tax (income + NICs)	−11,750	−5	28
Fall in VAT	−10,452	−13	25
Fall in stamp duty	−6,221	−44	15
Fall in CGT	−2,777	−68	7
Fall in Corp Tax	−2,777	−23	7
Other falls	−8,590		20

are incredibly severe, because they trigger secondary crises. As banks liquidate long-run assets to pay for short-term liabilities, lending collapses, business across all sectors is hit hard and tax receipts collapse. In their study of economic crises across the centuries, Rogoff and Reinhart[10] discover that a typical banking crisis brings with it asset market falls, house price declines of around a third over six years and unemployment rises of 7%. On average government debt explodes by some 86%, or nearly doubles. In the UK, tax revenues have collapsed across the board, but falls in personal taxes, consumption tax and stamp duty have accounted for over 70% of the decline, since 2007–8.

Focusing on the economic trends outlined above and the effects of the financial crisis, which together have contributed to a squeeze of middle earners' living standards, two weaknesses of such a political economy model have emerged.

First, deregulating in order to create an environment amenable to high-flyers in the financial sector required a far more robust system of checks and balances to protect it against the global financial contagion which almost destroyed the European banking system. At the time of the crash the financial services sector was around 10% of GDP.[11] The risk of this scenario is that, since 1800, the US, UK and France have experienced 40 banking crises between them. As Rogoff and Reinhart note in their study of 66 countries since the Napoleonic War, just four avoided a crisis between 1945 and 2007.[12]

Rather than seeing the disappearance of crises, then, what we observe in the UK is the recurrence of familiar patterns of financial liberalisation, faster international capital flows and asset price bubbles: in 18 of the 26 banking crises since 1970, the financial sector was liberalised in the preceding five years, generally sparking faster international capital mobility.

The crisis of 2008 followed this pattern, but on a staggering scale. In the UK and US during the 1980s and 1990s, deregulation of the financial sector multiplied offers of sub-prime loans to those who could ill afford them. By 2005, home equity withdrawals in the US peaked at an annualised rate of $1 trillion.[13] This in turn had been enabled by a second trend.

Paying for a sustained current account deficit required a flow of capital to match. During the period, America was running a current account deficit of around $600 billion. The capital came from Asia. After the Asian crisis of the late 1990s, surplus nations exported hard and saved harder. Some $7 trillion of forex reserves was amassed, and much of it headed towards US Treasury bills. Thus, by August 2005, Alan Greenspan was pondering a 'conundrum'. The Fed has raised interest rates from 1 to 3%. But the long-term rate on US Treasury bills was not rising, it was falling: from 4.9% to under 4%. From early 2001 to mid-2003, the Fed lowered interest rates by 5.5%, and kept them low. But as the Fed raised the headline interest rates between 2004 and 2006, from 1% to 5.25%, long-term rates and mortgage rates barely moved. Combined with faster international capital flows this helped fuel an extraordinary asset price boom.

While many wanted to believe that 'this time it is different', in fact, history was beginning to repeat itself. In the big five crashes in advanced economies since the late 1970s (Finland in 1991, Japan in 1992,

Norway in 1987, Spain in 1977 and Sweden in 1991), house prices boomed for between four and six years before a crisis. This time was no different, except that the asset bubble was a global phenomenon. In 2005 the *Economist* reported that the total value of residential properties had doubled to $40 trillion between 2000 and 2005, noting, 'it looks like the biggest bubble in history'. A shortfall in house building in the UK at the time added to the pressure, and against these rising asset prices, consumer debt spiked around the world. US private-sector debt rose from 123% of GDP in 1981 to 290% by 2008.

Exacerbating this risk, was the way in which banks were responding to rising asset prices by taking on dramatic new volumes of debt. In the US, financial sector debt rose from 22% of GDP to 117%. Among UK and European consumers and banks the pattern was similar. By June 2008, leverage ratios at European banks had grown gigantically; Credit Suisse stood at 3 to 1; ING stood at 49 to 1; Deutsche Bank stood at 53 to 1; and Barclays stood at 61 to 1.

As Mervyn King[14] recently pointed out, until the Second World War, UK bank balance sheets were stable at around 50% of GDP. But over the last 50 years, they have ballooned to five times the size of our economy. Alongside them has grown a shadow banking system $7 trillion in size. Worse, within the banks, risk grew. UK banks' liquid assets fell from 33% of banks' balance sheet to just 3%.[15] This was part of a vast expansion of private sector debt. Despite relatively low government debt, McKinsey estimates that UK debts expanded to 469% of GDP by 2008.[16] Between 2000 and 2008, bank debt grew by some $2.3 trillion; non-financial institutions' debt grew by $1.3 trillion and household debt grew $1.1 trillion.

Therefore, when the bubble began to burst, problems spread fast throughout the Western financial system. US house prices peaked in 2005, and by late 2006, US non-bank mortgage lenders were starting to go bust. Ten failed by the end of 2006, and 50 fell by the end of March 2007. In April 2007, New Century Financial collapsed, helping trigger the collapse of two hedge funds and Bear Stearns in June. In a short space of time, BNP Paribas suffered major losses (summer 2007) as did the German bank IKB. Similarly, Iceland's banking system totally collapsed. Ireland's system was totally underwritten by the government, and the UK's banking system was effectively nationalised. By 15 September 2008, Lehman Brothers had collapsed and in the weeks that followed, 'Each of [America's] big five investment banks failed, was sold or was converted into a bank holding company'.[17]

The lesson to draw from this story is that Governments cannot be neutral about what 'good growth' looks like. That was the fundamental mistake of new Labour's statecraft. If we assume that banking crises are a very real risk in the future, then economic policy must reflect this. Three conclusions are clear: governments should consistently act to curtail risky behaviour, and caution against deregulation that allows for excessive borrowing by public or private, personal or corporate actors; second, greater caution should be built-in to projections of future tax receipts; and third, investment decisions should be shaped in order diversify the economy, employment growth and the tax base.

Rather than 'more of the same', then, a new political economy and growth model are required. The next section outlines the key features of this model in the UK context. It is composed of three parts: it involves being full-blooded globalisers abroad, seeking a new consensus for growth; at home, it involves striking a new bargain with business on the one hand; and on the other, a new balance between civil society and the state.

A New Growth Model

The discussion above noted how many of the problems faced by the centre-left are due to the imbalanced way in which a pre-crisis form of capitalism operated, and the new kinds of inequality it created. The response to these issues can either embrace developments in the global economy that will emerge over the next decade, or turn away from globalisation back towards the nation-state.

In short, the costs of turning away from globalisation would be very great indeed. Doing so would preclude setting out a new global trade deal, invent new restrictions on foreign investors, impose impractical controls on the movement of people, and fail to lead an expansive, self-confident, outward-looking culture at home. Rather, recognising that globalisation is likely to change course dramatically over the decade ahead requires a new approach.

For the last 10 years the vehicle of global growth was the great American consumer, who prior to the crash powered an incredible 20% of global GDP. The financial crisis has destroyed approximately $8 trillion of American wealth,[18] meaning this consumer is unlikely to power GDP in the decade to come. According to McKinsey & Co, on average 'deleveraging' (paying down debt after a financial crisis) can take some 6–7 years.[19] The recovery in the US, hitherto, has been relatively jobless. It is simply not clear that levels of growth commensurate with large scale job creation are going to return to America soon.

With this in mind, it is clear that the kind of global growth that European social democrats need to help ignite reform at home must come from a larger range of nations. Goldman Sachs[20] forecast that by 2050, China, India, Brazil, Egypt, the Philippines, Indonesia, Iran, Mexico and others will account for 60% of global GDP. This revolutionary shift could push 2 billion people into the global middle class, around 70% of these in India and China. By 2050, the BRICs nations could make up four out of the top five economies.

These nations are Europe's new partners. But rather than forcing their way into these new markets like peaceful imperialists, European social democrats need to be full-blooded free-traders. Instead of 'zero-sum' conflicts such as the exchange rate level, European social democrats should pro-actively assist the kind of structural reform in developing countries that will create a vast new market of consumers for our exports. We should patiently construct a community of civilisations.

Positive-sum global growth diplomacy has to be the hallmark of a social democratic growth plan. It must lead the way in the debate to reform the International Monetary Fund, conclude the Doha round of trade agreements and global commitments to low carbon growth. Crucially, it must formulate an account of international financial reform that does not shut down the global financial system, but renders it less explosive.

Second, creating a more balanced economy in the coming years will require the government to formulate an advanced industrial policy for the twenty-first century, one that includes a competitive response as developing nations move up the value chain.

In the context of the UK this has a number of implications. Much is made of the 'imbalances' and 'dependency' of the British economy on financial services. Our future has to include financial services; Britain's financial services industry exports some £40 billion more than it imports. But a focus on the competitive performance of financial services is not enough. Other sectors must be stronger – not least because of the competitive challenge they will soon encounter from the East. India and China's productive capacity has expanded rapidly, but this is nothing compared to their future potential. As Brad DeLong and Stephen Cohen[21] argue, there is some $3–4 trillion lodged in sovereign wealth funds globally. While some of it is in countries such as Norway, around a third is held in Asia. A large proportion is invested in US Treasury bills, but given that their return is too low, before long it will flow into infrastructure and industrial policy, boosting the strength of China and India's production base.

Our ability to compete with these trends depends on the adequacy of our industrial policy. But as Josh Lerner and Dani Rodrik have argued,[22] industrial policy in the West is fraught with failures ranging from bad loans programmes to hi-tech businesses, to the French government's attempt to build a state-run electronics sector (which required subsidies of $4.6 billion by 1982). This contrasts with a power range of successes, from Silicon Valley to South Korean steel, to Dubai's Jebel Ali airport, to Brazil's aircraft industry, to Taiwan and Singapore's electronics industry.

Thus, the centre-left must engage seriously with the debate about industrial policy, not only embracing government investments, but seeking to change the structure and incentives of our banking system, national infrastructure, the relationship between industry and universities, and the skills of the workforce. Serious reform at the global level is vital. The centre-left simply cannot afford to turn inwards because the financial crisis was of a global scale. But nor does pursuing reform at the global level entail turning our attention away from domestic issues either. Indeed, being full-blooded globalisers abroad will mean little without a real unity of purpose at home, particularly in relation to the new inequality and the squeezed middle discussed earlier in the chapter.

Achieving a Unity of Purpose

Finally, the centre-left has to worry more about creating a new unity of purpose at home, if nations are to do well abroad.

Globalisation has moved ideas, people and capital around the planet, the effects of which are illustrated in The Pew Global Attitude Surveys. In the US, 53% believe free trade is good for America, down from 78% in 2002.[23] In Europe, only 21–30% say free trade is 'very good'[24] and large proportions feel immigration is bad. In seeking to develop a unity of its guiding purpose, the centre-left must attend to these attitudes, while re-conceiving the nature of the relationship between the state, market and civil society.

In the UK the Coalition's immigration cap, which seeks to limit numbers of foreign workers, is causing anxiety among businesses and universities who believe their projects will fail if foreign specialists cannot be accommodated. Foreign direct investment in the UK is worth over a trillion dollars (around 50% of GDP), and supports around a million jobs. As global markets boom, countries like the UK will only succeed through innovation. If immigration laws bar entry to the correct specialists, the UK will fail in this task. It is for this reason that a unity of purpose around globalisation is so important.

The problem of the squeezed middle and the new inequality outlined above is an acute one for the centre-left in the UK and elsewhere. Although some of the issues associated with this problem are related to globalisation, the two are not irreconcilable. Countries must recognise that a more globalised economy is the key to national growth, but this growth must reconnect with the squeezed middle. An agenda to do this must incorporate a number of parts.

First, supporting measures to boost productivity in non-traded industries (retail, logistics, distribution, tourism, construction) and exploring with business how rises in productivity are translated into wage gains. Second, where families want to work more hours to raise their standard of living, they should be given the freedom to do so.

But in order to facilitate this, new policies for child and social-care are needed. Third, the tax credit system must be revisited to ensure that income transfers are effectively targeted. Fourth, because it is a vital part of asset building, the ease with which families can acquire housing must be improved. Finally, the complex but important issue of pensions and savings should be addressed.

This presents a complex set of policy dilemmas, and therefore we must recognise that the state cannot do everything alone. In addition to this complexity, social democrats cannot afford to neglect the impact of globalisation, immigration and foreign investment on communities. Anxieties about immigration are concentrated by a wider insecurity about the decline of community, meaning a renewal of community spirit will be the *sine qua non* of a new self-confidence about globalisation. Again, these pressures are not Britain's alone, but are shared by the US and indeed the West as a whole. As the American political scientist Robert Putnam has put it, 'at the century's end . . . we have developed communities of limited liability . . . place-based social capital is being supplanted by function-based social capital'.[25]

The communitarian thinker Amitai Etzioni has recently argued that we need new ways of engaging in 'moral dialogue' with each other in order to fill the void that opened with the breakdown of the norms and traditions of the 1950s and 1960s. In reality, few of us wish to return to that period. Rather, Etzioni argues we should forge a new 'shared basis of good conduct', or what we might call 'shared standards'. Living in a country where individuals have different backgrounds, inspirations and ambitions is compatible with a country that also promotes 'shared standards'. While the right offers nothing better than to fall back on 'traditional institutions', social democrats are uniquely placed to achieve this unity.

The centre-left must promote what Putnam calls 'an era of civic inventiveness'. It is a challenge that the centre-left should approach with optimism, because it is one that was overcome at the end of the nineteenth century during industrialisation, and its associated migration from the countryside to the city. While the communities of the countryside broke up, new communities were invented in our cities, underpinned by a civic pride that held them together.

Social democrats are capable of mastering this challenge again. But it demands a constant exercise of imagination in every aspect of government to put community life first. Politically and organisationally this means rediscovering the social democratic roots of community organisation, and remembering that only so much change is delivered through the 'hard power' of elections. Much else can be delivered by the 'soft power' of community mobilisation. The UK government understands this to an extent, reflected in its Big Society programme. But this project commits the fallacy of opposing the state and society, when in fact they are partners.

Conclusion

Success in renewing the centre-left political programme demands that social democrats are not defined by the past. Rather, the principles and ideas that worked in the last decade must be applied to the future. This requires a statecraft that has the ability to spread new riches more widely, while rejuvenating old ideals of community life. The components of this new statecraft are: a collaborative effort to grow global markets and deepen economic interdependence; not a clash of civilisations, but a community of civilisations; a smart, twenty-first-century industrial policy; a new bargain with business; a new strategy of coalition building for our party, aimed not simply at winning the 'hard power' of elected office but mobilising the 'soft power' of social action.

As we set about this work we need to remember the revisionist method; clarify the nature of the ends and the means. The last time the UK Labour party took on substantial policy review of this scale, Roy Hattersley was Deputy Leader. He did a great service by writing *Choose Freedom*, a book aimed at clarifying ends and means. Hattersley argued against the Millsian liberals to formulate a positive conception of liberty and its associated political and economic rights that owed much to John Rawls.

A small evolution in thinking could give centre-left arguments today more focus. In communities up and down the UK, one sees that the great barriers to a more equal country are the 'power failures' that afflict modern Britain: the failure of power that stops young people getting a college place, although they have the aspiration and raw intelligence; the failure of power that stops a resident walking down a certain street; or the power failures that stop people getting a job, or the health care they need.

The writer who has written most lucidly about this challenge is Amartya Sen. His thought provides the means to challenge our old refrain about equality of opportunity, and focus more explicitly on the kind of 'powers' or 'capabilities' that people need in order to live a life they have reason to value in today's society: a good job which provides a sufficient income; membership of a of a strong, active community; mobility to access different places easily and aspirations for the future. As Sen notes, these are 'notions of freedom, in the positive sense: what real opportunities you have regarding the life you may lead'.[26] It is a strong foundation for overcoming the challenges faced by the centre-left today.

CHAPTER 14

Citizen Engagement and the Quest for Solidarity

Henry Tam

In order to tackle societal problems which would otherwise get worse, social democrats are generally more inclined to consider raising the level of collective resources committed to provide for members of society, compared with their political opponents on the right. Whereas the latter tend to maintain that the more resources are retained in private hands the better it is for everyone, the centre-left seeks to preserve a minimum standard of common well-being, especially for those with the least capacity to look after themselves.

In order to secure an electoral mandate to enhance the common good with an increased (or at least not reduced) level of collective resources, social democrats need to gain enough public support to steer government decisions more often than their rivals. However, since the fall of the Berlin Wall – an event which for many signified the ultimate end of collectivist challenges to free market politics[1] – the figures have not been favourable to this aim.

In the 10 most populous countries then in the European Union, between 1989 and 2010, social democratic parties were in power only 44% of the time.[2] Limiting our perspective to the most recent decade, coinciding with the rise of post-9/11 Islamophobia, the trend is even more disheartening, with social democratic parties in power 40% of the time. Indeed, of the four national elections held in these countries in 2010, social democratic parties did not manage to win a single one.

During the last two decades, social democrats have increasingly questioned whether wider changes in society now mean that their politics should be less orientated towards citizens' concern with the common good, and more on appealing to them as individuals and families. In the third way approach, for example, instead of taxing people more (especially the high earners who were keen to see tax levels on their expanding wealth reduced), government should focus on enabling businesses to make more money. Their growing prosperity would in turn benefit the poorer sections of society too.[3]

The third way's attempt to reorientate social democracy has been criticised on two levels. First, by blurring the once distinct social democratic concern with securing more collective resources for the common good, it is charged with failing to distinguish social democracy from the technocratic centre-right focus on helping businesses grow, and using a limited pot of public money as efficiently as possible. Second, in relegating redistribution to the margins of politics, it is challenged for its failure to recognise that an accelerating wealth gap undermines the well-being of both individuals and society.

The aim of this chapter is not to rehearse these two strands of criticism,[4] but to develop a third line of enquiry: namely, whether it is right to assume that there has been an irrevocable dissolution of the kind of civic solidarity needed for social democracy to thrive. Or whether it is the case that social democrats can rebuild a vibrant sense of common purpose amongst the citizenry to support their drive for greater use of collective resources to tackle social ills. And if so, how?

Is Solidarity Really Impossible to Recover?

Given the substantial economic, cultural and global transformations in recent decades, it may seem inevitable that individuals increasingly think about their own needs over and above broader collective issues. For example, in the workplace, the stable firm offering a job for life and a long-term relationship with one's fellow workers has given way to fast changing businesses bought, sold or simply threatened with extinction by corporate giants which treat anyone outside top management as dispensable for cost-cutting initiatives. At home, the extended family rooted in a local community has been displaced by small family units having to adapt constantly to parent(s) working more hours or relocating to secure new job opportunities.

However, the weakening of these social mechanisms for collaborative action may in fact mean that there is now a greater need for people to pool their resources in order to achieve shared objectives. The implication that the above transformations mean people should look above all to their own interests is not necessary. Rather than turning away from joint efforts, society's polarisation between a wealth-based elite and individuals with a much less secured quality of life could be the very reason why citizens should urgently unite to defend their interests in a way precluded by individualism.

More plausible than the assumption that people across Europe have opted for a more individualistic outlook over the past two decades is the claim that they have come to believe widely circulated messages that collective actions by the state can no longer be relied upon to address the problems they face. It is in response to such messages that they have come to count more and more on their own material resources.[5] It is a behavioural pattern which has become more commonplace in America since the 1980s and the Reaganite Republican philosophy of cutting down state provisions, giving more powers to business corporations, and blaming social problems on people's reliance on government instead of taking their own responsibility to solve them. Many of those growing up during that time were convinced that the future was about looking to their own interests and not trusting any form of public organisation. Between 1980 and 1990, the proportion of high-school seniors in America who believed that 'having lots of money' was personally important to them rose from 51% to 70%.[6]

In Europe, Thatcherite Britain led the way in following the American conservative model of redistributing power from the weak to the strong. By the mid-1990s, the UK had joined the US in having higher income inequality rates than all other developed countries in Western Europe and North America.[7] Correspondingly, social attitudes shifted in a self-centred, individualistic direction. According to the Eurobarometer poll (2001) of European Union countries, the UK had the second highest score in believing that people live in want because they are lazy or lack willpower (23%). Only Portugal had a higher score (29%) but an even higher percentage of the Portuguese attributed the problem of poverty to injustice in society (34%). In the UK, only 19% believed poverty was due to the prevalence of injustice in society. The UK was uniquely following the lead of the US.

Although America was not covered by the Eurobarometer poll, the World Values Survey (1995–7) asked its respondents (who include those living in the United States) if they believed people lived in need because of their 'laziness and lack of will power' or because 'society treats them unfairly'; 61% of Americans chose the former.

Coming to power in 1997, New Labour did not reverse the trends which privileged the prerogative of businesses to act with ever reducing collective intervention. Indeed, it reinforced them and even sought to promote them to the rest of Europe as an essential step in securing electoral power. According to the 20th British Social Attitudes Survey (2003), even Labour voters' support for channelling tax revenue towards welfare provisions had dropped – from 73% (1987 figures) to just 50%. The political messages they were getting emphasised the growing expectation for people to deal with their own problems in life rather than looking to the state to find solutions for them.[8]

By the time the 26th British Social Attitudes Survey (2010) was published, it was clear that support for collective action was on a downward trajectory. Public support for increased taxation and public spending had fallen from 62% (1997) to 39%. Those who felt that it was a civic duty to vote had dropped sharply over the last two decades to 56%. This reflects the 2005 (British) Citizenship Survey, which found that only about 21% of the public believed they had any influence over decisions affecting their country. In the UK General Election that year, more people abstained from voting (39%) than actually voted for the winning party (36%).

As the Anglo-American brand of plutocratic politics has spread across Europe in the last two decades, we can detect a similar shift from the readiness to back state action with citizens' collective support, to a greater acceptance of the deregulated market rather than the state to meet people's needs. The post-1989 drive to use the fall of the Berlin Wall as a springboard to discredit collective state action gathered momentum. The deregulation of business became a mainstream mantra. According to the Pew Global Attitudes Survey (2007), free trade was viewed positively by a growing number of people across Europe: for example, 65% in Germany, and 73% in Italy. Conversely, Europeans were increasingly inclined to think that the 'Government

TABLE 14.1 Respondents agreeing that their government has too much power

	2002 (%)	2007 (%)	Change in % points
Germany	61	74	+13
France	55	65	+10
UK	54	64	+10
Italy	64	73	+9

has too much control' (see Table 14.1 above for change in the percentage of people who agree with that statement).

Even when the highly deregulated financial system of the UK and US – the supposed source of those countries' economic vibrancy compared with 'old' Europe – brought about the massive economic crisis which plunged them into recession, there was no resurgent leadership to rally for stronger collective action against rising commercial powers. At a time when people should have been pulling together more than ever to tackle the problems they face, anxiety appeared to be pushing them apart. Consequently, and ironically, plutocrats again were able to seize the agenda and insist that corporate freedom was the only possible salvation to economic recovery: in the name of austerity, a consequence of irresponsible business practices, citizens were to have state support relentlessly reduced. Though such policies have begun to stir up resistance – in France where over 70% of the public is against Sarkozy's pension reforms – the intense opposition has not yet translated into a revival for the political left.

The disjunction between the need to exercise more collective control over irresponsible corporate forces and the prevailing reluctance to entrust the state with such control has reached a point where we must ask: Is it not the case that social democracy has suffered from the self-fulfilling prophecy that governments must concede to the expansion of market forces? In other words, by echoing the plutocratic fatalism which leaves no alternative but for individuals to adapt on their own (through better educational attainment, professional/vocational skills, entrepreneurial talent, readiness to sacrifice family and social relationships for work demands, etc.), we are unable to escape a world view that relegates civic solidarity to the margins of political actions. As a result, people protest against what affects them personally. They express their anger in the streets, without having established how they can actually reshape policies. They distrust political parties without appreciating the substantial differences which would be made to their lives if one side or the other wins power. The challenge, then, is to help the public see that there is an alternative, one which they must pursue together.

This is solidarity, not as an abstract ideal but a practical solution to overcoming threats which cannot be withstood individually.[9] Enabling the emotional and intellectual recognition that citizens must lend their collective support to curtailing the excesses of corporate powers for their own, their families' and their fellow workers' sake is the key to recovering extensive public backing for the social democratic cause. This in turn depends on facilitating communications to shape a genuinely shared agenda.[10]

Building Solidarity by Focusing on the Real Threats

Many have observed that people would stand together if they felt that their welfare and security were imminently threatened. When the threat is well disguised, however, it can be extremely difficult to rouse collective resistance. Year on year, people have less security in their jobs; they become more stressed about work pressures on their family life; the public safety net is shrunk, making them more vulnerable to private hire-and-fire decisions; more public services are contracted out to businesses which will run them in a way that would make the most profit regardless of the impact on the vulnerable; the environment continues to be exposed to pollution and climate-change-inducing emissions; and capacity for consumption is marketed ever more as the yardstick for self-esteem (and this applies increasingly to children). Alongside the 'free market' mantra propagated since the 1980s, big business has passed the blame for these social ills onto 'big government'. These same governments are blamed for mismanaging the economy by over-regulating the conditions under which they operate; how workers are treated; for diverting people from seeking work through too generous welfare provisions; for legislating to control unsafe products; and for spending too much public money on investigating tax evasion, fraudulent practices and other socially damaging activities.

Degree by degree, business elites are taking control of an ever-growing proportion of capital and revenue resources as their power grows over timid regulators, vulnerable workers and subordinate media outlets. In 2010, it was almost an expectation in the UK that while many workers had their wages frozen or faced redundancy, senior directors of the top 100 companies rewarded themselves with a 55% pay rise.

Instead of perpetuating the claim that corporate interests are over-constrained rather than a driver for power inequalities which threaten the well-being of the majority, social democrats should ensure citizens are aware of the real causes of contemporary problems: it is concentrations of wealth and power that push others towards greater vulnerability. For example, research shows that those with lower socio-economic status generally have shorter life expectancy than those with higher status.[11] Within organisations there was a gradient for life expectancy positively related to occupational class – in one case, with 17,000 staff, death rates from heart disease rose to four times as high amongst the most junior workers when compared to the most senior managers working in the same offices.[12]

Another study which covered over 500 cities across the US, UK, Canada, Australia and Sweden found that working-age men in cities with higher income differences tended to have higher death rates.[13] Within countries, income disparity could be translated directly into disparity in life expectancy. For instance, a boy living in the deprived Glasgow suburb of Calton will live on average 28 years fewer than a boy born in nearby affluent Lenzie. Similarly, the average life expectancy in London's wealthy Hampstead was 11 years longer than in nearby St Pancras.[14]

In addition to the effect on health, inequalities have been found to be linked to destructive attitudes and forms of behaviour. From studies which found that the US states with the highest income inequality had four times the homicide rates of those with the lowest income inequality,[15] to research across 39 countries from different continents which concluded that homicide rates were higher in countries with greater income inequality,[16] one encounters a recurring pattern. As

J. L. Neapolitan notes, '[T]he most consistent finding in cross-national research on homicides has been that of a positive association between income inequality and homicides'.[17]

Unfortunately, right-wing supporters of plutocratic interests have always been adept at deflecting public attention from the excessive concentrations of power, and channelling anger towards vilified scapegoats, typically the least powerful in society – benefit claimants, immigrants and asylum seekers. This is well illustrated in the Conservative-led Government's highly publicised policy to direct more resources to tackle benefit fraud, while discreetly cutting back on staffing levels at HM Revenue and Customs to deal with the problem of tax avoidance and evasion. In reality, benefit fraud committed by mostly poor claimants amounted to £1 billion (less than 1% of the total benefits budget) whereas tax avoidance and evasion, much of it carried out by large companies and wealthy executives, deprived the country of £100 billion.[18]

The need to counter the systematic misdirection of the public into overlooking the most serious threats to society's well-being became even more urgent after 2001. The 9/11 terrorist attack was rapidly used by the neo-conservative regime in America and their European allies to legitimise a culture of suspicion against Muslims and anything associated with 'foreign' non-conformity.

Far from conceding to the claim that people want to segregate us from the 'others', social democrats need to expose deliberate strategies to divert people from the real threats posed by those with concentrated power, and demonstrate how socio-economic iniquities corrode the common good. The banks which have taken billions of pounds of public money are able to use those funds to pay their executives large bonuses, while the Conservative-led Government is trumpeting its determination to cut non-EU (i.e. predominantly non-white) immigration. Immigrants have moved to the UK where they contribute to wider social and economic well-being through their skills, labour and the taxes they pay. In fact, those from an ethnic minority (including those who have settled in the country for more than one generation) tend to get paid notably less for what they offer compared with their white counterparts.[19]

It is essential for social democrats to prevent the right from continuing to present a distorted picture of society's pressing problems, and turn their attention to what collective actions are needed to address vested interests and inequality.[20] To do this effectively, however, they should make use of deliberative engagement to secure the committed involvement of citizens in shaping the reform agenda.

Extending Solidarity Through Deliberative Engagement

Deliberative engagement is a philosophy as well as a technique for involving citizens in setting priorities and shaping policies. Whereas the current Government's Big Society rhetoric is principally concerned with reducing the capacity of the state and leaving responsibilities for society's well-being to individuals, deliberative engagement is about strengthening *both* state and citizen. It does this by ensuring the latter can achieve more than they could otherwise as individuals by enabling them to steer collective state action, critically reflecting on what they have duly considered as informed citizens. To be effective, it needs to contain the following six elements:

1. Structured opportunities for individuals to talk about the things which are troubling them. This may be done through a generic event or, more likely, a process focused on one set of specific issues.
2. The identification of concerns is followed by facilitated discussions, under conditions of courtesy and reasonableness so that individuals are able to ask each other and invited experts questions to examine the real causes of the problems they face.
3. Anyone with a coherent proposal can share it with others, while options put forward can be challenged on grounds of effectiveness, feasibility and relative priority compared with options for tackling other problems.
4. There will be a transparent process for agreeing the priority actions to be taken with those present, signing up to commitments in return for the outcomes they now jointly seek to pursue.

5. The discussion is not concluded as a one-off meeting but is sustained by feedback on the implementation of the agreed actions and impact made, including any obstacles encountered in taking the actions forward.
6. The effects of the agreed plan of action are kept under review with further action developed under similar deliberative conditions to attain the agreed objectives.

In recent decades, processes bringing together these elements have been taken forward in many parts of the world, with the aim of giving ordinary citizens a much more informed way to influence public policies and provisions. Consensus Conferences have been run by the Danish Board of Technology to incorporate the considered views of citizens in its assessment of new, and often controversial, scientific and technological developments. Deliberative Opinion Polls, devised by James Fishkin, have been used in America and other countries to provide civic decision makers with a source of information based on what people think, not as isolated individuals lacking relevant knowledge, but as citizens deliberating together in light of the key evidence and testimony.[21] With the help of the World Health Organisation since the 1980s, the Healthy Communities Initiative has spread to many countries, enabling citizens to shape public health services. The Colorado Communities Health Initiative, for example, brought citizens together through a statewide council to steer legislators on the priority issues to address and projects to support.[22] Since the 1990s, Participatory Rural Appraisal has been used in over 100 countries across Latin America, Africa, Asia and Europe, whereby people who are supposed to benefit from development programmes get to play a central and informed role in shaping the design and delivery of those programmes.[23]

Although to date no country has systematically engaged its citizens in public policy development across the board, two examples may provide some indication of the wider potential of deliberative engagement in building the solidarity needed to sustain a social democratic reform agenda. The first is drawn from the experience of Latin America, where the spread of deliberative engagement practices has been a factor in the success of centre-left parties in winning power and delivering substantial reforms.[24]

In a region where plutocratic and military rule dominated for decades, it might be thought that any political campaign which relied on people appreciating what needed to be done for their common good would inevitably fail. Yet when the authoritarian regimes began to lose their grip on the people during the 1980s, a new generation of politicians and public officials recognised the need for trust and co-operation between citizens and a state with a historical democratic deficit. Many municipal authorities used the opportunity to take on more responsibilities and involve local people in decisions regarding their budgets and operations. Participatory budgeting – a technique which has subsequently spread across the world as a citizen-led approach to prioritising the spending of public funds – began in Brazil in 1989. Other practices which emphasised the use of dialogue and deliberation took root in Mexico, Uruguay, Venezuela, Guatemala and many other Latin American countries.

Another example is from the recent Labour Government which developed a programme for civil renewal and community empowerment between 2003 and 2010. The programme supported and promoted deliberative-engagement approaches between state and citizens across a range of policy areas in diverse localities in England. The Neighbourhood Management initiative enabled residents to prioritise neighbourhood improvements and delivered higher levels of satisfaction with street cleaning, policing and the area as a place to live compared with other similar neighbourhoods without the initiative. The Mental Health Commission engaged former service users on joint visits to mental health institutions, and with their support was able to improve services and tackle safety issues which would otherwise have been overlooked. Capital projects were taken forward with the involvement of the public in, for example, the development of Portsmouth's £9m Copnor Bridge, which was ready one month early and 10% under budget. Tenant participation was widely encouraged with savings achieved from tenant-supported efficiency savings ploughed back to enhancing caretaker services and tackling anti-social behaviour. Birmingham City Council and West Midlands Police engaged local people in designing community safety action plans which secured a saving of over £6m in return for a £600,000 investment for five selected neighbourhoods. All crime fell by 14% against a drop of 7% for comparator neighbourhoods in the city. There were many other examples of success.[25]

There is no guarantee that deliberative engagement always produces better results, yet it promotes a sense of collective efficacy, and has a higher rate of success in solving problems traditionally felt to be divisive. A wider embrace and more systematic application of this approach would go a long way towards generating the very solidarity needed to revive social democratic political reforms. Citizens, having been given the chance to reflect on what truly threatens their well-being, will back such reforms.

Towards a New Form of Social Democratic Activism

Social democrats accustomed to conventional methods of articulating their agenda may well question the replicability of deliberative approaches on a national, not to mention international, level. But herein lies one of the most critical gestalt challenges required for progressive consensus building. People no longer believe that satisfactory solutions to their problems can be formulated in an authority in London, Paris or Berlin. They distrust policymakers who suggest answers without consultation, or take their support for granted between elections. Instead of insisting the public must learn to understand their problems from the highest level, politicians and reform advocates must learn from engagement at people's everyday level. This means that instead of determining the overall political programme and trying to sell it in smaller packages to citizens, we begin by engaging citizens in identifying problems and shaping solutions, and using those outcomes as the building blocks for a bigger programme.

To bridge citizens' concerns and collective institutions, social democrats need to support the development of community-based organisations (CBOs) and work with them as partners in devising public policy. CBOs such as community co-operatives, local development trusts, neighbourhood associations or worker councils are familiar and accessible to those they aim to reach. They can facilitate deliberation in order to achieve consensus on the key collective actions that need to be taken. By building an ongoing relationship with them (as opposed to conducting a few one-off consultation events), social democrats can become part of the regeneration of activist engagement.

This is essential to counter right-wing/populist movements across Europe which, as with the Tea Party movement in America, feed on public anxiety and misdirect their concerns towards immigrants. With the help of CBOs, social democrats can enable disparate individuals to obtain a constructive opportunity to develop shared views as fellow citizens.

Furthermore, with the appropriate deliberative engagement practices, CBOs can make emotional connections with people's deepest concerns: how their fear of crime could be addressed; how to turn development proposals which could wreck their neighbourhoods into improvements which are meaningful to them; or how to channel scarce resources to meet their greatest needs. By applying the lessons offered by commentators on how the framing of political issues can affect the emotional response they engender,[26] social democrats can, for example, stop exploitative groups hijacking the trinity of 'God/Flag/Prosperity' as their exclusive totem, and reclaim them by invoking the equality of all before God, the patriotic dedication to not leaving anyone behind, and the entrepreneurial demand for a level playing field, in strengthening civic solidarity.

We may of course question the assumption that engaging citizens deliberatively would necessarily lead to the 'right' social democratic proposals. Two forms of risk in particular are clear. One derives from the possible dispersal of political power. If decisions are passed from a centralised state (which social democrats could control) to a plurality of local decision points, one consequence might be a fragmentation of policy objectives, therein limiting the sustainability of large-scale fiscal redistribution and universal welfare. However, the principle of subsidiarity works both ways. Where decisions which are more effectively taken at the local level should be devolved to smaller social units, those decisions which can only be taken at the national (or indeed, international) level (e.g. regulating national organisations or redistributing resources across different localities polarised by extreme inequalities) should remain there. Deliberative engagement in such cases would have a role in informing national decisions, but would not entail the state being deprived of its capacity to take them.

Where decisions are devolved there is another form of risk to be considered: namely, the possibility that citizens may opt for policies which conflict with social democratic goals. But just as democratic elections do not always produce favourable results for social democrats, nor can deliberative engagement guarantee one set of outcomes. Democrats believe that over time, with the conditions for fair elections increasingly strengthened, more outcomes flowing from voters' decisions will serve society's overall interests. Deliberative engagement is itself a tool to aid better understanding as to what different policy options really mean for citizens. It is argued that with the conditions for reflective participation steadily improving, the cumulative effect of deliberative engagement will nurture engaged citizens arriving at positions most consistent with their considered assessment.

What should not be taken for granted is the difficulty in overcoming the barriers to an informed, engaged citizenry. In practice, it would take sustained efforts to counter the distraction and distortion which could undermine participants attaining a better understanding of how their problems could be tackled. Yet these issues are not irreconcilable, and social democrats should not think that such efforts are not worth making, but rather that they are indispensable to a healthy democracy.

Some may go beyond the practical difficulties of removing the obstacles to authentic deliberation, and question whether citizens, even under conditions which facilitate full reflection on options for enhancing their well-being, may nonetheless select 'wrong' solutions. However, this challenge presupposes that the formulation of reform ideas in accordance with social democratic values can be achieved in isolation from the practical development of proposals carried out in accordance with social democratic commitment to openness, rationality and citizen participation. Since it cannot, deliberative engagement with the help of CBOs is actually the best chance we have of identifying a commonly owned social democratic agenda, supported by the very people who have engaged in its formulation.

It is because CBOs can help to join up civic concerns with a wider collective programme that they can play a crucial mediating role between supporters of social democratic actions and political parties which to varying degrees espouse social democratic values. Generally speaking, the vicissitudes of party politics do not offer citizens a stable base around which to rally against concentrations of power and vested interests. By contrast, CBOs provide a permanent forum for people to consider priorities for collective action, and to judge how best they could secure those priorities, without giving them false promises about what one party or another might deliver. Thus, instead of political parties assuming the electoral support of social democratic citizens, they have to demonstrate how their programme will address the latter's articulated agenda. If they fail to establish such a programme, or win power but fail to deliver on their proposals, the relationship between CBOs and the supporters for social democratic change would remain intact and continue to serve as a pressure point for progressive reform.

Finally, CBOs provide an independent perspective on the effectiveness of institutions responsible for collective action. Since the late 1970s, a twin strategy of attacking public institutions as ineffective and inefficient has developed in politics when parties are not in control. In enabling citizens to reflect on how some of the most difficult problems they face can be realistically tackled with the help of organisations capable of exercising collective power over their areas of jurisdiction, CBOs can serve to enhance much needed understanding of local authorities, national government, European institutions and UN bodies.

Instead of focusing solely on raising money for political parties, social democrats should help channel social investment into the development of CBOs concerned with building civic solidarity through deliberative engagements. Contrary to the 'state-shrinking' politics of substituting private charities for public provisions, the approach set out in this chapter would engender more informed support for state action. The more people are given a real chance to understand what the dismantling of public services entails, and to be involved in designing collective responses without which their lives would be further impoverished, the more likely they would lend their support to resisting the corrosive spread of market fundamentalism.

CHAPTER 15

Co-operation, Creativity and Equality: Key Concepts for a New Social Democratic Era

Tobias Dürr and Robert Misik

> *'Politics will become a contest between reformers and demagogues. It would be wise to get ahead of the curve, to take steps now before the worst of the reaction ensues'*
>
> —Robert Reich[1]

Ever since the exhaustion of the reformist élan at the end of the 1970s, social democratic and other parties of the centre-left have maintained a rather complicated relationship to the concept of social progress. Their de facto break with progress had its causes, and has consequences for the present and future of the centre-left. We shall discuss both aspects below. Central to our argument is the claim that the loss of an empathic understanding of social progress has heavily weakened the parties of the centre-left in the long term. 'Progressivism' when conceived merely as a nominal or tactical marketing ploy, and presented without genuine progressive urge and inspiration, is not an adequate substitute.[2] Only through the renewed practice of progress will social democrats and other parties regain their creativity, attractiveness and possibly even electoral majorities. But this new progressive thinking cannot be the old one. The progressive left-centre for our time must be based on the guiding principles of co-operation, creativity and equality.

What Progress Once Meant

In order to understand what the centre-left has lost, it is helpful to remember the societal configuration of almost half a century ago. In the reform era of the 1960s and early-1970s, it was confidently assumed that welfare state reforms combined with stable prosperity would lead to greater material equality and ensure a good life for all. Every citizen would have the opportunity to make something of his life. Economic growth and technological progress would thus go hand in hand and translate into social progress. At the same time, centre-left governments took steps to 'open windows'. More and more people were going to have access to a decent education, with the intention that that this would lift the general cultural level of Western societies, as well as give people the opportunity to improve their individual qualifications. Old habits and authorities were questioned, and an emancipatory spirit of egalitarianism swept through outmoded hierarchical organisations.

Not just in Germany, but in Sweden and in Austria, the progressive slogans of the time sounded similar: 'We are building modern Germany', Willy Brandt announced, while his Austrian colleague Bruno Kreisky intended to 'flood all areas of life with democracy'. As early as 1964, the rising young Swedish social democrat Olof Palme had postulated, 'Our goal is freedom, as far as possible, from the pressure of external circumstances. Freedom for the individual to develop his character. Freedom of choice for all human beings to shape their existence according to their own desires'.[3] And shortly before the SPD's historic election victory of 1969, Willy Brandt declared:

> In the opinion of a large proportion of our people the Social Democratic Party of Germany is as a party of progress. The days when political successes could be achieved with the slogan 'No experiments!' are over anyway. The majority of Germans feel the link between the preservation of peace, economic stability, reform of the education and training systems.[4]

In the same year, in his first major policy speech as the new Chancellor, Brandt insisted, 'We have not reached the end of our democracy, we are only now beginning in earnest'. With statements like these, Kreisky, Palme and Brandt summed up the progressive spirit of a whole generation of Western Europeans. Looking forward with confidence, they left behind the 'Dark Continent' (Mark Mazower) of the first half of the twentieth century.[5] The future was going to be brighter.

'Modernity + equality = freedom': this was the inspiring equation of the times.[6] And people took the message seriously. The majority were not cynical about politics, certainly not to a degree comparable to today's scale of disillusionment, frustration and contempt. The political leaders of the centre-left parties and their voters still cultivated a forward-looking and future-oriented disposition, in which they actually believed. They were convinced that their societies would be better places within 10 or 20 years, that it would be possible to realise an even higher level of equity and social equality, eliminate material grievances and widespread disparities in life-chances, and at the same time to introduce a greater degree of democratic participation. They entertained, in short, a full vision of progressive improvement of society.

Progress in Crisis

This political, social and cultural configuration came to an end for various reasons. One of these was that the reformist enthusiasm of the 1960s and early-1970s was something of a catch-up modernisation. Representatives of the centre-left had a fairly accurate idea of how the societal and political realities of their countries lagged behind the cultural changes which had been accelerating since at least the 1950s. At the same time, the centre-left parties kept a number of basic programmatic certainties and projects in their drawers, which they could now, as it were, check off one after another. Once this was done, the zeal for reform already began to wane. In addition to this, many voters soon started to feel overwhelmed by the hurricane of social and political transformation of the time. By the mid-1970s, one of the key publicly debated questions was how much change people could be expected to stomach. Only a few years earlier the horizon of progress had appeared wide open and almost everything had seemed possible, but by the mid-1970s liberal-conservative scholars beyond Germany were already asking anxious questions regarding to the general 'governability' or, as they feared, 'ungovernability' of Western societies.[7]

With the end of the post-war boom, the conditions for progressive distributive policy also worsened. The 'short dream of perpetual prosperity' (Burkart Lutz) had soon ended.[8] After the first oil price shock of 1973, rising unemployment forced a pragmatic refocusing of social democratic politics, and thus more programmatic self-restriction. Keeping working people in their jobs at almost any cost suddenly became the primary – sometimes even the sole – objective of centre-left governments.

With the neo-liberal turn of the late-1970s, initiated by the Thatcher revolution and the ideas of Reaganomics, many centre-left parties and their supporters began to feel that the existing welfare state was the best they could hope to achieve. Little more than defending their hard-won accomplishments seemed possible from now on. The historical perspective thus changed both among centre-left party leaders and their supporters. Suddenly it was no longer clear that tomorrow would be better than today. That children would be better off than their parents was no longer seen as an obvious fact. 'Since the mid seventies . . . we have become aware of the limits of the welfare state project – without any clear alternative being visible yet', the German social philosopher Jürgen Habermas soberly noted in 1985.[9]

What also mattered was the fact that politics is always an ideological struggle – a struggle for words and their meaning. Many terms were now reinterpreted, and the normatively charged concept of 'progress' was narrowed down to technological progress and economic dynamics. The term 'reform' which in the previous *Reformära* ('era of reform') had been taken to mean changes within society towards greater equality, more social security, greater prosperity and increased life-chances for all, gradually changed its contents. The word 'reform' was increasingly used to describe changes which from the perspective of many people meant the reduction of welfare policy and social security.

Thus, a fundamentally new situation had arisen. For Western political culture since the Enlightenment and the French Revolution, 'progress' had been a constitutive concept. Seldom is this principled position still postulated with confidence. 'The claim of inalienable human rights remains universal', the historian Heinrich August Winkler writes, 'and as long as [human rights] do not apply world-wide, the normative project of the West is unfinished'.[10] One could argue as a rule of thumb that without the principle of progress, there cannot be a 'West' in any normative sense. And, moreover, there can be no social democratic, centre-left or liberal politics without the regulative idea of progress.

It is clear that the idea, attitude and lifestyle of progress have become marginalised. The basic assumption of the possibility of a positive development of things or, as Habermas writes, the 'idea of infinite progress of knowledge and of progression to the socially and morally better',[11] has been called into question since the second half of the 1970s in Western European societies.

The long-term impact of this sea change can hardly be overestimated. As early as 1984, Habermas took account of the damage: 'The horizon of the future has shrivelled, and this has thoroughly changed both Zeitgeist and politics', he wrote, concluding that 'The future has a negative connotation'.[12] What was true back then applies more than ever today. The turbulent upheavals of the three decades of market hegemony have given rise to a deep-seated scepticism of progress and future. This is especially true in the case of the centre-left political family which into the 1970s was the most determined advocate of the idea of progress. A social democracy of fear?

Historically, social democrats have been the closest wedded of all political parties to the idea of progress. It is part and parcel of social democracy's collective DNA. But today the party that used to be a major force for renewal and optimism hardly appears to believe in the possibility of progressive politics or the feasibility of a better future. This view is shared in other left-of-centre parties, most of all among Greens. For many today, the idea of progress is discredited and frivolous. For some it is a public danger, and more than a few believe that due to the civilisational and ecological disasters of the twentieth century the concept has become totally obsolete. Meanwhile, more lenient observers today believe continued adherence to the principle of progress to be 'idealistic', not in the positive sense of the past but 'eccentric': well intentioned, even desirable perhaps, but refuted by history and unfeasible today. In short, outmoded and unachievable.

Anyone who today remains committed to the basic idea of progress – whether to its sheer necessity or its possibility – is likely to be suspected of naivety. Either they will be sneered at for their 'innocent optimism'

(Tony Judt) or, more likely, find themselves accused of not having drawn the proper lessons from the adversities of history. They will be lectured on the correct lessons of the twentieth-century experience, namely that some of the greatest crimes in the history of humankind were committed in the name of 'progress'.

Put simply, the experience of the European *Aufbauära* ('era of development'), starting in the 1950s, left a deep imprint on the minds of citizens – reforms would improve their living conditions. However, since the end of the 1970s, this has not been so clear. Often just the opposite has been the case. Where talk is about 'reform', the immediate assumption is that someone wants to take something away. In the political and economic discourse it has increasingly become conventional wisdom that economic dynamism necessarily presupposes the growth of material inequality. It is alleged that this has to be accepted because only then will 'the markets' work smoothly. If everyone just followed their aggressive self-interest, this would contribute to the general benefit, creating more wealth and prosperity. From this prosperity, albeit with an uneven distribution, even the underprivileged would benefit thanks to the famous trickle-down effect.

The philosophical basis of these calculations was a fundamentally altered view of humanity, a new hegemonic zeitgeist according to which social and economic inequalities are not at all bad and harmful, but in fact desirable. After all, they supposedly bring colour, variation and diversity into a world inhabited by human beings who are above all characterised by their competitive nature. Because each individual has only his own advantage in mind, the notion that in a society there could be such thing as a social progress towards greater equality was now considered not only completely naive, but also economically absurd.

To be sure, structural changes over the last three decades have objectively undermined the preconditions of the previously successful model of the centre-left. Among the factors at work have been demographic changes, a fundamental transformation of traditional industrial society due to rationalisation, an increasingly knowledge-intensive economy and global competition. Together they have irreversibly removed the conditions on which the nation-state-based welfare and progress model of the centre-left had fundamentally depended. But the centre-left parties did not respond appropriately to the transition into the 'post-industrial society'. Instead of systematically inquiring into the underlying causes of the ongoing crisis, they too often confined themselves to the treatment of symptoms.

The result was for the parties of the centre-left to adjust their rhetoric to changed circumstances. Two fundamentally different types of discourse emerged. Both were similar, however, in that they were purely reactive in character. Some said, 'Yes, we support these free-market reforms because we, too, believe that they will help make our societies more dynamic and increase the competitiveness of our economies. But unlike our political opponents we at least try to make sure that in the process as much fairness as possible remains in place'. Others tried to distinguish themselves as defenders of the old order, in effect telling their traditional electorate: 'Vote for us because if you do, things will get worse more slowly'.

In reality, nearly all centre-left parties combined these two rhetorical modes in one way or another. What they had in common was that they lacked a specific idea of their own on how to progressively improve society. But because of that they also lacked a clear political perspective, a particular cause that could have inspired citizens. Of course, it can be very honourable to defend hard-won rights and achievements of the past. The late Tony Judt does just this in *Ill Fares the Land* when he argues that:

> To put the point quite bluntly, if social democracy has a future, it will be a social democracy of fear. Accordingly, the first task is to remind ourselves of the achievements of the 20th century, along with the likely consequences of a heedless rush to dismantle them . . . The Left has something to conserve.[13]

This is undeniably true. Still, one will find it difficult to inspire a significant number of people to simply defend the status quo. The status quo also has its shortcomings, but what ultimately makes the defence of the status quo almost impossible to sell is the recognition that only positive goals can encourage people to join forces in order to achieve their goals collectively.

Progress! But What Progress?

It is time for a new era of progress. What is obvious, however, is that this era cannot be about recycling technocratic, or even authoritarian, varieties of progress from the nineteenth and twentieth centuries. After all, in no small measure it was an over-simplistic and sometimes vulgar understanding of progress in the past which contributed to the miseries of the present: widespread environmental problems, climate change and the dead ends of nuclear and fossil energy are just a few of the issues that spring to mind. Likewise, religious fundamentalism and terrorism can be understood as reactions to all too linear concepts of progress. A lot of the challenges we face today are the results of poorly conceived promises of progress made in the last century.

A teleological style of progressive thinking no longer works. Less than ever before can the cause of progress today be advanced as an over-arching project, moving towards a finishing point, studied through quasi-scientific means – like a tunnel that ends with a triumphant breakthrough into the glaring sunlight. Enlightened contemporary progressives have every reason to display some humility on that score. But what follows from this? Does it mean progressives should renounce the idea and practice of progress altogether, and instead devote themselves to a despondent muddling-through, designed – somehow, maybe, hopefully – to avoid the worst? The dilemma of progress, in which we find ourselves today as a result of too much vulgar progress in the past, is not at all easy to resolve.

In his latest book, *The Politics of Climate Change*, Anthony Giddens raises the question with regard to the undoubtedly greatest problem of our age:

> Our civilization could self-destruct – no doubt about it . . . Doomsday is no longer a religious concept, a day of spiritual reckoning, but a Possibility in our society and economy imminent . . . No wonder many take fright. Let's go back! Let's return to a simpler world! They are entirely understandable sentiments and have practical application in some contexts. Yet there can be no overall 'going back' – the very expansion of human power that has created deep problems is seeking the only means of resolving them, with science and technology at the forefront. There will probably be nine billion people in the world by 2050 – after which world population

> will hopefully stabilise, especially if the least developed countries make significant economic and social progress. Ways will have to be found of providing those nine billion people with a decent way of life.[14]

Giddens is right. If we are to overcome the misery already experienced as well as the problems still to arise during the twenty-first century, we will do so only with a clear commitment to a prudent kind of progress and renewal. Analogous to the sociologist Ulrich Beck's notion of 'reflexive modernisation', this could be called 'reflexive progress'.[15] In precisely this sense, centre-left parties are in need of a new historical horizon – not a 'utopia' in the register of 'socialism', nor a vision of a completely different society, but the goal of a society that works better, provides a more equal share in its existing wealth, leaves no one behind and allows all of its citizens to develop their talents. The centre-left requires a set of ideas as to how such a better community can be achieved over a period of time, say, 20 years. Moreover, it must tie these often pragmatic approaches together to produce a compelling story, a unifying narrative.

Equality Is Better for Everyone

It is instructive that Richard Wilkinson and Kate Pickett's study, *The Spirit Level: Why Equality is Better for Everyone*, has become such a success in Britain, Continental Europe and even the United States.[16] The furore around *The Spirit Level* must first and foremost be interpreted as a symptom of how widespread the desire for a plausible 'next big idea' really is. Based on thorough empirical research, Wilkinson and Pickett demonstrate that in almost every conceivable way societies will work better when they realise greater material equality among citizens. Societies of this kind are not only advantageous for the immediate 'beneficiaries' of redistribution, namely the underprivileged, but ultimately everyone. Everyone benefits when social institutions work better, everyone benefits when a society can rightly be called a 'community' and everyone benefits when the social stress decreases, which gross inequality and the never-ending race to outdo one another bring for all citizens.

Since the fiasco in the financial markets, we have known more clearly than before that it is not only society as a whole which functions better when we establish relative material equality, but the economy, too. Economies with gross inequalities squander their potential for growth. They accept that a considerable segment of citizens cannot develop their talents, thus restricting the people who can contribute to the welfare of the community as productive participants in the market. Moreover, gross material inequality tends to increase social instability. That is why unequal societies are economically inefficient in the long run, and particularly under the conditions of the current, increasingly knowledge-intensive capitalist market economy. Contemporary centre-left parties must therefore press for the implementation of various reforms – from tax policy to economic policy, from education policy to family policy, immigration and integration policies – with the aim of significantly increasing society's egalitarian character. It is that simple, or, as it were, that difficult.

To achieve this goal, a transformation of ideology and rhetoric is needed. Competition and individualism, efficiency and inequality have been the ideological catchwords that have dominated the past 30 years. Those who asked whether this was an acceptable way of understanding the world were typically dismissed as idealistic dreamers. We were told that people were simply competition-oriented by nature, caring only about their own advantage and material self-interest. This was why in the 'real world' there was supposedly no room for empathy or co-operation. If people continued to ask awkward questions, they were told they simply had no understanding of the modern economy. The lasting effect of this perception has been that social democrats and other 'moralising do-gooders' should never be left in charge of the machinery. For far too long too many people accepted this, even though such explanations contradict the better part of our everyday experience.

After all, most of us know very well that the best way to a good performance at one's workplace is an environment in which people co-operate amiably and constructively. We know, too, that our urge to work to the best of our ability tends to decline considerably in circumstances in which everybody works for himself and all work against each other. Many large companies have long understood that it does not necessarily make economic sense for them to cut costs at any price, to harm the environment or exploit suppliers in the developing world, because they need motivated employees at home who identify with their company without embarrassment.

To be sure, people do often compete against each other, and there are many good reasons for this. World-class footballers would not have got very far in their line of business if they found no pleasure at all in winning a tackle. Many people perform excellently, precisely because they are driven to win the upper hand in competition with others. But, of course, we know that something else is equally true – competition is not everything in life. Moreover, we know that we do not only help others in situations in which they pay us for doing so. We are not pure egoists. Sometimes we help out of an impulse of pure altruism, because our moral sense tells us that this is just the thing we should be doing.

Beyond the private realm, there are many fine gradations of this attitude, even in the spheres of business and economics. There are software engineers making good money working for Google, who spend their spare time volunteering as network administrators for their favourite non-governmental organisations. Everywhere in the societies of the West the established economics of buying and selling has long been complemented by something of an 'economy of favours' and mutual aid, which more and more people participate in as a matter of course. Who knows many people who make their career choices exclusively – or even primarily – on the grounds of 'optimisation of career opportunities' or achieving a maximum income? More frequently one encounters people who want a job they can experience as 'meaningful' or 'satisfying'. Not infrequently, people even accept a lower salary because they prefer an exciting, creative activity which suits their interests and talents.

Even if we concede that people very often and in many respects have an eye on their personal 'benefit', this benefit is certainly not limited to material profit, but includes idealistic and non-material interests. People do not just want to earn a lot of money, they also want to be respected and enjoy recognition. They may even rightly believe that it is in their longer-term, material self-interest not to continuously behave as ultra-competitive egoists, because if they do, at some point no one will want to do business let alone associate with them anymore. Thus, even in terms of individual benefit, many facets need to be taken into consideration.

In short, in the real world the supposedly ubiquitous homo economicus is a mysterious ghost. His existence is persistently asserted, but we very rarely encounter him face to face. Yet against better evidence people still believe that the world works according to the gospel of the neo-liberal prophets. Consequently, many interpret their discomfort as their own private malaise which, they are led to believe, carries no general relevance. As Richard Wilkinson and Kate Pickett write:

> Many people have a strong personal belief in greater equality and fairness, but these values have remained private intuitions which they fear others do not share ... The advantage of the growing body of evidence of the harm inflicted by inequality is that it turns what were purely personal intuitions into publicly demonstrable facts.[17]

Competition, individualism and inequality – these ideological props of the past era have not only proven to be dysfunctional for a stable, prosperous economy. They are also entirely inappropriate, given the technological development towards a knowledge-intensive network economy with its many interdependencies. Furthermore, in an emerging global order, no side can secure their own advantage in the long term by impairing the opportunities of others.

Progress Reloaded

What are the key concepts, then, on which a new progressive era can be based? Three come to mind: co-operation, creativity and equality. Co-operation is critical because more can be achieved when people work together – we simply are not exclusively competitive beings. Creativity matters, because we all want to do things to which we can attach meaning, because we want to develop our talents and because a society flourishes better when all people have the opportunity to do so. The concept of creativity contains the best of individuality, without the connotation of self-interest which has recently been attached to the term. Finally, equality is important because in the twenty-first century those societies which can offer their citizens egalitarian living conditions will also prove to be the more sustainable ones. 'Modern societies will depend on increasingly being creative, adaptable, inventive, well-informed and flexible communities, able to respond generously to each other and to needs wherever they arise', Wilkinson and Pickett point out. 'Those are not characteristics of societies in hock to the rich, in which people are driven by status insecurities, but of populations used to working together and respecting each other as equals.'[18]

Based on these utilitarian considerations alone, hundreds of thousands, if not millions, of citizens in our societies would sign up to a political agenda based on the principles of co-operation, creativity and equality. But many cannot yet locate the practical means to give their beliefs political efficacy. Political parties offer a limited number of programmatic points they can share, but for the most part the *res publica*, the public affairs, are characterised by the inability, the amateurism and the small-mindedness of those who inhabit the insular world of the party-political machinery.

Understandably, citizens tend to turn away from these apparatus parties. Yet this leads to a vicious circle, because as a result parties become even more lifeless. For this reason, a new progressive era will only be realised if citizens begin to take matters into their own hands. Just possibly, the traditional parties of the democratic left will be able to reinvent themselves one more time. Should they fail to do so, however, new political forces will have to form: broad-based progressive coalitions which, both as extra-party and extra-parliamentary movements, begin to create the political and organisational basis for a new progressive majority.

Business as usual is not an option for the parties of the centre-left, but neither is engaging reverse gear. Among the ranks of social democratic parties and traditional industrial trade unions today, more than a few would welcome a return to the 1970s, allegedly an era in which their world was still intact: unions were strong; the societies of the West were more socially and ethnically homogeneous; globalisation was an unthreatening abstract concept; the working life was still organised formally; and social democrats could even manage to win absolute majorities once in a while. On television, no one dared to make fun of a prime minister, teenagers politely made room for the elderly on the bus, and on 1 May people waved red flags (which even then was nostalgic).

Occasionally, a similar nostalgia exists in the milieu of the unorthodox, politically independent left. People in these circles have been convinced that everything is getting worse all the time, the logical conclusion being that 30 years ago, everything must have been better. From this perspective, whatever has happened since then can only be understood as a story of decline. Quite often, however, the leftists of the *Reformära* now glorified by their heirs criticised their own present in the very same words during the 1960s and 1970s.

The obvious truth is that even in the supposedly 'golden' 1970s, things were far from perfect. Many of the cultural, technological and economic transformations since then have made our lives richer and more vibrant. In any case, these processes of far-reaching social change cannot be reversed. Today only very few people in the Western societies earn their wages as manual labourers in factories, and more and more people are economically active in the service sectors of the knowledge society. Whether one considers this process as a good or a bad one, this is a simple fact. Such transformations influence people: they change their ideals, their biographies and their goals. Often these effects are ambivalent. In many respects, the majority of people lead a freer and more independent life today. At the same time, however, social atomisation, alienation, loss of roots, strain and mental homelessness have increased. As a consequence, people today often have to fend for themselves when they really are in need of solidarity; they live their lives as lone fighters, even though they would much prefer to work together with others.

A Better Tomorrow, Again

We cannot return to a glorified world of yesteryear. Rather, we must improve our world in our time. This will not work if we hang onto the language, rituals and types of political organisation of a bygone era.

We have to be at the height of our own times. We can turn our societies into places that are more just than today, in which all citizens have a fair opportunity to live successful lives. We cannot accept that some are left behind without hope or that others begin life as born losers. All citizens must be given the opportunity to make something of their lives, and no one should be trapped in living conditions which combine chronic poverty with lack of opportunity. Life is simply better for all in egalitarian societies, and for this reason we must organise our economy in a way that combines prosperity with stability and reduces the worst inequalities. The eternal treadmill of competition contaminates the lives of all. To address the present crisis we must stimulate our economies, and we should do this in a way that makes life better for ourselves and for future generations by investing heavily in the environmental upgrading of our societies. We need more democracy in our democracies, so people do not turn away from politics with indifference and disgust. We have to free our political systems from the captivity of the privileged and their lobbies. All of this is much more than a political agenda in the narrower material interest of the underprivileged. It is a worthy goal for all people everywhere.

CHAPTER 16

Afterword: The New Social Democracy?

Olaf Cramme and Patrick Diamond

We believe this book to be necessary since both of the dominant narratives about social democracy in Europe are patently flawed, or at least inaccurate. On the one hand, 'third way modernisers' have insisted that social democrats have no alternative but to embrace the inexorable logic of globalisation, liberalisation and public sector reform. The forces of history point only in the direction of Anglo-American neo-liberalism. On the other hand, there are those on the 'traditional left' who have sought a return to the verities of post-1945 social democracy, a settlement built on a unitary nation-state and a model of managed market capitalism which perished in the economic crisis of the 1970s. Neither of these narratives offers a credible future strategy for the centre-left.

The authors in this volume have assiduously avoided framing their arguments in such terms: instead they have sought to carve out new doctrines, new concepts and new interpretations on which a credible centre-left politics might be built and from which new ideas can emerge. The result is not a comprehensive policy programme for a new European social democracy, but a nuanced, reflective account of the options and choices available to centre-left parties who are operating in national contexts marked by varying traditions, circumstances and constraints.

If the financial crisis of 2007–8 marks the demise of 1980s neo-liberalism, it is unlikely to encourage the embrace of the state at the expense of the market. The very dominance of neo-liberalism over the last 30 years was built not only on the particular remedies it imposed on national governments, but its refrain that there is 'no alternative' to relentless marketisation in an age of global capitalism. Echoing Francis Fukuyama's 'end of history' thesis, it was argued by numerous commentators and policymakers that states had no choice but to submit themselves to neo-liberal policy regimes. The optimists believed that the era of boom and bust was finally over, and that the global economy was so dynamic and flexible that a breakdown in the international system was completely unthinkable.

Yet the global financial crisis, in Andrew Gamble's view, 'struck like an earthquake at the heart of the institutions, practices and beliefs of those years'.[1] The aftershocks of the crisis will be felt for years to come following the worst global depression since the 1930s, and the search is on for ideas and remedies that will enable the world to exorcise the spectre of a permanent breakdown in global capitalism. The central question resulting from the crisis is not whether it will rejuvenate traditional nation-state social democracy, but whether it can stimulate new programmes and strategies on which a revived system of egalitarian prosperity and social welfare might be constructed. The task for left-of-centre parties is to frame these responses such that social democracy might benefit from the new contingency in domestic and world politics, against a residual neo-liberalism that would frame the world financial crisis as one of the over-extended, social democratic state.

In undertaking such an enterprise, three animating themes appear immediately resonant. The first relates to the nature of global capitalism. Historically, social democracy has developed in conjunction with the capitalist system itself. In the post-war era, critics such as the British academic commentator David Coates argued that centre-left parties had become 'structurally dependent' on capitalism, while the historian Donald Sassoon has written that the fortunes of all social democratic parties have come to depend on developments within capitalism.[2]

In fact, capitalism continues to define the boundaries of what is politically feasible, since social democrats aim not to replace capitalism with an alternative economic system, but to reform the nature of the capitalist settlement. This makes it essential that centre-left parties understand the changing contours of capitalism, which sets the context and frame in which they strive to attain power. In recent decades, capitalism has been steadily transformed through new technologies, an acceleration of the trends towards globalisation, and a shift from manufacturing to services, in particular financial services. This has dismantled the forms of industrial age production that fuelled the post-war boom and financed the dramatic expansion of the state's role in welfare provision and social services. There are also many 'varieties of capitalism' that have emerged in the advanced economies of the world that ought to be considered. Grasping the scale of the structural transformation of capitalism has never been more urgent for the centre-left, which aims to bring about a more just, humane and efficient conception of a market capitalist economy.

The second theme alludes to the changing nature and form of the state. Again, social democracy has been historically dependent on particular forms of state power, but these appear increasingly problematic given the contemporary conjuncture we are experiencing. The size and complexity of the state makes it more and more difficult for citizens to understand who makes decisions and who should be held accountable. Decision-making power lies increasingly in the hands of experts, putting additional constraints on modern liberal forms of representative and participative democracy. Large-scale bureaucracies can fuel citizen disengagement and declining trust in the political system. As this book has shown, there are also pressures on the traditional social democratic conception of the welfare state, such as the ageing society and changing demography, that will hardly disappear. Indeed, the crisis will accelerate the impact of these long-range trends and forces on the affordability and efficacy of the contemporary welfare state.

A final theme relates to new cultural conflicts and cleavages that have undermined left-of-centre parties in Europe and the United States. These concern increasing ethnic heterogeneity, the free movement of labour and open migration systems, the rise of new forms of politicised and assertive Islamic radicalism, and an apparent conflict between 'cosmopolitan' and 'communitarian' interests. Many of the identities, solidarities and constituencies on which European social democracy was built are under increasing strain. New political actors on the far left and far right, as well as astutely positioned conservative and Christian democratic parties, will not hesitate to capitalise on these political pressures by crafting a populist narrative and programmatic response. In this context, providing citizens with a clearer sense of belonging, community and collective purpose in a rapidly changing world has to be at the forefront of this revitalisation in centre-left thinking. Markets that have no respect for traditional values and ways of living cannot be allowed to flourish untamed.

So there is a radical and expansive agenda for modern, left-of-centre politics to pursue. Inevitably, social democracy has to renew itself in every generation if it is to remain relevant and practical. It has always had to adapt in order to survive, but the challenge is to combine workable and credible policies with a clear vision of the kind of society that social democrats wish to bring about. Each of the themes referred to in this concluding chapter need to be subject to a rigorous credibility test: are social democrats capable of developing a governing strategy which can live up to these enormous challenges? With the 'golden age' of the nation-state irrefutably at an end, there is an urgent need for new methods, capacities and instruments at different levels of governance and the state. For social democrats, this means a fundamental change in mindset given the traditional fixation with the central levers of state power in building a fairer society in their own country.

Indeed, pride in building up the national welfare state allowed the left to assume the mantle of modern patriotism, coupled with a genuine commitment to internationalism. This was seen mainly in the post-Second World War era through the lens of harmonious and co-operative international partnership in the form of the Atlantic alliance. But in today's world, citizens have to be engaged in a more sophisticated and complex understanding of interdependence and sovereignty. As this volume has sought to demonstrate, retreating from an increasingly demanding and complex international agenda is simply not an option. The centre-left must instead regain ownership of it: from European integration to climate change, as well as responding to the humanitarian crises that continue to afflict our world.

In short, this is the terrain on which social democratic parties have to forge compelling electoral strategies, political identities and policy agendas. The purpose of this book is to develop new frameworks and new concepts through which such a task might be undertaken, bringing ideas back into the mainstream of European social democracy. Success is not inevitable: contingency and events conspire against the best ideas. But without ideas there is no hope.

Notes

PREFACE

1. Béland, D. *What is Social Policy? Understanding the Welfare State.* Cambridge: Polity, 2010, p. 12.
2. Dahrendorf, R. Die Chancen der Krise. Über die Zukunft des Liberalismus, Stuttgart: DVA, 1983.

CHAPTER 1 From Fatalism to Fraternity: Governing Purpose and the Good Society

1. Judt, T. *Ill Fairs the Land*, London: Penguin, 2010.
2. See Gray, J. 'The Sons of Ralph Miliband', *The Guardian*, 2010.
3. Gamble, A. 'Social Democracy' on 'Social Europe', 2010.
4. Organisation of Economic Co-ordination and Development (OECD), *OECD in Figures: 2005 edition*, 2005.
5. See Darendorf, R. *The Modern Social Conflict: The Politics of Liberty*, London: Transaction Books, 2007.
6. See Sassoon, D. *One Hundred Years of Socialism: The Western European Left in the 20th Century*, London: I.B.Tauris, 1996.
7. Cramme, O. and Diamond, P. *The Politics of Evasion*, London: Policy Network, 2009.
8. See Jones, T. *Remaking the Labour Party from Gaitskell to Blair*, London: Routledge, 1996.
9. Clift, B. 'Social democracy and globalisation: the cases of Britain and France', *Government and Opposition*, 37(4), pp. 466–500, 2002.
10. Keynes, J. M. *The General Theory of Employment, Interest, and Money*, London: Prometheus, 1997.
11. Sassoon, D. *One Hundred Years of Socialism: The West European Left in the Twentieth Century*, New York: The New Press, 1998.

12. Howell, D. *British Social Democracy: A Study in Development and Decay*, Manchester: Manchester University Press, 1980.
13. Callaghan, J. *The Retreat of Social Democracy*, Manchester: Manchester University Press, 2000.
14. Merkel, W., et al. *Social Democracy in Power: The Capacity to Reform*, London: Routledge, 2004.
15. See OECD. 'Growing Unequal? Income Distribution and Poverty in OECD Countries', 2008.
16. Hall, P. 'The dilemmas of contemporary social science', in *boundary* 2, 34(3), winter 2007.
17. Merkel, W., et al. *Social Democracy in Power: The Capacity to Reform*, London: Routledge, 2004.
18. Padget, S. *Social Democracy in Europe*, London: Routledge, 2000.
19. Sassoon, D. *One Hundred Years of Socialism: The Western European Left in the 20th Century*, London: I.B.Tauris, 1996.
20. Przeworski, A. *Capitalism and Social Democracy*, Cambridge: Cambridge University Press, 1985.
21. Coates, D. 'Chickens coming home to roost: New Labour at the eleventh hour', in *British Politics*, 4(4), 2009, pp. 421–433.
22. Blanden, J., Gregg, P. and Machin, S. 'Intergenerational mobility in Europe and North America', Sutton Trust report, April 2005.
23. Saggar, S. *Pariah Politics*, Oxford: Oxford University Press, 2008.
24. Reich, R. *The Wealth of Nations*, Stanford: Stanford University Press, 1994.
25. International Labour Organisation (ILO), Global Wage Report 2008–9, 2009.
26. Organisation of Economic Co-ordination and Development (OECD), *OECD in Figures: 2005 edition*, 2005.
27. Hacker, J. *The Great Risk Shift*, Yale: Yale University Press, 2007.
28. Share of total wages and salaries in total value added: (a) total labour compensation, including employers' social security and pension contributions and imputed labour income for self-employed persons; (b) GDP-weighted average of the following countries: Austria, Belgium, Denmark, Finland, France, Germany, Ireland, Italy, the Netherlands, Spain, Sweden and the United Kingdom. Source: OECD estimates using the OECD Economic Outlook database, 2009.
29. Gamble, A. 'Social Democracy Beyond the Nation-State', in O. Cramme and P. Diamond (eds), *Social Justice in the Global Age*, Cambridge: Polity Press, 2009.

30. Gamble, A. 'Social Democracy Beyond the Nation-State', in O. Cramme and P. Diamond (eds), *Social Justice in the Global Age*, Cambridge: Polity Press, 2009.
31. Smith, M. 'Defining New Labour', in S. Ludlum and M. Smith (eds), *Governing as New Labour: Policy and Politics under Blair*, London: Palgrave MacMillan, 2004.
32. See Goodhart, D. 'Solidarity and Diversity', *Prospect*, 2002.
33. See Gray, J. *After Social Democracy: Politics, Capitalism, and the Common Life*, London: Demos, 1996.
34. See Denham, J. 'The Fairness Code', *Prospect*, 2004.
35. Gamble, A. *The Free Economy and the Strong State*, London: Macmillan, 1987.
36. European Commission, 'Economy, Finance and Tax Report', June 2010.
37. Hutton, W. *The State We're In*, London: Random House, 1996.
38. Hacker, J. *The Great Risk Shift*, Yale: Yale University Press, 2006.
39. Kay, J. *The Truth About Markets*, London: Penguin Books, 2003.
40. Flinders, M. 'The Future of the State', in I. Maclean and V. Uberoi (eds), *Options for Britain II*, London: Palgrave MacMillan, 2010.
41. Giddens, A. *The Politics of Climate Change*, Cambridge: Polity Press, 2010.

CHAPTER 2 Social Democracy in a Global Era

1. See, for example, Mosley, L. 'Globalization and the State: Still Room to Move?', *New Political Economy*, 10(3), 2005, pp. 355–362.
2. Bourdieu, P. *Acts of Resistance: Against the Tyranny of the Market*, The New Press: New York, 1998.
3. See, for example, Held, D. *Global Covenant: The Social Democratic Alternative to the Washington Consensus*, Cambridge: Polity Press, 2004.
4. Morales, M. A. 'Have Latin Americans turned left?', in J. G. Castañeda and M. A. Morales (eds), *Leftovers: Tales of the Latin American left*, Routledge: London, 2008.
5. Norris, P. 'Global Governance and Cosmopolitan Citizens', in J. S. Nye and J. D. Donahue (eds), *Governance in a Globalizing World*, Washington DC: Brookings Institution Press, 2000.
6. Martell, L. *The Sociology of Globalization*, Cambridge: Polity Press, 2010, ch. 6.
7. Gamble, A. 'Moving beyond the National: the challenges for social democracy in a global world', in O. Cramme and P. Diamond (eds), *Social Justice in the Global Age*, Cambridge: Polity Press, 2009, ch. 7, 125.

CHAPTER 4 The Mechanics of Markets: Politics, Economics and Finance

1. Further, see Gamble, A. 'Debt and deficits: the quest for economic competence' in this volume.
2. This account relies heavily on Kay, J. *The Truth About Markets*, London: Allen Lane the Penguin Press, 2003.
3. Notably in Hayek, F. A. *Law, Legislation and Liberty*, Vol. 1, *Rules and Order*, Chicago: University of Chicago Press, 1973.
4. See Hall, P. A. and Soskice, D. *Varieties of Capitalism*, Oxford: Oxford University Press, 2001.
5. See Kay, J. 'The future of markets', *Economic Affairs*, 2010.

CHAPTER 5 Social Democracy at the End of the Welfare State?

1. Atkinson, A. 'The distribution of earnings in OECD countries'. *International Labour Review*, 146(2), 2007, pp. 41–60.
2. IPCC. Fourth Assessment Report, available at: http://www.ipcc.ch/publications_and_data/ar4/wg3/en/spmsspm-d.html, consulted 14.10.10, 2007.
3. Stern, N. The Economics of Climate Change, HM Treasury, available at: http://www.webcitation.org/5nCeyEYJr, consulted 14.10.10, 2006.
4. New Economics Foundation. Growth isn't Possible, available at: http://www.neweconomics.org/publications/growth-isnt-possible, consulted 14.10.10, 2010.
5. EU. Renewed Social Agenda, available at: http://ec.europa.eu/social/main.jsp?catId=547, consulted 26.02.09, 2008.
6. Palier, B. *A Long Goodbye to Bismarck?* Amsterdam University Press, Amsterdam, 2010.
7. OECD. Economic Outlook, No. 87, Paris, 2010.
8. Taylor-Gooby, P. and Stoker, G. 'The Coalition Programme: A new vision for Britain or politics as usual?'. *Political Quarterly*, 82 (1), 2011, pp. 4–27.

CHAPTER 6 Equality, Social Trust and the Politics of Institutional Design

1. See my article 'Dead and Alive in Social Democracy' published in INROADS: *The Canadian Journal of Opinion*, 28, 2011. There are interesting exceptions, most notably in some developing countries, see for example

Sandbrook, R., Edelman, M., Heller, P. and Teichman, J. *Social Democracy in the Global Periphery,* New York: Cambridge University Press, 2006. For an overview of the current political debate see Meyer, H. 'European Social Democracy in Crisis', *Political Insight,* 1(2), 2010.

2. See for example Wilkinson, R. G. and Pickett, K. *The Spirit Level: Why More Equal Societies Almost Always Do Better,* London: Allen Lane, 2009.
3. It may be added that there are a lot of interesting research results in this area that are not policy-relevant, such as what type of electoral systems different countries adopted a hundred years ago.
4. *Just Institutions Matter: The Moral and Political Logic of the Universal Welfare State,* Cambridge: Cambridge University Press, 1998; *Social Traps and the Problem of Trust,* Cambridge: Cambridge University Press, 2006; and *The Quality of Government: Corruption, Inequality and Social Trust,* Chicago: University of Chicago Press, 2011.
5. Personally, I am interested in generous and high-quality systems for vocational training and education (also known as Active Labour Market Policy) since this gives people hurt by unemployment caused by global economic competition a chance to come back. Another strong candidate, not least from a gender equality system, is a universal high-quality preschool (day care) system.
6. Increased equality in work and family life are also important, but for reasons of space I leave these out. I have treated these issues in other publications which I will be happy to send by email upon request.
7. Rawls, J. *A Theory of Justice,* Oxford: Oxford University Press, 1971.

CHAPTER 7 Progress and Social Policy: Two-and-a-Half Cheers for Education

1. Blair, T. *A Journey: My Political Life,* New York: Knopf, 2010, p. 104. See also Reich, R. B. *The Work of Nations,* New York: Knopf, 1991; Giddens, A. *The Third Way,* Cambridge: Polity Press, 1998; Esping-Andersen, G. 'Equal Opportunities and the Welfare State', *Contexts,* Summer 2007; Morel, N., Palier, B. and Palme, J. *What Future for Social Investment?,* Stockholm: Institute for Futures Studies, 2009; Hemerijck, A. *Changing Welfare States,* Oxford: Oxford University Press, 2012.
2. For more discussion see Wolff, E. N. *Does Education Really Help?* Oxford: Oxford University Press, 2006; Kenworthy, L. *Jobs with Equality,* Oxford: Oxford University Press, 2008, ch. 9.
3. A prominent recent argument for education as a key to reducing inequality is Goldin, C. and Katz, L. *The Race between Education and Technology,*

Cambridge, MA: Harvard University Press, 2008. For a critique see Kenworthy, L. 'Reducing Inequality: Education to the Rescue?', *Consider the Evidence*, available at: lanekenworthy.net/2009/04/14/reducing-inequality-education-to-the-rescue, consulted 27.01.12, 2009.

4. Some other alternatives include average years of schooling in the working-age population; the share of the working-age population having completed tertiary education; the share of the adult population who lack basic literacy skills. Using any of these alternatives would not alter the conclusion.
5. OECD, *Education at a Glance*, 2010; Luxembourg Income Study, 'LIS Key Figures', available at: www.lisproject.org; Atkinson, A. B., Piketty, T. and Saez, E. 'Top Incomes in the Long Run of History', Working Paper 15408, National Bureau of Economic Research, 2009.
6. Sen, A. *Development as Freedom*, Oxford: Oxford University Press, 1999.
7. Jan, O. Jonsson and Robert Erikson are sceptical that expansion of university slots in Sweden improved equality of opportunity, though they caution that this finding might be specific to Sweden. Jonsson, J. O. and Erikson, R. 'Sweden: why educational expansion is not such a great strategy for equality – theory and evidence'. See also Lind, M. 'The fantasy of a vast upper-middle class', *Salon*, available at: www.salon.com/news/opinion/feature/2010/08/03/myth_upper_middle_class, consulted 27.01.12, 2010.
8. Heckman, J. J. 'School, Skills, and Synapses', Working Paper 14064, National Bureau of Economic Research, 2008; Cunha, F. and Heckman, J. J. 'Investing in Our Young People', Working Paper 16201, National Bureau of Economic Research, 2010.
9. Alexander, K. L., Entwisle, D. R. and Olson, L. S. 'Lasting consequences of the summer learning gap', *American Sociological Review*, 2007, pp. 167–180.
10. Nisbett, R. *Intelligence and How to Get It: Why Schools and Cultures Count*, New York: W. W. Norton, 2009, p. 40.
11. It certainly does for individuals. The question is whether a better-educated society will tend to have higher mobility.
12. Breen, R. and Jonsson, J. O. 'Explaining change in social fluidity: educational equalization and educational expansion in twentieth-century Sweden', *American Journal of Sociology*, 2007, pp. 1775–1810; Björklund, A. and Jäntti, M. 'Intergenerational income mobility and the role of family background', in Salverda, W., Nolan, B. and Smeeding, T. M. (eds), *The Oxford Handbook of Economic Inequality*, Oxford: Oxford University Press, 2007.

13. Harding, D. J., Jencks, C., Lopoo, L. M. and Mayer, S. E. 'The changing effect of family background on the incomes of American Adults', in S. Bowles, H. Gintis and M. Osborne (eds), *Unequal Chances: Family Background and Economic Success*, Russell Sage Foundation and Princeton University Press, 2008; Milburn, A., et al, *Unleashing Aspiration: The Final Report of the Panel on Fair Access to the Professions*, available at: www.bis.gov.uk/assets/biscore/corporate/migratedd/publications/p/panel-fair-access-to-professions-final-report-21july09.pdf, consulted 27.01.12, 2009.
14. Blanden, J., Gregg, P. and Machin, S. 'Integenerational Mobility in Europe and North America', Center on Economic Performance, 2005, available at: cep.lse.ac.uk/about/news/IntergenerationalMobility.pdf; Williams, D. 'Social mobility and the rise of the politariat', *Local Economy*, 2009.
15. For more discussion see Jencks, C. and Tach, L. 'Would equal opportunity mean more mobility?', in Morgan, S. L., Grusky, D. B. and Fields, G. S. (eds), *Mobility and Inequality*, Stanford, CA: Stanford University Press, 2006; Breen, R. 'Social mobility and equality of opportunity', upublished, Yale University, 2010.
16. Crouch, C., Finegold, D. and Sako, M. *Are Skills the Answer?*, Oxford: Oxford University Press, 1999; Kenworthy, L. *Jobs with Equality*, Oxford: Oxford University Press, 2008, ch. 9.
17. Esping-Andersen, G. *Social Foundations of Postindustrial Economies*, Oxford: Oxford University Press, 1999.
18. Blau, D. M. *The Child Care Problem: An Economic Analysis*, New York: Russell Sage Foundation, 2001; Waldfogel, J. *What Children Need*, Cambridge & London: Harvard University Press, 2006.
19. Kenworthy, L. 'Institutions, Wealth, and Inequality', in *The Oxford Handbook of Comparative Institutional Analysis*, Oxford: Oxford University Press, 2010.
20. Baumol, W. J., Litan, R. E. and Schramm, C. J. *Good Capitalism, Bad Capitalism, and the Economics of Growth and Prosperity*, New Haven, CT: Yale University Press, 2007.
21. OECD, *Education at a Glance*, 2010; Lochner, L. 'Non-Production Benefits of Education: Crime, Health, and Good Citizenship'. Working Paper 16722, National Bureau of Economic Research, 2011.
22. Causa, O. and Johansson, A. 'Intergenerational Social Mobility', Economics Department Working Paper 707, OECD, 2009; Van der Werfhorst, H. G. and Mijs, J. J. B. 'Achievement inequality and the institutional structure of education systems: a comparative perspective', *Annual Review of Sociology*, 2010, pp. 407–428.

CHAPTER 8 Social Cohesion, Culture Politics and the Impact of Migration

1. Levels, M., Dronkers, J. and Kraaykamp, G. 'Het belang van herkomst en bestemming voor de schoolprestaties van immigranten. Een cross-nationale vergelijking', in F. van Tubergen and I. Maas (eds), *Allochtonen in Nederland in Internationaal Perspectief*, Amsterdam: AUP, 2006; Levels, M. and Dronkers, J. 'Verschillen in wiskundekennis in hoog ontwikkelde landen van Europa, Australië en Nieuw-Zeeland tussen eerste en tweede-generatie migrantenleerlingen uit verschillende herkomstregio's en autochtone leerlingen', in S. Waslander and R. Bosman (eds), *Over kansen, competenties en cohesie*, Assen: Van Gorcum, 2006; Levels, M. and Dronkers, J. 'Educational performance of native and immigrant children from various countries of origin', *Ethnic and Racial Studies*, 31(8), 2008, pp. 1404–1425.
2. Van De Werfhorst, H. G. and Van Tubergen, F. 'Ethnicity, schooling, and merit in the Netherlands', *Ethnicities*, 7(3), 2007, pp. 416–444; Duquet, N., Glorieux, I., Laurijssen, I. and Van Dorsselaer, Y. *Wit krijt schrijft beter: Schoolloopbanen van allochtone jongeren in beeld*, Antwerpen-Apeldoorn: Garant, 2006; Phalet, K., Deboosere, P. and Bastiaenssen, V. 'Old and new inequalities in educational attainment: ethnic minorities in the Belgian census 1991–2001', *Ethnicities*, 7(3), 2007, pp. 390–415.
3. Jonsson, J. O. and Rudolphi, F. 'Weak performance—strong determination: school achievement and educational choice among children of immigrants in Sweden', *European Sociological Review*, 2010.
4. Duquet, N., Glorieux, I., Laurijssen, I. and Van Dorsselaer, Y. *Wit krijt schrijft beter: Schoolloopbanen van allochtone jongeren in beeld*, Antwerpen-Apeldoorn: Garant, 2006.
5. Mark Elchardus, Eva Franck, Saskia De Groof, Dimokritos Kavadias. The acceptance of the multicultural society among young people. A comparative analysis of the effect of market driven versus publicly regulated educational systems. Unpublished manuscript, Vrije Universiteit, Brussels, 2011.
6. Janssens, R., Carlier, D. and Van de Craen, P. 'Het onderwijs in Brussel', *Brussels Studies*, Issue 5, 2009.
7. Sassen, S. *The Global City: New York, London, Tokyo*, Princeton: Princeton UP, 1991.
8. Koopmans, R. 'Trade-offs between equality and difference: immigrant integration, multiculturalism and the welfare state in cross-national perspective', *Journal of Ethnic and Migration Studies*, 36(1), 2010, pp. 1–26.
9. Vinocur, J. *The International Herald Tribune*, 14 December, 2005.

10. FORUM, *Een vreemde in eigen land. Ontevreden autochtone burgers over nieuwe Nederlanders en de overheid*, Amsterdam: AUP, 2010.
11. Schoo, H. J. *De verwarde natie: Dwarse notities over immigratie in Nederland*, Amsterdam: Prometheus, 2000.
12. Elchardus, M. Etnisch vooroordeel als verwerkte kwetsbaarheid, in M. Elchardus and J. Siongers (eds), Vreemden. Naar een cultuursociologische benadering van etnocentrisme. Lannoo Campus, 2009, pp. 61–78; De Groof, S. and Elchardus, M. Kwetsbaarheid, anomie, autoritarisme en etnocentrisme, in M. Elchardus and J. Siongers (eds), Vreemden. Naar een cultuursociologische benadering van etnocentrisme. Lannoo Campus, 2009, pp. 79–98.
13. Hainmueller, J. and Hiscox, M. J. 'Educated preferences: explaining attitudes towards immigration in Europe', *International Organization*, 61(2), 2007, pp. 399–442.
14. Diamond, P. and Radice, G. *Southern Discomfort Again*, London: Policy Network, 2010, pp. 25–35.
15. FORUM, *Een vreemde in eigen land*, 2010.
16. Recent research appears to confirm, on the basis of quantitative data, what the in-depth qualitative analyses had already revealed. Robert Putnam and Lauren McLaren have shown that immigration tends to cause problems of social and political trust and may lead to a decline in social cohesion. See Putnam, R. D. 'E Pluribus Unum: diversity and community in the twenty first century. The 2006 Johann Skytte Prize Lecture', *Scandinavian Political Studies*, 30(2), 2007, pp. 137–174; McLaren, L. M. *Cause for Concern? The impact of immigration on political trust*, London: Policy Network, 2010.
17. Elchardus, M. and Smits, W. *Het grootste geluk*, Leuven: LannooCampus, 2007, pp. 104–124.
18. See Elchardus, M. 'Class, cultural re-alignment and the rise of the populist right', in A. Erskine, M. Elchardus, S. Herkommer and J. Ryan (eds), *Changing Europe: Some aspects of identity, conflict and social justice*, Aldershot: Avebury, 1996; Evans, G. A., Heath, A. F. and Lalljee, M. 'Measuring left-right and libertarian-authoritarian values in the British electorate', *The British Journal of Sociology*, 47(1), 1996, pp. 93–112; Evans, G. A. and Heath, A. F. 'The measurement of left-right and libertarian-authoritarian values: a comparison of balanced and unbalanced scales', *Quality and Quantity*, 29(2), 1995, pp. 191–206; Stubager, R. 'Education-based group identity and consciousness in the authoritarian-libertarian value conflict', *European Journal of Political Research*, 48(2), 2009, pp. 204–233; Stubager, R. 'Education effects on authoritarian-libertarian values:

a question of socialization', *The British Journal of Sociology*, 59(2), 2008, pp. 327–350; Cuperus, R. *De wereldburger bestaat niet: Waarom de opstand der elites de samenleving ondermijnt*, Amsterdam: Bert Bakker, 2009.

19. Houtman, D., Achterberg, P. and Derks, A. *Farewell to the Leftist Working Class*, New York: Transaction Publishers, 2008.
20. Paul Scheffer, Het land van aankomst. De Bezige Bij, 2007.
21. De Lange, T. *Staat, markt en migrant: De regulering van arbiedsmigratie naar Nederland 1945–2006*, The Hague: Boom Juridische Uitgevers, 2008.
22. Bonjour, S. 'Insider of buitenstaander?', Rotterdam: Tijdschrift Migrantenstudies, 2007, available at: www.kennislink.nl.
23. Vermeulen, H. and Penninx, P. *Immigrant Integration: The Dutch Case*, Amsterdam: Het Spinhuis, 2000.

CHAPTER 9 Identity, Community and the Politics of Recognition

1. This involved Prime Minister Gordon Brown making insulting remarks during the General Election Campaign about a Labour supporter (Mrs Gillian Duffy) who had raised concerns about immigration with him, and these being inadvertently recorded and subsequently broadcast.
2. Lind, M. *Republican Liberty and the Future of the Centre-Left*, London: Policy Network, available at: http://www.policy-network.net/publications_download.aspx?ID=7251, consulted 27.01.12, 2010.
3. Goldthorpe, J. H. *Social Mobility and Class Structure in Modern Britain*, Oxford: Clarendon Press, 1980.
4. Hall, S. 'A Sense of Classlessness', *Universities and Left Review*, 5, 1958, available at: http://www.amielandmelburn.org.uk/collections/ulr/05_26.pdf, consulted 27.01.12.
5. Sennett, R. and Cobb, J. *The Hidden Injuries of Class*, New York: Vintage, 1973.
6. Hoggart, R. *The Uses of Literacy: Aspects of Working Class Life*, London: Chatto & Windus, 1957.
7. For an insightful discussion of the contemporary political implications of these changes see Kelly, G and Pearce, N. 'Wanted: an old, new left', *Prospect*, available at: http://www.prospectmagazine.co.uk/2010/09/wanted-an-old-new-left, consulted 27.01.12, 2010.
8. Denham, J. 'Labour's lost millions revisited', *The Guardian*, available at: http://www.guardian.co.uk/commentisfree/2010/may/13/labour-fairness-denham-election, consulted 27.01.12, 2010.

9. Houtman, D., Achterberg, P. and Derks, A. *Farewell to the Leftist Working Class*, London: Transaction, 2008.
10. Citrin, J. and Sides, J. 'Immigration and the imagined community in Europe and the United States', *Political Studies*, 56(1), 2008, pp. 33–56; and Garner, S. 'Home truths: the white working class and the racialization of social housing', in K. P. Sveinsson (ed.), *Who Cares about the White Working Class?*, London: Runneymede Trust, 2009, pp. 45–50, and 'The Entitled Nation: how people make themselves white in contemporary England', *Sens Public*, available at: http://www.sens public.org/spip.php?article729, consulted 27.01.12, 2010.
11. See, for instance, Pearce, N. 'Fair rules: procedural fairness and public services', in J. Margo and N. Pearce (eds), *Politics for a New Generation: The Progressive Moment*, London: IPPR, 2007.
12. See Kenny, M. 'The political theory of recognition: the case of the white working class', *British Journal of Politics and International Relations*, 2011.
13. Department of Communities and Local Government, *Community Futures Overview*, London: DCLG, 2009.
14. Cowles, J., Garner, S., Lung, B. and Stott, S. *Sources of Resentment, and Perceptions of Ethnic Minorities among Poor White People in England*, London: National Community Forum/Department for Communities and Local Government, available at: http://www.communities.gov.uk/documents/communities/pdf/1113921.pdf, consulted 27.01.12, 2009.

CHAPTER 10 The Power of European Integration: Choice and Purpose for Centre-Left Politics

1. See, for instance, 'Ansichten über die Europäische Vereinigung', Survey published by the Konrad-Adenauer-Stiftung, October 2010; Survey by Infratest dimap of 20 May 2011 on 'Political parties and the Euro'. Also see results of the elctions to the European Parliament, despite their contested meaning: the past two decades have shown a steady increase of the relative majority of the centre-right group (EPP) whereas the share of the centre-left (PES) has continously declined.
2. For an informative and well-referenced account, see Dimitrakopoulos, D. G. 'Introduction: social democracy, European integration and preference formation', in D. G. Dimitrakopoulos (ed.), *Social Democracy and European Integration*, London: Routledge, 2011.
3. Dimitrakopoulos, 2011, pp. 5–6.
4. Gustavsson, S. 'European transnational constitutionalism: end of history, or a role for legitimate opposition?', in E. Özdalga and S. Persson (eds),

Contested Sovereignties. Forms of Government and Democracy in Eastern and European Perspectives. London: I.B.Tauris, 2010.

5. Hay, C. 'Globalisation, 'EU-isation' and the space for social democratic alternatives: pessimism of the intellect: a reply to Coates', *British Journal of Politics and International Relations*, 2002.
6. Kriesi, H., Grande, E., Lachat, R., Dolezal M., Bornschier S., Frey T. 'West European Politics in the Age of Globalization', Cambridge: Cambridge University Press, 2008.
7. Bartolini, S. 'Political parties, ideology and Populism, in the post-crisis Europe', discussion paper presented at the 8th Annual European Seminar of ELIAMEP 'Adjusting to the Crisis: Policy Choices and Politics in Europe', Poros, 7–10 July 2011.
8. See for example O'Rourke, K. H. 'A Tale of Two Trilemmas', Institute for New Economic Thinking, 2011, p. 14f.
9. See Moschonas, G. 'Reformism in a 'conservative' system: the European Union and social democratic identity', in J. Callaghan, N. Fishman, B. Jackson, M. McIvor. (eds), *In search of Social Democracy, Responses to Crisis and Modernisation,* Manchester University Press, 2009.
10. Moschonas, Reformism in a conservative system, p. 181ff. Also Scharpf, F. 'Solidarität statt Nibelungentreue', *Berliner Republik*, 2010.
11. Scharpf, F. 'Monetary Union, Fiscal Crisis and the Preemption of Democracy', LEQS Annual Lecture Paper, London School of Economics, May 2011.
12. Runciman, D. 'Socialism in One Country', London Review of Books, 2011.
13. OECD aggregate data of social expenditures between 1980 and 2007.
14. Monti, M. 'A new Strategy for the Single Market', Report to the President of the European Commision, May 2010.
15. Hacker, J. S. and Pierson, P. *Winner-Take-All Politics: How Washington Made the Rich Richer – and Turned its Back on the Middle Class*, Simon & Schuster, USA, 2010.
16. Vandenbroucke, F., Hemerijck, A. and Palier, B. 'The EU Needs a Social Investment Pact', Opinion Paper, Observatoire Socia Européen, May 2011.
17. Koll, W. and Hallwirth, V. 'Strengthening the Macroeconomic Dialogue to tackle economic imbalances within Europe', in A. Watt and A. Botsch (eds), *After the Crisis: towards a Sustainable Growth Model*, Brussels: ETUI, 2010.

18. See, for instance, Rixen, T. and Uhl, S. 'Europeanising Company Taxation – Regaining National Tax Policy Autonomy', Friedrich-Ebert Stiftung, 2007.

CHAPTER 11 Back to the Future: Towards a Red-Green Politics

1. Available at: http://www.neweconomics.org/publications/21-hours.

CHAPTER 12 Globalisation challenges to Centre-Left Internationalism

1. See Chapter 1, Diamond, P. 'From Fatalism to Fraternity: Governing Purpose and the Good Society'.
2. Held, D. and McGrew, A. *Globalisation/Anti-Globalisation*. Cambridge: Polity Press, 2007.
3. Interview given to the Swedish writer Kay Glans for the Glasshouse Forum.
4. In a report for the Financial Times, available at: http://www.ft.com/cms/s/0/fd54377c-f104-11df-bb17-00144feab49a.html#axzz1NNYWUWAE.
5. Quoted in ibid. FT report above.
6. See Jacomb, M. *Europhiles risk ignoring the jobless tide*, The Financial Times, 19 Dec, 2010.
7. Bobbitt, P. *Terror and Consent*, London: Penguin, 2008.
8. See speech by Blair, T. *Chicago Council on Global Affairs*, Apr 23, 2009. Available at http://www.tonyblairoffice.org/speeches/entry/tony-blair-speech-to-chicago-council-on-global-affairs, consulted 27.01.12.

CHAPTER 13 The Squeezed Middle and the New Inequality

1. Clinton, B. 'The struggle for the soul of the 21st century', *DLC Blueprint Magazine*, 15 November 2001, available at: http://www.dlc.org/ndol_ci.cfm?&kaid=124&subid=307&contentid=3917, consulted 27.01.12.
2. ONS. *Economic Review*, 2010, p. 12, available at: http://www.ons.gov.uk/ons/rel/elmr/economic-and-labour-market-review/no--8--august-2010/economic-review.pdf, consulted 27.01.12.
3. Krugman, P. *Conscience of a Liberal*, New York/London: W. W. Norton & Company, 2007.
4. Reich, R. *Supercapitalism*, New York: Knopf, 2007.
5. Bernstein, J. *Crunch*, San Francisco: Berrett-Koehler, 2008.
6. HMRC, 'Tax and NIC receipts and taxpayers', available at: http://www.hmrc.gov.uk/stats/tax_receipts/menu.htm, consulted 27.01.12.

7. Internal HMT figures.
8. Parliamentary answers to Liam Byrne MP, 24 January 2011.
9. HMT, Pre-Budget Report, 2009, p187, available at: http://www.hm-treasury.gov.uk/pbr_archive.htm, consulted 27.01.12.
10. Reinhart, C. M. and Rogoff, K. S. *This Time Is Different: Eight Years of Financial Folly*, Princeton, 2009.
11. Second Bagehot Lecture, Buttonwood Gathering, New York City, 'Banking: From Bagehot to Basel, and Back Again', 25 October 2010, available at: http://www.bankofengland.co.uk/publications/speeches/2010/speech455.pdf, consulted 27.01.12. King later points out that this overstates the size of the banking sector.
12. Reinhart, *This Time Is Different*, 2009.
13. Roubini, N. *Crisis Economics: A Crash Course in the Future of Finance*, Allen Lane, 2010, p. 18.
14. King, M. Second Bagehot Lecture, Buttonwood Gathering, New York City, 'Banking: From Bagehot to Basel, and Back Again', 25 October 2010, available at: http://www.bankofengland.co.uk/publications/speeches/2010/speech455.pdf, consulted 27.01.12.
15. King, M. 'Banking: From Bagehot to Basel, and Back Again', p. 4.
16. McKinsey & Co. 'Debt and deleveraging: the global credit bubble and its economic consequences', p. 20, available at: http://www.mckinsey.com/mgi/publications/debt_and_deleveraging/index.asp, consulted 27.01.12.
17. Sorkin, A. R. *Too Big to Fail: Inside the Battle to Save Wall Street*, Allen Lane, 2009, p. 529.
18. Krugman, P. 'The Slump Goes On: Why?', *New York Review of Books*, 2010, available at: http://www.nybooks.com/articles/archives/2010/sep/30/slump-goes-why, consulted 27.01.12.
19. McKinsey & Co. 'Debt and deleveraging: the global credit bubble and its economic consequences', p. 13.
20. Goldman Sachs. Global Paper 170, 'The Expanding Middle', p3. Goldman Sachs define middle class as those with incomes of $6,000–$30,000 per year.
21. DeLong, B. and Cohen, S. *The End of Influence*, Basic, 2010.
22. Available at: www.economist.com/debate/days/view/541, consulted 27.01.12.
23. 'Public support for increased trade, except with South Korea and China', The Pew Research Center for the People & the Press, November 2010,

available at: http://www.people-press.org/2010/11/09/public-support-for-increased-trade-except-with-south-korea-and-china, consulted 27.01.12.

24. Pew Global Attitudes Survey, June 2008, p. 18, available at: www.pewglobal.org/files/pdf/260.pdf, consulted 27.01.12.
25. Putnam, R. *Bowling Alone*. p. 184.
26. Sen, A. 'The standard of living', in G. Hawthorn (ed.), *The Standard of Living*, Cambridge: Cambridge University Press, 1987, p. 36.

CHAPTER 14 Citizen Engagement and the Quest for Solidarity

1. Including theorists ranging from Fukuyama to Dahrendorf.
2. Measured by which party held the Prime Minister's office (or that of the President in the case of France) in West Germany/Germany, UK, France, Spain, Italy, Portugal, Belgium, the Netherlands, Greece and Sweden.
3. See Giddens, A. *The Third Way*, Cambridge: Polity Press, 1999 and *The Third Way & Its Critics*, Cambridge: Polity Press, 2000 and Tam, H. 'What is the third way', *The Responsive Community*, Summer, 2001.
4. These arguments can be found in Cramme, O and Diamond, P. *Social Justice in the Global Age*, Cambridge: Polity Press, 2009; Tam H. (ed.), *Progressive Politics in the Global Age*, Cambridge: Polity Press, 2001; Baker, D., Epstein, G. and Pollin, R. *Globalization and Progressive Economic Policy*, Cambridge: Cambridge University Press, 1998.
5. On how the presentation of public policies can affect public attitudes see Chong, D. and Druckman, J. N. 'Framing theory', *Annual Review of Political Science*, 10, 2007, pp. 103–126.
6. Bachman, J. G., Johnston, L. D. and O'Malley, P. M. *Monitoring the Future: Questionnaire Responses from the Nation's High School Seniors, 1990*, Ann Arbor, MI: Institute for Social Research, 1993.
7. Luxembourg Income Study, available at: www.lisproject.org, 9 June 2003.
8. See Soss, J. and Schram, S. F. 'A public transformed? Welfare reform as policy feedback', *American Political Science Review*, 101, 2007, pp. 111–127.
9. Here see Quentin Skinner's argument that it is perfectly consistent to maintain that we should each protect our own 'negative' liberty and seek to bind ourselves by collective constraints to make us act together so as to defend that liberty which each of us values individually but could not secure separately. See Skinner, Q. 'On justice, the common good and the

priority of liberty', in C. Mouffe (ed.), *Dimensions of Radical Democracy*, London: Verso, 1992.

10. The notion of 'facilitated communication' has parallels with but is not identical to Habermas's thinking on ideal communicative conditions, or Rorty's ideas on practical persuasion. See my chapter on co-operative enquiry in Tam, H. *Communitarianism*, Basingstoke: Macmillan, 1998.
11. Donkin, A., Goldblatt, P. and Lynch, K. 'Inequalities in life expectancy by social class 1972–1999', *Health Statistics Quarterly*, 52, 2002, pp. 15–19.
12. Rose, G. and Marmot, M. 'Social class and coronary heart disease', *British Heart Journal*, 45, 1981, pp. 13–19.
13. Ross, N. and Dorling, D., Dunn, J. R, et al. 'Metropolitan income inequality and working age mortality', *Journal of Urban Health*, in R. Wilkinson, *The Impact of Inequality*, London: Routledge, 2005.

    It was hardly surprising that when Hurricane Katrina hit New Orleans, the city with the worst income inequalities in America, the rich had by and large moved out of the city, and the poor were left behind to suffer the devastation. Nearly 2,000 people died, and thousands remained displaced from their homes five years after the disaster.
14. Report by the World Health Organisation's Commission on the Social Determinants of Health, 2008.
15. Daly, M., Wilson, M. and Vasdev, S. 'Income inequality and homicide rates in Canada and the United States', *Canadian Journal of Criminology*, 43, 2001, pp. 219–236.
16. Fajnzylber, P., Lederman, D. and Loayza, N. 'Inequality and violent crime', *Journal of Law and Economics*, 45(I), 2002, pp. 1–40.
17. Neapolitan, J. L. 'A comparative analysis of nations with low and high levels of violent crime', *Journal of Criminal Justice*, 27(3), 1999, pp. 259–274.
18. The £1 billion benefit fraud estimate came from the Department of Work and Pensions, the £100 billion tax avoidance and evasion figure is based on calculations by the Tax Justice Network (the Treasury has separately estimated the tax gap to be between £97 billion and £150 billion).
19. According to 'An Anatomy of Economic Inequality in the UK', 2010, Pakistani and Bangladeshi Muslim men and Black African Christian men, for example, were predicted to earn around 13–21% less than British White men who have similar qualifications and other relevant characteristics; while Chinese men could expect to suffer a pay penalty of 11%.
20. For an overview of the threat posed by power inequalities, see Tam, H. *Against Power Inequalities*, London: Birkbeck College, 2010, available at: http://www.equalitytrust.org.uk/resources/against-power-inequalities.

21. For a consideration of Fishkin's approach, see Fishkin, J. and Laslett, P. *Debating Deliberating Democracy*, Oxford: Blackwell Publishing, 2003.
22. Siriani, C. and Friedland, L. *Civic Innovation in America*, Berkeley: University of California Press, 2001.
23. See Singh, K. 'Handing over the stick: the global spread of participatory approaches to development', in M. Edwards and J. Gaventa (eds), *Global Citizen Action*, Boulder: Lynne Rienner Publishers, 2001.
24. See Selee, A. 'Deliberative Approaches to Governance in Latin America', 2008, available at: http://www.deliberative-democracy.net.
25. The 2006 cross-government report 'Together We Can' set out what each Secretary of State of the Government considered the key achievements in empowering citizens to shape their respective policies.
26. See Westen, D. *The Political Brain*, New York: Public Affairs, 2007; Frank, T. *What's the Matter with America?* London: Vintage Books, 2006; Duncombe, S. *Dream: Re-imaging Progressive Politics in the Age of Fantasy*, New York: The New Press, 2007.

CHAPTER 15 Co-operation, Creativity and Equality: Key Concepts for a New Social Democratic Era

1. Reich, R. *Aftershock: The Next Economy and America's Future*, New York: Knopf, 2010, p. 8.
2. On this see Marquand, D. 'After progress', in P. Diamond and R. Liddle (eds), *Beyond New Labour: The Future of Social Democracy in Britain*, London: Politico's, 2009, pp. 3–16.
3. See Palmgren, H. *Olof Palme: Vor uns liegen wunderbare Tage – Die Biografie*, München: btb Verlag, 2010, p. 339. Also see Petritsch, W. *Bruno Kreisky – Die Biografie*, Wien: Residenz Verlag, 2010; Merseburger, P. *Willy Brandt 1913–1992: Visionär und Realist*, München: DVA, 2002.
4. Brandt, Willy. German federal election campaign, 1969.
5. Mazower, M. *The Dark Continent: Europe's Twentieth Century*, London: Penguin, 1999.
6. Palmgren, *Olof Palme*, 2010.
7. See Hennis, W., Kielmansegg, P. G. and Matz, U. *Regierbarkeit: Studien zu ihrer Problematisierung*, Stuttgart, 1977.
8. Lutz, B. *Der kurze Traum immerwährender Prosperität: Eine Neuinterpretation der industriell-kapitalistischen Entwicklung im Europa des 20,* Jahrhundert, Frankfurt am Main: Campus, 1984.

9. Habermas, J. *Die Krise des Wohlfahrtsstaates und die Erschöpfung utopischer Energien, in: ders., Die neue Unübersichtlichkeit*, Frankfurt am Main: Suhrkamp, 1985, pp. 141–163.
10. See Winkler, H. A. *Geschichte des Westens: Von den Anfängen der Antike bis zum 20. Jahrhundert*, München: Beck, 2009.
11. Habermas, J. *Die Moderne – ein unvollendetes Projekt, in: ibid., Zeitdiagnosen: 12 Essays*, Frankfurt am Main: Suhrkamp, 2003 (first published 1981).
12. Habermas, J. *Die Krise des Wohlfahrtsstaates*, 1985, p. 143.
13. Judt, T. *Ill Fares the Land: A Treatise on Our Present Discontents*, London: Allen Lane, 2010, p. 210.
14. Giddens, A. *The Politics of Climate Change*, London: Polity, 2009, p. 228.
15. See Beck, U. *Anthony Giddens and Scott Lash, Reflexive Modernization: Politics, Tradition and Aesthetics in the Modern Social Order*, London: Polity Press, 1994.
16. Wilkinson, R. and Pickett, K. *The Spirit Level: Why Equality is Better for Everyone*, London: Allen Lane, 2009.
17. Wilkinson and Pickett, *The Spirit Level*, 2009, p. 247.
18. Ibid., p. 270.

CHAPTER 16 Afterword: The New Social Democracy?

1. Andrew Gamble, The Spectre at the Feast: Capitalist Crisis and the Politics of Recession, London: Palgrave Macmillan.
2. David Coates, 2000, Models of Capitalism: Growth and Stagnation in the Modern Era, Cambridge: Polity Press; Donald Sassoon, 1996, One Hundred Years of Socialism: The West European Left in the Twentieth Century, London: Fontana Books.

Index

A

American consumer, 213
Anglo-American neo-liberalism, 251
Anti-immigrant sentiment, 78
  Welfare states and, 78
Anti-market dogmatism, 39
Anti-migrant groups, 78
Anti-migrant movement, shift towards, 77–78
Anti-Muslim parties, 125, 140
Anti-Muslim sentiment, 140
Anti-Semitism, 142
Arab League, 199
Argentina, globalisation in, 31
Asian crisis, 210
Assertive/relevant policy agenda
  Quest for, 172–174
Atlantic alliance, 254
Atomic weapon, 200
Aufbauära, 240
Australia, socioeconomic status and life expectancy, 225
Austria
  Progress in, 236
  Social democratic project across, 8

B

Banking crises, 210
Barber, Tony, 193
Beck, Ulrich, 81
Benefits, 83
Berlin Wall, fall of, 219
Big Society programme, 84, 217
BNP Paribas, 211
Bonus culture in investment banks, 71–72
Bottom-up internationalism, 37
Britain
  Capital and revenue resources in, 225
  Economic success, 207
  Eurobarometer poll (2001) of, 221–222
  Health, education and police services, 206
  Income inequality in, 221
  Markets mechanics, centre-left predicament, 63
  'More regulation' mantra in, 66
  Neo-conservative regime in, 226
  Racial discrimination in, 226
  Social democratic project across, 8
  Socioeconomic status and life expectancy, 225
  Trade union movement in, 29
British economy
  Imbalances and dependency, 214
British Labour Government, 187
British Labour Party, 63
British Liberal Democratic Party, 190
Brown's Government
  Global financial crisis, 177
Bureaucratic discretion, 105

C

Canada
  Socioeconomic status and life expectancy, 225
Capitalism, structural transformation of, 252–253
Capitalist economy
  Economic competence, 52
  Economic development models, 63
  Europe, 1970s crisis of, 4
Capitalist success, 187
Care responsibilities damage, 77
Centrally directed economic systems, 62
Centre-left governments, 203
Centre-left politics, 169
Child care centres, 118
China
  Boom in world trade, 204
  Productive capacity, 214

Christian democracy, 75, 78
  Status-protection, 75, 79
Christian democratic parties, 79
Christian democratic pro-family parties (CDU), 136
Civil society approaches, 84
Class-based 'majoritarian' social democracy, 12
Climate change, 254
  Centre-right approach to, 178
  Challenge of, 180
  Impact on daily lives, 80
  Inter-Governmental Panel on, 80
Colonialism, European legacy of, 137
Colorado Communities Health Initiative, 228
Common Consolidated Corporate Tax Base, European Commission's proposals, 174
Communist manifesto, 191
Community-based organisations (CBOs), 230–233. *See also* Social democratic activism
Community method, 168
Community policies, 87
'Compassionate', 175
Conservative–Liberal Democrat coalition, 89
Corporate governance practices, 112
Corporatism
  Labour market and, 79
Corruption, 104, 105
  Nigeria, 101
  Pakistan, 102
Crisis, progress in
  Catch-up modernisation, 237
  Centre-left parties, reaction of, 241
  Civilisational/ecological disasters of 20th century, 239
  Demographic changes, factors for, 240–241
  Economic dynamism and material inequality, 240
  European *Aufbauära* experience, 240
  Humanity, altered view of, 240
  Long-term impact, 239
  Marginalised positive development, 239
  Market hegemony, 239
  Neo-liberal turn of late-1970s, 238
  New hegemonic zeitgeist, 240
  Oil price shock of 1973, 237–238
  Politics as ideological struggle, 238
  'Post-industrial society,' transition into, 240–241
  Post-war boom, end of, 237–238
  Social and political transformation, 237
  Social democrats view on, 239
  Trickle-down effect, 240
  Western political culture, 238–239
  Western societies, 'ungovernability' of, 237
Crunch, 205
C2s, 203, 206
Cultural diversification, 145
Cultural explanations, 130, 131
Cultural nationalism, 166

D

'Deleveraging', 213
Deliberative engagement
  Advantages of, 230
  Capital projects, involvement in, 229–230
  Civil renewal and community empowerment, 229
  Consensus Conferences for, 228
  Deliberative Opinion Polls for civic decision, 228
  Key elements for, 227–228
  Neighbourhood management initiative, 229
  Participatory budgeting technique, 229
  Public policy development and, 228
Demand
  Social spending and, 79
Democratic Party, 190
Democratic reforms, 91
DE worker, 206
Disposable income
  Treasury analysis of, 204
Diversity, vibrant, 138–140
Dutch Institute for Multicultural Affairs, 133
Dutch language, 130

E

Economic activities, 160
Economic and employment strategies, 82
Economic and Monetary Union (EMU), 158
  Financial crisis, 173

Economic competence
Centre-left strategies
Aim of, 46
Distinctions between, 46
Markets, 49–50
Planning, 47–48
Social democracy, 46
Welfare, 48–49
Dependent factors, 45
Economic security/opportunity indicators, 45
Economy management, framework for, 58–59
Financialisation as strategy, 58
Golden age, illusory hopes of
Economy, neo-liberal framework, 50–51
International economy in 1990s, 50–51
Social democratic governments and 2008 crisis, 51
Sweden/US, recessions in, 51
Market complementing
Deficit reduction strategy in US, 55–56
Green growth, programmes for, 56
Monetary and fiscal interventions combination, 55
in Recession, 55
Regions/sectors, targeted assistance to, 56
Market conforming
Constraints, working within, 55
Drawback of, 55
Socialism and, 54–55
Treasury View, endorsement of, 54–55
Market resisting and market substituting
Capital/labour/goods, controls on, 56–57
Currency union divisions, 57
National protectionism, 56–57
Market transforming
Drawback of, 58
Public into private, 58
Radical decentralisation and redistribution, 58
Moral and political economy, 51
Big government and centre-left, 52
Capitalist economy, progression in, 52
Centre-left's reasons for, 53–54
Deficit financing, necessity of, 53
Government role and spending levels, 53
Hayekians and Keynesians dispute, 52–53
in Public and private sectors, 52
Political success, component of, 45
Economic competition, globalisation, 76
Economic crisis, 79
Europe, 81, 223
Global, 1, 36
Mid-1970s, 10, 251
Pressures of, 80
State borrowing and, 79
Economic equality, 96, 103
Economic globalisation, 78
Economic growth, 120–121, 183, 203
by Education, 121
Employment, 13
Goal of, 80
Green agenda, 91
in High income countries, 183
Market-driven, 109
Model of, 15
Opportunity, 45
Success in achieving, 63
and Technological progress, 236
Economic inequality
Focus on, 23
Measures of, 95
Economic insecurity, 205
Economic liberalism, 163
Economic protectionism, 166
Economic theory, 109
Economy of favours, 245
Education
Economic growth, 121
Employment by, 119
Intergenerational mobility, 117
Reform, 13–14
Secondary and tertiary completion, 115
System, 127
Features of, 140
Educational failure, problems of, 128
Educational performance, 127
Electoral coalition, 178
Electoral defeat, analyses of, 203
Electoral success, 175
Embourgeoisement, 145
Employers' ability, 119
Employment, 118–120
by Education, 119
Strategies, economic, 82

Equality
Competition and performance, 245
Economic resources/social status, 97
Education policy/family policy, 244
Employee's personal benefit and, 245–246
Ideology, transformation of, 244
Immigration and integration policies, 244
Individualism and competition, 244
Inequalities, economies with, 244
Mutual aid and 'economy of favours,' 245
Problem of, 97–98
Reciprocity, 99–102
Social instability and, 244
Society as community, 243
Stay clear of paternalism, 108–109
Tax policy/economic policy, 244
Workplace environment and productivity, 244–245
Equality-enhancing policies, 101
Ethnic diversification, 145
Ethnic prejudice, 142
Eurobarometer data, 193
Europe
Boom in world trade, 204
British politics and Thatcherism
Conservative Party, cultural shift of, 21
Electoral dominance, reasons for, 21
Electoral opinion surveys in 80s/90s, 20
Thatcherite Conservatism, advent of, 20
20th British Social Attitudes Survey (2003), 222
26th British Social Attitudes Survey (2010), 222
Centre-left renaissance, prospect of, 1–2
Citizenship Survey, 222
Completion of, 196
Cultural conflicts in, 253–254
Economic crisis and political tide in, 1
Immigration trauma, 125
Integration failure in, 126
Closed labour markets, 128–129
Overstretched education systems, 126–127
Market-friendly policies in, 35
Neighbourhood Management initiative, 229
New social democratic reckoning
Public expenditure management, 22
Thatcherite approach, potency of, 21–22
World economy, shape, 22
Political economy and common good
Corporate governance models, 22–23
Deep global recession, strategy for, 22
Economic inequality, focus on, 23
Income volatility, 23
Management and workers, power imbalance, 22–23
New growth theory, 23–24
Regulated competitive markets, 24
Swedish Meidner Plan, 23
Politics of nostalgia and politics of despair
Economic liberalism and, 2–3
Existing ideals/institutions preservation, 3–4
in 'Golden age,' 2–3
Neo-liberalism, efficacy of, 3
Post-war Attlee Government, 2–3
Third way social democracy, 2–3
Weakness of, 3
Welfare state and social protection expenses, 3
Post-war social democracy, 2
Regulatory capture in, 70
Single European capital market in, 71
Social democracy, electoral performance, 1–2
Capitalist crisis in 1970s, 4
Centre-left, governance of, 4
Doctrinal modernisation process, 5
European market, integration of, 4
Germany, SPD in, 5
Globalisation, rise of, 5–6
Ideological revisionism, 4
Material interests clash, 6
Neo-liberal globalisation, 4
PvdA in the Netherlands, 5
Socialist Party (PS) in France, 4
Social solidarity decline, 5–6
Swedish SAP, 5
Social democratic project
in Britain and Austria, 8
British Labour Party and, 8
Centre-left parties, historical experience of, 10
Divergent traditions, sweep of, 7
Economic efficiency and social justice, impact on, 9
France, state-centric model in, 8–9
German model, 8–9

Market and state, relationship between, 10
New Labour's globalised model, 8–9
Policy shift and values dilution, 10
Politics, interpretation of, 11
in Scandinavia, 8
Second World War end, 8
Social inclusion, 9–10
in Sweden, 8
Traditional social democratic parties, 9–10
European banking system, 210
European Central Bank (ECB), 168
European centre-left parties, 134, 165
European Commission, 168
European countries, public expenditure, 90
European Court of Justice, 164
European Economic Community (EEC), 159
European electorates, 163
European GDP, 170
European governments
Fiscal policy, 158
Taxation, 158
European immigration societies, 137
European integration, 166
Europeanisation, 164
European labour movement, 189
European Market, 76
European Parliament, 168
European policymaking, 162
European social democracy, 88
European societies, 125, 126
European Union
Centre-left politics, 169
Conservative system, 168
Demarcation *vs.* integration, 169
Electoral and political liability, 162
Fundamental moment, 158
Future of, 195–198
Jurisdiction, role of, 163
Living constitution, 163
Macro-economic co-ordination mechanism, 173
Political alignment of, 156
Political emotions/ideological contention, 157
Politics choice and purpose in, 169–171
Post-sovereign-debt-crisis, 167
Protector against globalisation, 161
Regulatory authority, 167
Renewed Social Agenda, 81
Social democratic politics, weakness of, 159
Social Investment Pact, 172
Social policy, 164
European welfare state. *See also* Welfare state settlement
Economic crisis, 81
Extreme right, rise of, 77–78
Immigrants, 129
Settlement, defending, 78–81
Social democracy, 75–91
Uncertain future, 85
European welfare systems, 83
Europe's post-industrial societies, 126
Euro-zone crisis, 72
of Sovereign indebtedness, 157

F

Faith schools, 128
Fed, interest rates, 210
Federazione Ipiegati Operai Metallurgici (FIOM), 189
Financial crisis
2008–9, 75
Fiscal policy, 158
Flexicurity, 119–120
France
Recession, 89
Sarkozy's pension reforms in, 223
Social democracy, electoral performance
Socialist Party (PS) in, 4
State-centric model in, 8–9
Freedom Party, 78
Free market, 65–66
French model of *laïcité*, 140
French Revolution and progress, 238–239

G

Gender equality
in Workplace, 87
The General Theory, 53
German bank IKB, 211
Germany
Pew Global Attitudes Survey (2007) in, 222–223
Progress in, 236
Recession, 89

Germany (*Continued*)
Social democracy, electoral performance, 5
Social democratic project across German model, 8–9
Gini coefficient, 112
Global growth, 213
Globalisation, 63, 77, 251
Centre-left failed, 179
Challenges to centre-left internationalism, 187–201
of Economic competition, 76
European Union, future of, 195–198
Global security, 198–201
Immigration and integration, 193–195
Implications of, 161
Imposition on European countries, 195
Politics of, 188–193
as Protector, 161
as Threat, 77
Winners and losers of, 132–133
Globalisation Adjustment Fund, 165
Global North–South divide, 85
Global security, 198–201
Global social democracy. *See also* Social democracy
American unilateralism, rejection of, 36
Bilateralism and multilateralism, 36
British Social Attitudes surveys, 33–34
Citizenship/constitutional power/democracy, 33
Europe, market-friendly policies in, 35
Financial crisis, responses to, 35
Global fora, 33, 36
International problems in, 32–33
Latin America, image of, 33–34
Lula's Workers' Party in Brazil, 35
Nuclear proliferation, nations' view on, 36
Obama, reflationary approach of, 36
Rich countries, immigration in, 34
Social and cultural bases for, 33–34
Social democrats' responsibility, 33
World trade/climate change talks, nations role in, 34
World values surveys, 34
Global welfare
Aid efforts, 85
Idealist politics of, 85–86
Goldthorpe, John, 145
Government institutions, 104
Gramsci, Antonio, 152–153
The Great Risk Shift, 15
Green growth, 56
Green New Deal, 162

H

Hall, Stuart, 145–146
Hoggart, Richard, 146
Homo economicus, 99
Human nature, understanding of, 99–102
Hungarian parliament, 78
Hussein, Saddam, 199–200

I

Ill Fares the Land, 241
Immigrants, 126. *See also* Migrants
and Low-skilled workers, conflict between, 79–80
Welfare states and, 78
Immigration, 141, 193
Integrated, 194
Muslim, 194
Trauma, 125
Wealthy states, 195
Incentives, individual
Social democracy, 82–84
Strengths and weaknesses, 83–84
Income-distribution, 76
Income inequality, 111–114
Aspects of, 112
by Education, 113
Education, relationship, 113
India
Boom in world trade, 204
Production base, 214
Individual incentives, focus on, 82–84
Strengths and weaknesses, 83–84
Industrial policy, 213
Institutional design, social trust, 103–106
Institutional trap, 168
Interest-based political mobilisation, 96
Intergenerational mobility, 116
Education, 117
in Sweden and Finland, 116
Inter-Governmental Panel on Climate Change, 80
Internationalism, 32
Inter-related social trends, 144–145
Intragenerational mobility, 120
Ireland, markets mechanics in, 67
Ireland's system, 211

Islam
Islamic identity, 140
Islamic radicalism, 253
Islamist terrorism, 194, 200
Solely extremist positions, 140
Islamophobia, 142
Italy, Pew Global Attitudes Survey (2007) in, 222–223

J

Japanese bubble, 72
Jewish communities, 194
Jobbik, 78

K

Kevin Rudd's Labor Government, financial crisis, 177
Knowledge-based growth, 82
Knowledge intensive economy, 240–241, 244

L

Labour market
Corporatism and, 79
Integration, 130
Policies, 141
Labour parties, 177
New Labour's globalised model, 8–9
Labour's statecraft, fundamental mistake of, 212
Left-of-centre parties, 197
Liberalisation, 251
Libya, intervention in, 199
Lula's Workers' Party in Brazil, 35

M

Macro-economic conditions, 118
Make work pay programmes, 82, 83
Market capitalism, conflicts of, 75
Market-centred response
to Financial crisis, 88–89
Market complementing
Deficit reduction strategy in US, 55–56
Green growth, programmes for, 56
Monetary and fiscal interventions combination, 55
in Recession, 55
Regions/sectors, targeted assistance to, 56
Market conforming
Constraints, working within, 55
Drawback of, 55
Socialism and, 54–55
Treasury View, endorsement of, 54–55
Market correcting, 165
Market failures, 64
Market resisting
Capital/labour/goods, controls on, 56–57
Currency union divisions, 57
National protectionism, 56–57
Market responses, bankrupt financial institutions, 89
Markets
Aim of, 50
Collectivist social democracy, 50
Emergence of, 49
Pro-market ideology, 49–50
Welfare social democracy and, 50
Markets mechanics
Banking crisis of 2008, 61
Centre-left predicament
Britain, post-war era, 63
Centrally directed economic systems, 62
Economic development, capitalist models, 63
Economic strategies, 62
Market fundamentalism, 63
Nationalisation and bank restructuring, 63
Planned economies, 62
Soviet Union, economic dominance, 62
Western Europe, 62
Corporations/financial markets relationships, 74
Finance, influence of
Anglo-American financial centres, 69
Company regulators, issues with, 70
Conglomerates growth and financial risks, 69
in Continental Europe, 69
Financial markets, herd behaviour in, 72
Investment bankers, importance to, 70
Investment banks, bonus culture in, 71–72
Japanese bubble and Euro-zone crisis, 72
Large companies/financial markets relations, 70–71
Market fundamentalist ideology conflation, 69
Mispricing and market dislocation, 72–73

Markets mechanics (*Continued*)
Public companies, objective of, 71
Ratchet of state intervention, 72–73
Single European capital market in Europe, 71
US and Europe, regulatory capture in, 70
Financial crisis, regulations for, 61–62
Financial services regulation, goals, 73–74
Planning and
Centrally directed economy, 64
Failures of, 64–65
Market fundamentalism, 64
Self-interested individuals in, 64
Pro-market/anti-market positions, 61
Reform, objectives of, 73
Right and market fundamentalism
Britain, 'more regulation' mantra in, 66
Complex modern economies, 65
European financial crisis, 67
Failed financial companies, slush fund for, 66
Free market, 65–66
Investment and retail banking link, 66–67
in Ireland, 67
Postponement, 67
Society, risks in, 65
Universal banking tradition, 66–67
Social markets
Financial innovation, results of, 68–69
Financial system, capital allocation in, 67–68
Market fundamentalism, 68
Strengths and weaknesses, 68
Market substituting
Capital/labour/goods, controls on, 56–57
Currency union divisions, 57
National protectionism, 56–57
Market transforming
Drawback of, 58
Public into private, 58
Radical decentralisation and redistribution, 58
Market wage, 110
Marxist theories, 99
Mass migration, problematic aspects of, 136
May Day, 183
Medicean incomes, 192
Meritocratic homogamy, 132
Micro-economic instruments, 169
Middle-class democracy
Institutional foundation of, 172
Migrants. *See also* Immigrants
Educational opportunities of, 140
Moderate Progress Within the Bounds of the Law, 177
Monopolies, 107
Monti, Mario, 171
Moral desirability, 80
Moral dialogue, 216
Moral economy, 51
Big Government and centre-left, 52
Capitalist economy, progression in, 52
Centre-left's reasons for, 53–54
Deficit financing, necessity of, 53
Government role and spending levels, 53
Hayekians and Keynesians dispute, 52–53
in Public and private sectors, 52
Morality, values and symbols, 181
Moroccans, 131
Multiculturalism
Welfare states and, 78
Muslim youth, violent revolt of, 140

N

National Security Council, 201
Neo-classical economic theory, 96
Neo-Liberal Europeanism, 166
Neo-liberalism, 3, 39
Neo-revisionism
Anglo-American economy, 15
Centre-left ideas, rethinking, 12
Centre-left politics, dilemmas for, 17
Class-based 'majoritarian' social democracy, 12
Core of, 12
Economic insecurity/anxiety addressing, 13
Economic prosperity, rising tide of, 15
Education reform, 13–14
European Union (EU), limitations of, 13
Inclusive economic growth model, 15
Income and wealth inequality, 13
International leadership and policy coordination, 17
Labour market mobility, 14
Manufacturing and service-orientated economy, 15

Modernisation strategies, flaws in, 16
National income, wage share in, 15–16
Nation-state social democracy, challenges to, 16–17
Post-crisis challenges, 17–18
Social liberalism and conservative values, 14
Third way as dominant strategy, 11–12
Netherlands, social democracy in, 5
Netherlands Institute for Social Research (SCP), 131
New Labour's globalised model, 8–9
New social democracy. *See also* Social democracy
Anglo-American neo-liberalism, 251
Anti-market dogmatism, 39
Capitalist system and, 252–253
Centre-left thinking, revitalisation in, 253–254
Cosmopolitan/communitarian interests, conflict between, 253–254
Cultural conflicts, 253–254
Economic efficiency and social justice, 39
Equality
Competition and performance, 245
Education policy/family policy, 244
Employee's personal benefit and, 245–246
Ideology, transformation of, 244
Immigration and integration policies, 244
Individualism and competition, 244
Inequalities, economies with, 244
Mutual aid and 'economy of favours,' 245
Social instability and, 244
Society as community, 243
Tax policy/economic policy, 244
Workplace environment and productivity, 244–245
Financial crisis of 2007–8, 251–252
Global depression since 1930s, 252
Global financial crisis, aftershocks of, 252
Humanitarian crises and, 254
Industrial age production forms, 252–253
Industrial strategy enforcement, 41
Large-scale bureaucracies and citizen disengagement, 253
Market and state, interpenetration of, 39
Marketisation of UK, 41
Modern patriotism and internationalism, 254
National economies, regulation/rebalancing of, 41
Neo-liberalism, 39
Dominance of, 251–252
Post-1945 social democracy, 251
in Post-war era, 252
Public sphere, market logic in, 40–41
Reformist élan, exhaustion of, 235
Social progress concept, 235. *See also* Progress
State power, dependence on, 253
'Third way modernisers' and democrats, 251
UK higher education, case of, 40
Nigeria, corruption, 101
Nisbett, Robert, 116
Nostalgia, 134

O

Oil price shock of 1973, 237–238
Opportunity-centred social democracy, 81–82. *See also* Social democracy

P

Participatory budgeting technique, 229
Party of European Socialists (PES), 168
Peace, 165
Peak oil, 179
Pensions
Reforms to, 83
Pew Global Attitude Surveys, 215
Philip Snowden solution. *See* Market conforming
PISA's standardised tests
of Secondary school pupils, 127
Planning, 62
Centrally directed economy, 64
Collectivist political economy, forms of, 47–48
Economic competence and, 47–48
Failures of, 64–65
Free market capitalism, 47
in Industrial societies, 47
Market fundamentalism, 64
Market mechanisms replacement, 47
Productive assets, substantial public ownership, 47
Self-interested individuals in, 64

Policy consequences, 140–142
Policymakers, 160
Political challenge
Reframing, 176–177
Political correctness
Cocoon of, 136–137
Political disaffection, 203
Political economy, 51
Big Government and centre-left, 52
Capitalist economy, progression in, 52
Centre-left's reasons for, 53–54
Common good and
Corporate governance models, 22–23
Deep global recession, strategy for, 22
Economic inequality, focus on, 23
Income volatility, 23
Management and workers, power imbalance, 22–23
New growth theory, 23–24
Regulated competitive markets, 24
Swedish Meidner Plan, 23
Deficit financing, necessity of, 53
Government role and spending levels, 53
Hayekians and Keynesians dispute, 52–53
in Public and private sectors, 52
Political equality, 103
Political inequality
Measures of, 95
Political institutions, design of, 96
Political legitimacy, 98
The Politics of Climate Change, 242–243
Portugal, Eurobarometer poll (2001) of, 221–222
Positive-sum global growth diplomacy, 213
Poverty, 95
Private health-insurance systems, 109
Privatisation, 63
Procedural justice, 100
Pro-European policy, 168
Progress. *See also* New social democracy
Broad-based progressive coalitions, 247
Co-operation and, 246
and Creativity, 246–247
in Crisis
Catch-up modernisation, 237
Centre-left parties, reaction of, 241
Civilisational/ecological disasters of 20th century, 239
Demographic changes, factors for, 240–241
Economic dynamism and material inequality, 240
European *Aufbauära* experience, 240
Humanity, altered view of, 240
Long-term impact, 239
Marginalised positive development, 239
Market hegemony, 239
Neo-liberal turn of late-1970s, 238
New hegemonic zeitgeist, 240
Oil price shock of 1973, 237–238
Politics as ideological struggle, 238
'Post-industrial society,' transition into, 240–241
Post-war boom, end of, 237–238
Social and political transformation, 237
Social democrats view on, 239
Trickle-down effect, 240
Western political culture, 238–239
Western societies, 'ungovernability' of, 237
Cultural/technological/economic transformations, 248
Drawbacks and consequences of, 248
Economic growth and, 235–236
Equality, importance of, 246–247
Future, economy organisation for, 248–249
in Germany/Sweden/Austria, 236
Globalisation and, 247–248
Human power expansion and, 242–243
Party-political machinery, 247
Political systems, desired freedom for, 248–249
Reflexive modernisation notion, 243
Reform era of 1960s/early-1970s, 235–236
Religious fundamentalism and terrorism, 242
Social democratic parties and traditional industrial trade unions, 247–248
Society improvement and, 237
Technocratic and authoritarian, 242
Thinking, teleological style of, 242
Unorthodox/politically independent left, 248
Welfare state reforms, 235–236
Progressive Governance, 188
Progressivism, 235
Progress Party, 193

Public expenditure, 89, 90
  European countries, 90
Public policy, 184
Public sector reform, 251

Q

Quilliam Foundation, 194

R

Racism, 142
Rationalisation
  and Industrial society transformation, 240–241
Reaganomics, 238
Recession, 89
  Market complementing in, 55
  Political economy and common good, strategy for, 22
  in Sweden/US, 51
Reciprocity, 101
  Human orientation, 99–102
Reconciliation, 165
Red-green politics, 175
  Explaining world to people, 177–179
  Persuaders for change, 184–185
  Political challenge, reframing, 176–177
  Returning to our roots, 180–184
  Tripartite strategy, 181
Reflation, 42–43
Reflexive progress, 243
Reform, 238
Reformära, 238
Reformist élan, exhaustion of, 235
Renewed Social Agenda, 81, 258n5
Responsibilities, 82–84
  Decentralising, 84–85
  Social democracy and, 82–84
  Strengths and weaknesses, 83–84
Revisionist social democracy. *See also* Social democracy
  Economic egalitarianism, 18–19
  Equality, structural context, 19
  Fairness and equity norms, 19–20
  Overarching/universal egalitarian principles, 19
  Policy programmes, reformulation of, 18
  Post-war social democracy, 'golden age' of, 18–19
  State capacity and social democracy, 20
  Superficiality, 18
Rights-based thinking, 148
Robin Hood tax, 162

S

Sachs, Goldman, 213
Scandinavia, 139
  Social democratic project across, 8
Scandinavian states, 193
Scandinavian-style preschools, 118
Schnapper, Dominique, 191
Scholars, 161
Self-governing legitimacy, 163
Skill-orientated employment structure, 119
Social bad, 101
Social democracy, 44, 82, 87, 138, 140, 158, 162, 170, 174
  Capital flight, possibility of, 29
  Electoral performance, 1–2
    Capitalist crisis in 1970s, 4
    Centre-left, governance of, 4
    Doctrinal modernisation process, 5
    European market, integration of, 4
    Germany, SPD in, 5
    Globalisation, rise of, 5–6
    Ideological revisionism, 4
    Material interests, 6
    Neo-liberal globalisation, 4
    PvdA in the Netherlands, 5
    Socialist Party (PS) in France, 4
    Social solidarity decline, 5–6
    Swedish SAP, 5
  in Europe, 198
  of Fear, 241
  Global
    American unilateralism, rejection of, 36
    Bilateralism and multilateralism, 36
    British Social Attitudes surveys, 33–34
    Citizenship/constitutional power/democracy, 33
    Europe, market-friendly policies in, 35
    Financial crisis, responses to, 35
    Global fora, 33
    International problems in, 32–33
    Latin America, image of, 33–34
    Lula's Workers' Party in Brazil, 35
    National social democratic parties in power, 34–35
    Nuclear proliferation, nations' view on, 36

Social democracy (*Continued*)
Obama, reflationary approach of, 36
Rich countries, immigration in, 34
Social and cultural bases for, 33–34
Social democrats' responsibility, 33
World trade/climate change talks, nations role in, 34
World values surveys, 34
Global capital and
Argentina and Venezuela, globalisation in, 31
in Developing countries, 31–32
Globalisation, social effects of, 31
Global left, international solidarity across, 32
Inflation and deficits, government control on, 30–31
Internationalism, 32
Mixed economy, shift from, 32
Modernisation as globalisation, 30
Global political rudder
Civil society, governing strategy in, 43
Financial regulation, lack of, 42
Going downwards and going sideways, 43
Ideological identity for, 42
Looking upwards, 43
Modernisation and, 42
Reflation, 42–43
Working-class people, conditions of, 41–42
Guiding values of, 137
as Hybrid ideology
British liberal tradition and labour movement, 6
Class politics, 6
Economic/social liberalism, rise of, 7
Keynesian political economy and redistribution, 6
Neo-conservatism, 7
Welfare universalism, 7
Individual incentives and responsibilities, 82–84
in International politics
Anti-statist approach, 37–38
Associational society, equality and collective provision, 38
Bottom-up internationalism, 37
Conflict-based approaches, 36–37
Formal global governance, 36–37
Ideas/practices for, 38
Justice movements and, 37
National laws building, 37
New social democracy, content of. *See* New social democracy
World capitalism development, 38
Material approach, 86–88
Neo-revisionism, rise of
Anglo-American economy, 15
Centre-left ideas, rethinking, 12
Centre-left politics, dilemmas for, 17
Class-based 'majoritarian' social democracy, 12
Core of, 12
Economic insecurity/anxiety addressing, 13
Economic prosperity, rising tide of, 15
Education reform, 13–14
European Union (EU), limitations of, 13
Inclusive economic growth model, 15
Income and wealth inequality, 13
International leadership and policy coordination, 17
Labour market mobility, 14
Manufacturing and service-orientated economy, 15
Modernisation strategies, flaws in, 16
National income, wage share in, 15–16
Nation-state social democracy, challenges to, 16–17
Post-crisis challenges, 17–18
Social liberalism and conservative values, 14
Third way as dominant strategy, 11–12
in Nordic countries, 79
Opportunity-centred, 81–82
Reorientation of, 220
Revisionist. *See* Revisionist social democracy and state power
Aim of, 27
Centralised bureaucracy effects, 24
Citizen-state relationship, 26
Civic sphere, vibrancy of, 26–27
Economy and social welfare, factors for, 24–25

European republican tradition, 26
Social citizenship rights preservation, 25–26
Trade union movement in UK, 29
Welfare state and, 75–93
Social democratic activism
America, Tea Party movement in, 231
Authentic deliberation, obstacles removing, 232
CBOs, development of, 230–231
Citizens' concerns and collective institutions, 230
Civic solidarity as sole concern, 233
Collective action, priorities for, 233
Europe, right-wing/populist movements, 231
Fair elections and deliberative engagement, 232
People's concerns, emotional connections with, 231
Policy objectives, fragmentation of, 231–232
Progressive consensus building, 230
Reform ideas, formulation of, 232
Risk in, 231–232
and 'State-shrinking' politics, 233
Subsidiarity, principle of, 231–232
Social democratic critics, 168
Social democratic electoral success, 187
Social democratic encounter, with diversity, 134–136
Social democratic heritage, 139
Social democratic parties, 189
Response of, 125
Working-class electorate of, 135
Social democratic policy
Failure of, 161
Key components of, 122
Social democratic politics
EU predicaments, 162–169
European integration, economic logic of, 163–165
Europe's political fragmentation, 165–167
EU's institutional architecture, idiosyncrasies of, 167–169
Social democratic pro-Europeanism, 159
Weakness of, 159–162
Social democratic welfare state
Crisis of, 77
Social insurance, 79
Social democrats, 85, 111–114, 144, 181, 182, 188, 192, 197, 217
Goal of, 120
Principle of common monetary unit, 197
Responsibility to protect, 201
Social equality, 103
Social Europe, 165, 171
Social fraud, 131
Social inclusion, 121–122
Social inequality, measures of, 95
Social insurance administrator, 104
Social insurance welfare, 79
Social Investment Pact, 173
Socialist cycling clubs, 182
Socialist walking groups, 182
Socially vulnerable, 135
Social malaise-separating myths
Nostalgia, 133–134
and Reality, 129
Real loss, 133–134
Strange land
Threatening minorities and strangers, 130–132
Winners and losers of globalisation, 132–133
Social-market Europeanist, 166
Social markets
Financial innovation, results of, 68–69
Financial system, capital allocation in, 67–68
Market fundamentalism, 68
Strengths and weaknesses, 68
Social mobility, 116–118
Social outcomes, 122
Social policy, 104, 164
Social provision and welfare state, 80
Social solidarity, 96, 102–103
Social spending
Demand and, 79
Social trust, 102–103, 104
Social welfare policies, 110
Social workers, MPs, 179
Societal community, membership, 135
Socio-economic conditions, 126
Socio-economic marginalisation, 131
Socio-economic status (SES), 115
Children, 116
Solidaristic justice, 100

Solidarity
Business, deregulation of, 222–223
Citizens' concern, orientation towards, 219–220
Collective resources, 219
Deliberative engagement
Advantages of, 230
Authoritarian regimes of 1980s, 229
Capital projects, involvement in, 229–230
Civil renewal and community empowerment, 229
Consensus Conferences for, 228
Deliberative Opinion Polls for civic decision, 228
Government's Big Society rhetoric, 227
Key elements for, 227–228
Neighbourhood Management initiative, 229
Participatory budgeting technique, 229
in Public health services, 228
Public policy development and, 228
Economic/cultural/global transformations, 220
Electoral mandate security, 219
in Europe, 221–222
Family, relationship changes in, 220
Free trade, positivity for, 222–223
Government power, views on, 222–223
Increased taxation and public spending, public support for, 222
Individualistic outlook, inclination to, 221
Plutocratic fatalism, 223–224
Post-9/11 Islamophobia, rise of, 219
Reaganite Republican philosophy, 221
Real threats, focus on
'Big government,' mismanagement of, 224–225
Capital and revenue resources, 225
Contemporary problems, causes of, 225
Destructive attitudes and income inequality, 225–226
Job security and, 224–225
Neo-conservative regime in US and UK, 226
Pollution and climate-change-inducing emissions, 224–225
Public, systematic misdirection of, 226
Reform agenda, citizen involvement in, 227
Socio-economic status and life expectancy, 225
Third way approach, 219–220
UK and US, economic vibrancy in, 223
Wealth-based elite and individuals polarisation, 220–221
Workplace, relationship changes in, 220
Soviet Union, economic dominance, 62
The Spirit Level: Why Equality is Better for Everyone, 243
Squeezed middle, 203–217
Disappearance of crises, 210
Economic success, 207
Financial crisis, 203
Good growth, 212
Income groups, 203
Meaning of, 204–206
New growth model, 212–215
Phenomenon of, 204
Tax revenues, 209
Collapse of, 209
Overall fall in, 209
UK tax receipts
Breakdown of, 208
Rise in, 207
Unfolding crisis of living standards, 206
Unity of purpose, 215–217
Value of residential properties, 211
Western financial system, 211
State borrowing
Economic crisis and, 79
Strange land
Threatening minorities and strangers, 130–132
Substantial justice, 100
Super capitalism, 205
Sweden
Economic competence, recessions in, 51
Electoral performance
Swedish SAP, 5
Progress in, 236
Recession, 89
Social democratic project across, 8
Socioeconomic status and life expectancy, 225
Swedish Democrats, 78
Poll, 193
Systemic problems, welfare state, 76–77

T

Tactical responses, 175
Tax
  Benefits, 187
  on International financial transactions, 86
Taxation, 158
Tax-cutting agenda, 90
Technical problems, welfare state, 76
Thatcherite Conservatism, 189
Thatcher revolution, 238
The death of the American Dream, 205
Tobin tax, 86
Trade, rebalancing, 86
Trade unions, 184
Transfer union, 157
Treasury, 204, 205
Treasury View, endorsement of, 54–55
Triangulation, 177
  Tactic of, 178
Trickle-down effect, 240
'True Finns', 167
Turkish community, 131

U

UK
  Coalition's immigration cap, 215
  Disappearance of crises, 210
  Economy, 205
  Labour's tenure, 207
UK Coalition Government, 195
Unemployment, social risks of, 76
Unions, 184
Universal banking tradition, 66–67
UN Security Council, 188
USA
  Boom in world trade, 204
  Cultural conflicts in, 253–254
  Deficit reduction strategy in, 55–56
  Destructive attitudes and income inequality, 225–226
  Economic competence, 51
  Individualistic outlook, inclination to, 221
  Marketisation of, 41
  Neo-conservative regime in, 226
  Regulatory capture in, 70
  Socioeconomic status and life expectancy, 225
  Sub-prime mortgage crisis, 157
  Treasury bills, 210
  World Values Survey (1995–7) in, 221–222

V

Venezuela, globalisation in, 31
Vulnerability, 129
  of Native people, 132

W

Wages, 83, 205
Wage-setting arrangements, 112
Washington consensus, 164
Weaponry, chemical and biological, 199
Welfare
  Countervailing powers/institutions establishment, 48
  Key elements and aim, 48–49
  Keynesian thinking business cycle, 49
  State as noncapitalist sphere guarantor, 49
Welfare states, 128
  Anti-immigrant and, 78
  Characteristic of, 75
  Defending, 78–81
  Future, 85–88
  Settlement, challenges to, 75–77
  Social democracy and, 75–93
  Social provision and, 80
  Systemic problems, 76–77
  Technical problems, 76
Welfare state settlement
  Challenges, 75
    2008–9 financial crisis, 75
    Systemic problems, 76–77
    Technical problems, 76
  Defending, 78–81
  High-spending, 78
  Politics of
    Decentralising responsibility to citizen level, 84–85
    Individual incentives and responsibilities, 82–84
    Opportunity-centred social democracy, 81–82
  Unattractive alternative, 88–91
  Uncertain future, 85
    Globalisation in politics, 85–86
    Material interests, alliances, 86–88
Welfare to work programmes, 82, 83

Western economies, 192
Western financial system, 211
Western liberal-democratic values, 132
Western political culture
  Enlightenment and progress, 238–239
Winner-take-all markets, development of, 112
Women's employment, 86–87
Working-class community, 144–149
Working-class movement
  Internationalisation of, 87–88
World Trade Organisation, 86

X

Xenophobia, 129, 131, 133

Z

Zero-sum conflicts, 213